B E Y O N D

T A L E N T

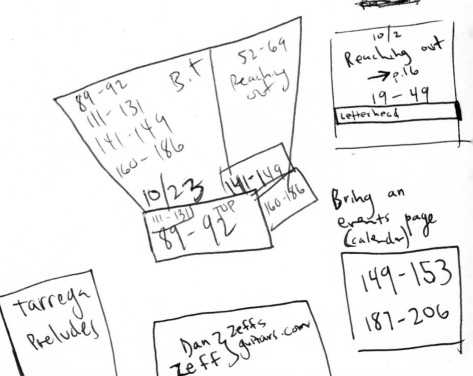

B E Y O N D

T A L E N T

Creating a Successful Career in Music

Angela Myles Beeching

OXFORD

UNIVERSITY PRESS

2005

OXFORD

UNIVERSITY PRESS

Oxford   New York
Auckland   Bangkok   Buenos Aires   Cape Town   Chennai
Dar es Salaam   Delhi   Hong Kong   Istanbul   Karachi   Kolkata
Kuala Lumpur   Madrid   Melbourne   Mexico City   Mumbai   Nairobi
São Paolo   Shanghai   Taipei   Tokyo   Toronto

Published by Oxford University Press, Inc.
198 Madison Avenue, New York, New York 10016

www.oup.com

Oxford is a registered trademark of Oxford University Press

Library of Congress Cataloging-in-Publication Data
Beeching, Angela Myles.
Beyond talent : creating a successful career in music / Angela Myles Beeching
p. cm.
Includes bibliographical references and index.
ISBN-13 978-0-19-516913-3; 978-0-19-516914-0 (pbk.)

1. Music—Vocational guidance   I. Title.
ML3795.B42   2004
780'.23—dc22   2004006114

"The Relaxation Response" from *The Relaxation Response* by Herbert Benson, M.D.
with Miriam Z. Klipper. Copyright 1975 by William Morrow & Company, Inc.
Reprinted by permission of HaperCollins Inc.

9   8   7   6   5

Printed in the United States of America
on acid-free paper

Preface

In order to make your dream of a successful music career a reality, you need more than talent. Talent fuels the engine of success, but it's not the whole vehicle! In order to get where you want to go, you need the wheels of ambition, a frame and support structure for your dream, the knowledge and experience to handle the ride, and a direction and route. Want to be in control of your future? This book helps put you in the driver's seat. This is a guide for serious performers looking to advance their careers. Although geared primarily toward classical artists, this guide contains information useful to all musicians interested in career advancement.

As the director of the Career Services Center at New England Conservatory of Music, one of the world's top music schools, I've advised hundreds of talented students, alumni, and faculty. In addition, I've worked with scores of professional musicians at national arts conferences and workshops. I've counseled classical, jazz, world, and some pop musicians on a range of issues. Clients have sought advice on CD and website projects, building audiences, contract issues, starting a concert series, finding or changing artist management, concert programming, commissioning new works, finding grants, supplementing their performance careers with other work. I've advised musicians whose long-term goals were to be presidents of music schools, those who wanted to start their own music schools, people who wanted to study and work in Europe or raise money to buy a new instrument.

Although every musician's situation is unique, there are some themes that I've found constant. Many of the musicians I meet have never discussed their career issues with a knowledgeable professional. Even established artists often find it difficult to get practical information on how to deal with the "business" side of the music industry. Many musicians get little or no guidance on how to manage their careers, promote themselves, or on how to move from dreaming to planning to doing. Most musicians pick up music business skills and information in a hit-or-miss fashion. And unfortunately, many musicians fail to establish themselves in the professional world because they lack the information and skills to create new opportunities for themselves.

Is This Book for You? ■

Are you curious what it takes to establish yourself as a performer? Are you interested in how to move forward toward your goals? Would you like to set goals for yourself and then accomplish these? Would you like to find more performances, build your reputation, and attract more audience to your concerts? If so, this is the book for you!

There are no typical "career paths" that musicians take to find success—not the kind that people studying medicine or engineering can generally take. Successful musicians tailor-make their own career paths, and these paths most often require an entrepreneurial approach. This book is designed to help fill these needs.

What This Book Includes ■

Drawing on my years of experience as a music career counselor and as a cellist, this book offers concrete detailed information and explanations for how musicians can make their way in the professional marketplace. It is spiced with the accumulated wisdom of the faculty, alumni, and guest speakers who regularly present career strategy workshops at New England Conservatory.

Each chapter contains background information, specific how-to directions, and real-life stories. The examples are real, although in some cases, I've changed the names and a few of the specifics to safeguard people's privacy. There are exercises for determining long-term and short-term goals and the practical steps to achieve these goals. The book includes detailed instructions for booking and publicizing performances and explains how to build a local reputation and a fan base. In addition, there are chapters that cover fundraising, grant writing, networking, marketing CDs, and producing the necessary press materials and mailing lists.

Some of the information and suggestions may be brand new for you. Other more familiar material may help you evaluate your current methods, confirm your good habits, or offer an alternative to the methods you've been using. Some of the information may seem like rocket science, while other sections are common-sense approaches and good manners—the kinds of things we can all use an occasional reminder about.

This is not a "one size fits all" approach. There's no one "right" career path for all musicians—we are individuals! So I've included throughout the book a range of ideas and suggestions for you to consider using.

This book will show you how to:

- Find and create performance opportunities
- Produce professional-quality promotional materials
- Attract media attention to build your reputation and audience
- Raise funds for your music projects
- Design your own career success plan to reach your long-term goals

How Is This Book Organized? ■

As much as possible, topics are presented in a first-things-first, step-by-step basis. For instance, how to create promotional materials is discussed before how to book performances. So, although chapters can certainly be read on their own or out of order, the book is designed to take the reader through a linear, career-mapping process. Taking the journey from chapter 1 to the end should help you develop perspective and a more holistic approach to advancing your career.

Where Do the Musician Examples Come From? ■

This book is full of examples of real musicians solving real issues in their careers. For the examples that come from my confidential career advising work, to protect the anonymity of clients, I've altered their names but left their stories and promotional material examples intact. You will also find other examples, not requiring anonymity, where musicians' stories include their actual names.

These examples include musicians working in a range of genres and serve to illustrate a wide range of career issues and possible solutions. There is much that musicians can learn from the innovation and creativity of artists outside their genre and I've found that some of the best ideas come from examining an issue from very different vantage points.

A New Perspective ■

Most musicians would understandably rather spend their time rehearsing and performing than concern themselves with the details of concert promotion, scheduling, finances, and so on. Many musicians steadfastly try to avoid dealing with any of the business aspects of the music industry. But whether out of fear or ignorance, musicians who "stick their heads in the sand" do so at the risk of their careers.

Without a real understanding of business issues, of resources available to them, musicians routinely miss out on opportunities. So, instead of viewing the business side of the music world with contempt or as a necessary evil, I recommend musicians become savvy about the business side of music.

After all, if you want to have an audience, if you want to perform publicly and be paid for it, you will need to get informed about the process. Unless you have someone you'd trust with your life taking care of your career (even mothers won't do this!) you need to get savvy about the industry. After all, it's *your* career, your life, your happiness, so these issues are *your* business.

Caution: This Book May Challenge Some of Your Assumptions about the Nature of Your "Job" as a Musician ■

Many people believe their "job" as musicians is to practice and perform. Period. That as accomplished professionals they will be protected from the "crass" world of commerce and the everyday details of handling finances, logistics and publicity. And that the details of managing their own career will be magically handled by someone else.

Unfortunately, these fantasies lead to a kind of black-and-white thinking, a music versus business dichotomy, and an unfortunate "us versus them" attitude. To illustrate this dichotomy, the two columns that follow list some contrasting thought associations musicians have between the artistic and business sides of their careers. These are purposely exaggerated to make clear the contrasts. This illustration is based on the questions, attitudes, surprises, and points of resistance I've encountered in advising hundreds of musicians on their profession. Notice that there are both positive and negative associations in each column. Keep in mind that for most musicians, even if they don't consciously think like this, they harbor trace elements of this thinking, and it can trip them up.

Your challenge is to deal effectively with both sides of your career, since they are both necessary for success. How do you practice and rehearse and still find the time and energy to be an entrepreneur, to take care of business? The answer, for most successful musicians, is to work hard at finding an appropriate balance, to pay careful attention to priorities, and to use effective time-management skills.

To set the record straight, the job of a musician involves far more than just practice and performance. A musician's job is multidimensional. Working musicians typically wear different hats in the course of their workweek and over the course of their work lives. Beyond practicing and performing,

Thought Associations

Is your unconscious pitting one side of your career against the other?
How do you think about the artistic and business sides of your career?
Do any of these associations resonate with you? What others can you add?

Music as Art	*versus*	*the Business of Music*
Good (clean, pure)		Bad (dirty, crass, beneath the dignity of an artist)
Us (musicians, people who "get it")		Them (everyone else)
True calling		"Selling out"
Realm of imagination, creativity		Tedium, overwhelming amounts of detail
About practicing, performing		About dealing with money, "administrivia"
Feel at home		Experience discomfort, distrust
Idealistic (unrealistic?)		Practical (limited in imagination?)
Ideas		Action
Art for its own sake		Music as a profession
Self-satisfaction		Take one's audience & community interests into consideration
Music for oneself		Music with an audience
Expect/wait for assistance (no guarantee)		Do It Yourself, artist in charge
Sense of entitlement		Entrepreneurial spirit

musicians often find or create performance opportunities for themselves: they self-manage their careers. They may also raise money for musical projects, and handle contracts, publicity, and administrative work for their ensembles. Musicians typically spend a portion of their work lives teaching, because they want to help influence the next generation. Musicians also advocate for K-12 arts education and for public funding for the arts. They often serve the community as advisory board members for arts organizations. It's typical for musicians to have ongoing multiple projects that may combine performing, recording, teaching, and other arts-related professional activities.

People often attribute career success to fate or destiny. They say it's a matter of being in the right place at the right time, or getting "discovered," or just being lucky. Unfortunately, this kind of thinking can keep people frozen, thinking that success will be handed to them. This book may cause you to shift your perspective so that *you* are the architect of your future. You can determine, through your attitude and behavior, your luck and your success. This book is all about how.

Acknowledgments

Many people were a great help to me in the writing of this. Thank you to my agent, Ann Rittenberg, and my editor, Kim Robinson, and her assistant, Eve Bachrach. And thank you to a host of terrific readers and friends, appearing here in alphabetical splendor:

Stephen Beaudoin

John Blanchard

Howard Block

Janet Bookspan

Mark Broschinsky

Kathy Canfield

Nancy Christensen

Carrie Cheron

Adrian Daly

Ed Donahue

James Falzone

Catherine Fitterman

Jack Garrity

The Jamaica Plain Prose
    Writers' Group

Jeffrey James

Tanya Maggi

Patrick Maxfield

Michael McGrade

Rick McLaughlin

Derek Mithaug

Jennifer Morris

Lisa Nigris

Barbara Owens

Eric Platz

Gwen Powell

Steve Procter

Omar Roca

Jean Rife

Nancy Shear

Peter Spellman

John Steinmetz

Sue Stockton

Bob Sullivan

Steve Wogaman

Judith Ciampa Wright

Jacob Yarrow

Phillip Ying

Contents

BEYOND

TALENT

Prelude:
Confessions of a
Career Counselor

Generally, accomplished musicians attribute their success to a combination of talent, luck, hard work, and the help of a few key mentors. When asked if they had a concrete plan for their career path, most successful musicians will say no.

Either they had no plan at all or they had only a vague vision. They stumbled onto opportunities. There were stretches of time when their lives made no sense, when they seemed directionless. They bounced from project to project relying on their instincts and following the "path" of their artistic integrity. Miraculously, it all worked out pretty well. Accomplished musicians often find the idea of career planning in music to be strange. They may think, "How can you plan for success when you can't control luck or talent?"

I want to come clean about some inherent problems with the concept of career paths. It's a problem inherent to books such as this and to my profession, career counseling.

The Truth about Career Paths ■

It's blasphemous for me to admit, but the real way people go through life is *not* with a handy map and directions. They don't usually set goals and plan carefully and work systematically toward success. Why? Because there's so much in life we can't control and so much of our career direction depends on exploration. Life is fluid and so are careers.

Musicians usually experience their careers as a series of projects, such as recordings, work with various ensembles, commissioning or grant projects, involvement with specific repertoire, residencies, and so on. These projects may overlap and connect but just as often they don't.

In short, we go through life as though there *is* no path, as though we're in a dense forest and we're simply making our way as best we can. It's often only in looking back over years that we can fashion a story line out of our own history. And as a narrative construct, our career path is subject to varied interpretations. We describe our own past in different ways, depending on our mood, our audience, the year, and our current circumstances.

It's impossible to see clearly the cause and effect of all the choices we make, small and large, each day. But that is the stuff our projects, paths, careers, and lives are made of. An idea leads to a conversation, a connection, a project, and through the course of these projects our career emerges.

Career counselors advocate making plans, writing down goals, exploring opportunities, and taking practical steps toward completing projects. I say and write these things and I believe them. To a degree.

We "pretend" that life will work logically, that action A will lead to a probable outcome B. But everyone knows that life almost never works according to our plans. You can't account for luck, for being in the right or wrong place and time. And there's your personal life and your health—these have huge impacts on careers. And there's the fact that any one of our projects can take us away from our original plan, take us off course, and lead us to a new goal, a new path. That's what's fascinating about life—you don't get to know in advance how things will turn out.

I started playing the cello at age eight and I was hooked. I wanted nothing more than to play music. In grad school I came to believe the best thing ever would be to get a tenure-track college teaching job so I could teach and perform. I got a doctorate, won several fellowships, and had two different tenure track positions. If someone had told me at age twenty or age thirty that I would end up running a career center and publishing a career guide and that I'd love this work, I'd have laughed and said they were full of it. Life has a way of throwing curve balls at us. It keeps things interesting. If things always went according to plan, we'd be bored.

So, yes, I still advise setting goals, and making plans, because there are practical ways to get from point A to point B in your career. But realize that your life, the good stuff, is all about the journey.

Coming Clean as a Career Counselor ∎

On my desk at work I have a useful tool of the trade. It's a magic wand. And sitting on top of my computer monitor there's a plastic tiara for the really tough days. With my magic wand I wish I could make people's dreams come true, give them the lucky break they need, and create the life work they'd love.

But the reality is, we each have to find our own way. But we don't have to do it alone. In life, we all get to learn from our mistakes and we get many opportunities to learn from and to help each other.

In a sense, this book is my best magic wand offering to you. Yes, the world needs artists of all kinds, but our opportunities are often the ones we create for ourselves.

Five Trade Secrets Revealed ■

With the information from the chapters here, you have a great advantage over most musicians—you have the tools to build your success.

Of course, information isn't all that's needed. You need to supply the talent, motivation, and determination. Are you ready? As an added boost, here are five professional career counseling 'secrets' you can use on your own. (A version of this piece was originally published in the *National Business Employment* weekly.)

As a career counselor, I typically spend a fair amount of time during a session listening to and watching the client. This is part of practicing the first great career counseling secret:

Secret #1

Look for the light in the eyes. Job searches can be long and frustrating; clients may be depressed and uncertain of their next career move. In a typical session, the career counselor encourages the client to talk about past accomplishments and about the choices they're considering. The trick comes in watching the client while they talk, noticing when their eyes light up, when they are charged with energy and enthusiasm. It's obvious when a client is talking about a career direction or opportunity they really find engaging. The light in their eyes is the clue to their passion.

Although it's not easy to watch for the light in your own eyes, your friends and colleagues can give you valuable feedback. You can also listen for the enthusiasm in your own voice when discussing career issues that capture your imagination—you'll "hear" your eyes light up. Make sure you know what types of work you find most rewarding and satisfying. Identifying areas of interest is essential to planning a good career move.

Once a client identifies areas of interest, the next thing is to figure out an action plan. Unfortunately, many people get stuck in the process right here because of all the "stuff" that's in their way: the "shoulds, buts, and if onlys." This brings us to the second career counseling trade secret:

Secret #2

We often create our own obstacles. Identify your baggage—the actual and perceived obstacles that block your road to success. Getting a client to acknowledge or discover what is actually standing in the way can be difficult. Sometimes I simply ask, "What do you think is really holding you back from moving forward with your career?" The answer may be a litany of rationalizations and extraneous issues. The actual obstacle may be depression, or a lack of information about the new career area, or the client may be chasing someone else's dream (a spouse's, or a parent's). You may need to do a bit of soul-searching to identify your obstacles, but once you can clearly see them, you can devise strategies to get around them, or get over them.

After identifying obstacles, it can be relatively easy to figure out the next logical action steps needed, and this leads to career counseling secret #3.

Secret #3

The first steps are the most important. A job search or a career change is exhausting emotionally, physically, and mentally; fear of failure may paralyze one's career momentum. Making a good start is key. Break down your goal into small practical action steps, such as phone calls you need to make, resources you need to gather, networking appointments you can arrange. To avoid becoming overwhelmed, use short weekly "to-do" lists with practical action steps. Action steps should be simple, measurable, and pragmatic. To keep your motivation up, it's important to succeed in your first action steps and feel the resulting sense of accomplishment.

How can you tell if your action steps are appropriate? Feedback from people working in your field is very helpful—get connected to the people "in the know" and get the information you need. Networking and researching are marvelous ways to expand your opportunities.

Although it's very important to get the best information to make the best decisions, you also need to trust yourself and your intuition, which is the substance of the fourth secret.

Secret #4

You already have the answers. That's right, a career counselor is not the one who supplies the "answers," it's you. Although talking through your ideas and plans with an objective professional can help, you are the person who ultimately knows what's best for you.

To move ahead effectively, our conscious decisions and actions need to be in sync with our "gut" instincts. Our values and intuition, our gut instincts, determine the countless daily small-scale decisions we make. These "small" decisions (how we spend free time, what projects we follow through on, who we network with) cumulatively determine our career direction. Make sure you're tuned into your gut instincts.

Although career counselors always look for ways to motivate their clients and keep them pushing forward, when push comes to shove, the truth is . . .

Secret #5

People move ahead when they're good and ready, and not a moment sooner. Clients may look and sound like they're ready for a career move, they may have a great plan, resources, support, and opportunity. It doesn't matter. If they're not ready emotionally or psychologically, they won't budge. To move forward, you have to be ready and willing—no one can do it for you.

So with these do-it-yourself techniques, do you really need a career counselor? My best advice is to tap into all the resources and support you have available to you. Check out what's free and low cost in your community: a local job resource center, public library, or college career center may all offer great services, including career counseling. Having these five career counseling "tricks" up your sleeve may help you make better use of whatever resources you have. The more you can do for yourself, the better, because in the end, you are the architect of your future.

1

Mapping Success
in Music

Some musicians dream of playing first chair in one of the world's top orchestras. Some dream of being a soloist or part of a well-known touring ensemble. Others yearn for a multilayered career playing Broadway shows, and doing studio recording and teaching. Some want to teach at the college level and perform, tour and record with their own ensemble. As you're reading this, you're probably reflecting on your own particular dream of a successful music career. Having the dream is important, but what comes next?

Many musicians get frustrated or stuck at various stages in their careers. Careers are developed over time, not hatched overnight. Career development is about process. As a music career counselor, my job is to help people determine the best next steps forward to advance their careers. And long-term career goals are realized through every day choices about the use of time, energy and money. Whether you're just starting out or are in mid-stream, these everyday choices are critical. The journey of a thousand steps really does begin with one.

Emerging artists often have a very narrow view of success. They may see success as being a soloist with a top orchestra, singing with the Met, or being a universally famous recording artist. But there are only a handful of folks who achieve careers in this category. And while there's nothing wrong with "going for gold," it can be a problem if you view anything short of this as failure. With a narrow view of success, musicians unconsciously limit their career options, and their satisfaction and fulfillment in their work lives.

Success for many accomplished professional musicians is less about fame and money and more about maintaining artistic integrity, contributing to the musical life of their community, and doing work that is intellectually and emotionally satisfying. It's important to think about how you're defining success and what kind of fulfillment you're seeking. Careers are about process, a journey that we create ourselves.

What Does It Take to "Make It"? ■

Winning and keeping an orchestra job demands skills and talents different from those needed to lead a jazz ensemble, or teach at a conservatory, or be a studio player, or a film composer. In considering your options and goals, what's important is to create a niche in the professional world that works for you.

■

Critical Factors Determining Success in Music

Talent *plus* **hard work** are necessary but *are not sufficient by themselves* to yield career success.

Winning Attitude: You are motivated and focused. You're resilient: you can handle rejection.

Sales Skills: You communicate and present yourself well; your enthusiasm is contagious. You can articulate your strengths to prospective employers / performance presenters.

Support System: You have emotional support and encouragement from several people, your career goals and plans do not put you in conflict with those close to you.

Strategy: You have a concrete plan of how to reach your short- and long-term goals; you have the skills and experience necessary to implement your plan.

Do you have all these factors working for you? If some areas need work, consider yourself in good company. No one has the total "perfect package." Knowing what needs improving is the first step to making positive change. The following chapters detail practical ways to enhance or develop these factors.

Musicians who do well professionally and have the least trouble with the realities of the music profession are those who have most of these six factors, or who have an overabundance in one area that compensates for a lack in another. It's not easy, though, to see our own deficiencies.

■

Case Study

A talented pianist, Helen, has built a good local reputation as a chamber musician and accompanist and has received a number of favorable reviews. However, she's passive in her approach to career issues and shies away from dealing directly with the business side of music (such as concert promoters, press). Helen does not actively seek advice from colleagues and supporters. She is frustrated by the fact that she's not getting as many concert dates as she'd like, does not have a manager, and is not commanding the fees she feels she deserves. Helen blames the unfair music industry, the competitive market, and the dwindling audience for classical music. She doesn't see how her own behavior and attitude may be holding her back.   ■

Musicians, like most people, can be fond of complaining. It's easier to gripe about a lack of opportunities than to take control of your life. What could Helen do differently? Like most of us, Helen could make better use of her existing support system, cultivate new collaborators and improve her self-management (until she can attract a manager). Identifying our shortcomings is essential to making improvements. Talking to others can be a great way to gain some perspective. You may recognize a bit of Helen in you. There's a bit of Helen in all of us.

To help Helen and others, I've presented the following basic principles for advancing music careers. I call these the ten success principles. See how many of these you use now and consider adopting the others. They don't necessarily demand a lot of time or effort. They do require adjusting your perspective, and perhaps modifying some of your habits and going beyond your comfort zone.

Ten Success Principles ■

There are many practical steps you can take to advance toward your career goals. In observing musicians make their way in the world, I've noticed certain kinds of thinking and behavior that works well. I've distilled these habits into the ten principles below. These are lifestyle habits, ways to think about and deal with the world. Outlined below, these principles are covered in greater detail and with examples in later chapters.

1. *Know yourself.* Know both your strengths and weaknesses. Know what you have to offer the professional world. Get feedback from colleagues, teachers, mentors. Their perspective and advice can help you to formulate the best career path.
2. *Know about the music industry.* Get savvy: Your research can include talking to colleagues and mentors and reading the arts pages regularly in your local newspapers. Know what other musicians at your career stage are doing, what types of performance work they are finding. Reading this book is a great start!
3. *Schmooze! (Network):* get out and exchange information and ideas with other musicians. When you share career and job information with oth-

ers, they reciprocate. Networking happens everywhere: at rehearsals, backstage at concerts, in supermarkets, gas stations, and at most social gatherings. Even if you're shy, you can find a style of networking to suit your personality. Chapter 2 examines networking in depth.

4. *Research your options.* Start by simply reading other musicians' bios for ideas about grants, competitions, festivals, and performance opportunities. Bios can be found on musicians' websites, CD liner notes, and in concert programs. Read local newspapers, check websites. Find out who is playing where, to get ideas on what you can do. Read the relevant music journals, available at your library, bookstore, or music store. Information leads to opportunities. Make it a habit. Set aside time once a week to catch up on what's going on in your profession.

As graduate student composers, Kohji Nakano from Japan and Lior Navok from Israel both made the time each week to research and follow up on opportunities. Kohji found competitions open to international students. Applying and winning a few of these led to commissions, summer seminars, and premieres of his works. Lior produced a CD of his own works, researched the appropriate radio stations and critics, and sent the CD out. The CD got radio airplay and was reviewed favorably in several publications and all this led to commissions for new works and plans for the next CD.

---

5. *Cultivate an attitude:* be positive, resilient, flexible, and professional. Keep your ego in check; you need to be able to deal well with both rejection and acceptance. It's human nature. People want to work with others who are pleasant, optimistic, and inspiring. Remember: Your attitude is a big part of your professional image.

6. *Assess your interpersonal skills. Clean up your act.* We've all suffered disappointments and difficulties in life. Get whatever kind of help you need but make sure you are not inflicting your personal difficulties on others. The more you can be at ease with yourself and with others, the more you can benefit from and appreciate the world you inhabit. Make sure you are contributing positively to a healthy working and living lifestyle.

The music industry is a very small relationship-driven world. Make sure you are a good colleague, because the person you snub today may be the person who doesn't hire you tomorrow. Be considerate, polite, and helpful. People will remember your thoughtfulness, your optimism, and your enthusiasm, and they will respond in kind.

Tips on Tuning Up Your Interpersonal Skills

- Before going to sleep each night, review your day in your mind. Think about your behavior and your interactions with people that day. Ask yourself, if you had a chance to do it over again, what would you do differently? Be honest. Envisioning new patterns of behavior is the first step to making change.
- Ask for feedback from trusted colleagues and friends. If you're unsure of how you're coming across or about how you handled a particular situation, ask a colleague for objective feedback.

7. *Think like an entrepreneur.* Put your imagination and creativity to work in the business side of your music career; spend time brainstorming with friends and colleagues; there may be career opportunities in unexpected places. These days, people are forming partnerships with other individuals and with organizations to utilize diverse skills, conserve resources, and boost creativity. There may be unexpected career opportunities you can create or help develop: concert series, after-school arts programming, or innovative partnerships with other performing, presenting, or educational organizations.

Many musicians create their own performance opportunities and develop their own audiences. The Ten O'Clock Classics (http://www.toc.org), is the brainchild of pianist Ronen Segev. While a student at Juilliard, he started organizing these performances at unexpected locations including Crunch Fitness Clubs, bars, bookstores, offices, and at the legendary disco club Studio 54. The series is named for the starting time of the group's initial performances, 10 P.M.

8. *Have a gimmick, a hook.* In order to get bookings and media attention, and an audience, you'll need to be able to communicate what is distinctive about you and your music-making. What makes you exceptional? Do you perform any specialized or unusual repertoire? Have you given concerts with innovative programming or performed in unusual settings? This topic will be discussed further in chapter 3.

Cellist Reinmar Seidler did a few concerts in South America and wanted to follow up on these leads. In order to increase his marketability and expand the scope of his touring, he put together a press packet with detailed descriptions of lecture/demonstrations and clinics he could offer to music schools along with his concerts. His workshop topics included early music performance practices for string players and healthy physical approaches to the instrument. He offered a unique package and it resulted in more bookings as well as more college-level teaching experience for his résumé.

9. *Have both short-term and long-term goals.* Articulating your goals is important. You can't get somewhere if you don't know where you're going! Having realistic short-term goals, for this week or month, will help to keep you focused and motivated. Meeting your short-term goals is the best way to work toward your long-term goals.

10. *Feed your soul.* How do you reenergize and rekindle your inspiration? What inspires you? What helps you recharge your imagination? What helps keep your spirit alive? Make sure you have room in your life for some kind of balance. Whether it's your spiritual side, your family life, communing with nature, or favorite hobbies, remind yourself of these regularly. Make sure that you are living a full and satisfying life.

    Keep in mind why you got involved in music in the first place. Your most basic motivations for being in music are crucial factors in keeping you moving forward in your career. Your motivation—what music means to you—should help sustain you throughout your professional life.

Part of the process of moving forward in your career involves fine-tuning your goals, assessing your strengths and discovering and exploring new opportunities. The kind of musician who puts these principles into action can be described as an entrepreneur. Cultivate your entrepreneurial skills and you'll be cultivating your career.

The Entrepreneurial Musician ■

Finding your niche within the professional music world may mean creating a niche for yourself. Creating niches is what entrepreneurs do. They "think outside the box" and see opportunities when others see obstacles.

Technically, an entrepreneur is a person who organizes, operates, and assumes the risk for a business venture. These days, people in all professions are creating new opportunities for themselves, instead of just waiting to apply for advertised job openings. Consider this: in the United States in the year 2000, there was a new business born every 54.9 seconds and in 2001, 78 percent of all jobs in the United States were in companies with fewer than ten employees (according to the Small Business Administration). Whether you're starting your own ensemble, a private teaching studio, contracting other musicians for gigs, or marketing your own CD, *you too are running a business*, and that makes *you* an entrepreneur.

Many musicians don't view themselves as business people or entrepreneurs, yet musicians are the quintessential "multipreneurs." Successful musicians may perform with various groups, teach both privately and at schools, record, compose or arrange and may assist in the administration of an arts organization. A satisfying successful musician's work life may include four to five concurrent "part-time" jobs. The diversity of ways you can contribute to society is one of the great things about being a musician.

How Does One Find or Create New Opportunities?

The first step is to get curious about what is out there. Talk to lots of musicians and gather information about existing opportunities (that's where your networking pays off). Look for ways your talents and experience might complement the needs of another person or organization. Collaboration can be a beautiful thing. Don't limit your possibilities: Think broadly about how your music might work in a variety of contexts.

What's Needed to Succeed, beyond Excellent Musical Skills and Training?

Characteristics of successful entrepreneurs include flexibility, resiliency, and the ability to find opportunities in the midst of difficulties or challenges. Entrepreneurs are innovators, creative problem-solvers who can attract people and resources to their projects. Able to assess their assets and set attainable goals, entrepreneurs are disciplined, persistent and learn from their mistakes.

Oboist Jennifer Montbach started Radius Ensemble (http://www.radiusensemble.org), a chamber group with its own concert series, so that she could program the music she wanted and experiment with reaching a broader audience. Within its first two seasons, Radius had already received great reviews, developed an impressive website and a database of followers, and was playing to full houses. The work involved forming a nonprofit organization, finding funding, writing program notes, press releases, not to mention all the practice and rehearsals! The payoff for her was seeing her vision realized.

There are certain general entrepreneurial characteristics, personality traits and skills that successful musicians often possess—*beyond* their musical skills.

Not every successful musician has all these, but they often have a high percentage. See how many of these traits you possess now and remember, it's never too late to start acquiring new skills or new qualities. Later chapters will cover how to develop these skills and how to cultivate these personality traits.

Entrepreneurial Checklist

Skills to Manage Your Music Career

❑ Interpersonal skills
❑ Writing skills
❑ Public speaking / presentation skills
❑ Negotiation skills

❑ Budget/finance skills
❑ Teaching skills and experience
❑ Research skills

❑ Publicity skills
❑ Computer skills

❑ Desktop publishing skills
❑ Grant writing/fund-raising skills

Personal Qualities for Success

❑ Determination
❑ Ability to handle rejection
❑ Imagination, creativity

❑ Flexibility, openness to new ideas
❑ Personal integrity
❑ Intellectual curiosity
❑ Ability to learn from one's mistakes
❑ Conscientiousness, reliability
❑ Good follow-through, detail-oriented
❑ Willingness to extend oneself
❑ Optimism

The sum of all your skills and qualities (musical and otherwise) determines your potential. Skills and qualities can be learned, improved and cultivated, so make a note to yourself about what needs attending. Now that you've done a bit of assessment, you're ready to design a plan.

Your Career Plan: Setting Goals ■

Goals are dreams with deadlines. Effective career plans start with specific goals. In working to make your dream come true, having achievable goals and specific strategies for reaching these goals is essential. Having a plan is a way to get you moving toward your goals. Without planning and action, you are relinquishing control of your future.

■
_____

"Ever heard about the Harvard study of business school grads? The study monitored graduates of an MBA program from 1979 to 1989. Researchers found that ten years after graduation the three percent who had written goals were making 10 times as much money as the other 97 percent combined."

– Annette Richmond, "How to develop more effective short-term goals"on www.career-intelligence.com

Even if financial success is not your top priority, the moral here is that writing your goals down is a way of committing yourself to a specific direction; it is a powerful method of focusing your energy and attention.

The most basic planning is to articulate your long-term and short-term goals. Write these down. You can revise and fine-tune your goals, as you gain more experience in the industry. People change, so their goals and plans need to change with them. You may find yourself revising your plan even as you work through the rest of this book, finding out more about yourself and the music industry. That's just fine because the process of researching and assessing your options and your interests contributes to your career health.

Let's imagine your long-term goal is to lead your own jazz quartet, playing international tours and recording CDs. Let's say you have your own band and so far you've played a few local jazz clubs. A reasonable short-term goal for the next year might be to arrange a small regional tour of jazz clubs, to give you more performance experience and the experience in promoting and booking your group.

Having short-term goals and strategies can keep you on track to your long-term destination. Goals help you benchmark your progress and help keep your morale up. The key then is to determine specific strategies. How do you get started organizing the tour? The following chapters are designed to help you fine-tune your own individual career success plan, to make it work for you.

■ Suggestions for Moving Ahead ■

1. Write your own definition of success. What would success be like in your future career? Is it being famous, wealthy, something else?
2. What specifically do you love about performing?
3. What specifically do you love about being a musician?
5. What is your long-term goal?
   Describe in detail the life you'd like to be leading ten years from now. Where do you see yourself living? What kinds of work are you doing? What is your income level? What is your family situation?

6. What is your short-term goal? To progress toward your long-term goal, what would you want to realistically accomplish one year from now?
7. What do you want to accomplish this month that will advance you toward your short-term goal?
8. What's on your to-do list for this week?

2

Making Connections: Schmoozing for Success

It's All about People Skills ■

Networking, or "schmoozing," simply means being neighborly, being open, and being interested in meeting new people. It's about *exchanging* information and ideas while getting to know people. It should be a two-way street, not all about you. Notice your conversation when someone introduces you to someone new. You probably ask the new person about their life, work, and their interests, and you reciprocate, sharing about yourself and your interests. That's networking, connecting with people. If you "click" there'll be the potential to turn a meeting with a stranger into an acquaintance, a trusted colleague, mentor or friend.

When I discuss networking with musicians, I often get as a response, along with a look of revulsion, "I hate pushy people, I hate small talk," or "I can't do this, I'm too shy." But you don't have to be extroverted, egotistical, or pushy to network. You simply need to be curious about people, willing to talk one-on-one, and willing to say a bit about who you are and what you'd like to be doing.

Effective networking is the number one tool for advancing a music career. Most musicians find out about auditions, jobs, performance opportunities and grants through their network of colleagues, mentors, friends and acquaintances. Networking is especially important in the small world of music where reputations and connections are critical to career building. The contacts you have *right now* include people who can help move your career forward.

■

Guitarist Bob Sullivan has been freelancing since his teens. He estimates that 99 percent of the work he gets—everything from pit orchestra work for musicals, to premiering new chamber works with contemporary ensembles, to many wedding gigs—comes from word of mouth, from networking. Referrals come from colleagues Bob has performed with, from contractors, conductors, former students, people in other fields who happen to know him, and people who have hired Bob for weddings and corporate functions. And when he gets a call for a gig or for a teaching opportunity and he's overbooked or not interested, he in turn refers this work to others, both to his colleagues and to qualified students.

It's easy to overlook the obvious. We don't think to ask all our friends, colleagues, former teachers and family members for suggestions or contacts. Some musicians feel embarrassed at being up-front about what they'd like to be doing professionally. But, if you don't state what it is you want to do, no one can help.

So, instead of "It's not what you know, it's who you know," it's really "not who you know, but *what you do about it*" that counts. Networking basically means being open and friendly to potential new contacts, mentors, employers and friends. It means getting out and meeting these people at concerts, conferences, and association meetings. These folks may be helpful in your career, but you need to get to know them first.

Sarah M., a vocalist who does a lot of contemporary classical music, came to see me because she was looking to get a better teaching position. We discussed options, places to look for job openings, and ways she might collaborate with other musicians at various schools for performances and master classes. When we started talking about networking, her face went blank; she said she didn't know anybody who could offer her work and she really didn't see how talking to friends might help.

We talked more about the idea of having her friends who teach at various colleges invite her to do master classes, or lecture-demonstrations at their school or summer program. By calling her contacts, re-connecting, finding out what they are up to, and telling people she's looking for more opportunities, she'll be boosting her morale and expanding her options. Sarah's current teaching position allows for doing exchange concerts or master classes with colleagues at other schools. These kinds of collaborations can result in larger opportunities, maybe a joint festival, or a teacher exchange. It's a way to build a résumé and reputation. Networking takes some time to payoff, but it's worth it. Sarah is now at work planning a summer music institute, collaborating with new colleagues from other schools. This project, and her expanding network, may eventually lead to the new position she seeks.

Younger musicians often think that people in positions of power are not interested in speaking with them. Not true. Established professionals often enjoy sharing their insights with emerging artists, and may be flattered to be sought out for advice. Alumni from your university or conservatory are a great source for influential networking contacts. You simply adjust your networking methods to fit the situation; it comes down to how you approach people.

As an undergraduate saxophone student, Michael L. made it a habit to write 3 letters per day to networking contacts, concert presenters, contractors, conductors, etc. In these letters he introduced himself, described his experience, and requested to be considered for future performance opportunities. By the time he graduated, he had already established himself as a professional freelancer.

Having good networking skills means having good people skills. We are not born with these skills; we need to learn them and work at them. Even schools like MIT are providing courses and seminars for students to practice networking, pitching a business idea to an investor and working a room. These people skills are necessary in all fields, but especially in music. Improving your people skills simply starts with becoming more aware of how you interact with others.

To prepare for my first college-level music teaching interview (a tenure-track job teaching cello at a university), I asked my graduate music department chair to do a mock interview with me. When I came to his office, he shook my hand and I introduced myself the way you would at a job interview. I was shocked when he then told me I had a *terrible* handshake! No one had ever told me or shown me how to give a good handshake (not wimpy, not bone-crushing, just firm and definite, while maintaining good eye-contact). This was an important lesson and I'm grateful to this day for it. You don't get a second chance to make a first impression.

Your Network

If you don't already have a working list of your contacts, start one now. List the people you know. Include relatives, people you've met traveling, your family dentist, doctor, lawyer, accountant, mailman, friends, neighbors, hairdresser, mechanic, colleagues, former classmates, teachers, coaches, mentors, business acquaintances and people who book performances in your area. Go through your address books to gather these names. Make the list as complete as possible.

You'll be surprised how many people you know. Statistics tell us that people "know" between one hundred and one thousand other people. These are already some of your most valuable contacts—these people can connect you with others who may be influential in your career. Don't screen out people because you think they may not be able to help your career—you don't know who knows whom. These are people who make up your audience, your potential advisory committee, your contributors for fund-raising projects, and so on. You need to have an organized way to contact them and add new names as you make new acquaintances. Your network is your support system.

You can create your list on paper or in various electronic versions. Include all the info you have: name, phone, e-mail, postal address, website if applicable. Eventually, you'll want to have this in a computer database form so you can print out labels for mailings and send a simple e-mail newsletter about upcoming performances. You can organize your list into categories, such as a local mailing list for announcing upcoming performances, or a wider list for sending newsletters, or for fund-raising projects. But the important thing is to get started, and paper is fine for that.

Mailing Lists

A mailing list is simply the segment of your network list used to send concert invitations and notices (e-mail and U.S. post) about upcoming performances. Your mailing list is your network list, used for a specific purpose.

Jazz musicians seeking bookings in clubs are typically asked about the size of their mailing list. A club manager wants to know how many people a band can draw. A band without a mailing list is a band without an audience, so the club manager has no incentive to book the group, however good they may be.

For all up-and-coming musicians, a mailing list is essential for drawing audiences to performances. Posters and calendar listings in local newspapers are not enough. Think about it, you are much more likely to attend a concert if you know the performer and if you've received a personal invitation.

Because your network list probably includes people in a wide variety of locations, being able to segment your list by state or Zip Code is important. This is why you want to have your list in a computer database, making it simple to find, segment, and update listings, as well as print labels as needed.

To enlarge your mailing list, use a guest sign-in book at your performances and offer a giveaway (perhaps a refrigerator magnet with your ensemble's logo) for anyone who signs in. Be clear that people signing up with an e-mail address will receive your newsletter about future performances.

■

Most networking happens on a very casual basis. People meet at concerts, bump into old acquaintances, introduce them to the people they're with. When the conversation turns to, "so what are you up to these days?" you have to be ready to say, "I'm working on finding more performance opportunities for my ensemble, we've been looking to perform at community centers, schools, and churches. We're looking for more ideas and leads, so if you have any ideas, or people I should contact . . ." And usually, you get good suggestions! The more people you know, the more options you'll have.

I regularly meet with musicians to work on a résumé, bios, or other promotional materials to apply for grants or jobs. Typically, I ask how they found out about this opportunity. Easily 75 percent of the time, they got a lead on an opportunity from someone they know, a colleague or a mentor. Whether they thought of it this way or not, that's networking.

■

You Never Know

Calico Winds, a quintet based in LA (http://www.calicowinds.com), found their manager by networking. As members of Chamber Music America (http://www.chambermusic.org), they had sent an announcement to the CMA membership about an upcoming performance. The artist manager Lisa Sapinkopf got the notice. She'd previously heard good things about the group and had recently been looking for a "back up" group for possible bookings when another of her groups had a scheduling conflict. One thing led to another and Lisa ended up signing Calico Winds to her roster. So their mailing list—their networking—led to Calico Winds getting professional management.

■

Networking Basics ■

If you share useful information and leads with others, they will likely return the favor. Start your networking by first reconnecting with the people you already know. Sarah M., the vocalist, recently started her networking by calling three friends she'd performed with in the past. They were living in different parts of the country. They were glad to reconnect with her and were interested in what she was up to. They had no job leads to offer (yet), but were very interested in collaborating on her summer institute project and had ideas for finding grant money and commissions for composers to invite to the institute. They also had suggestions for other people she should contact for more leads. So Sarah is off and running.

Cultivate your contacts by getting to know them beyond their work lives. People love to talk about themselves, to give their opinions, so practice striking up conversations unrelated to the music industry, such as a new film, book, or a local hero. When Sarah reconnects with old friends and acquaintances, they don't just talk music or career issues, they talk about family, mutual friends, other interests. When she gets a new contact, she asks about mutual friends or similar experiences. She demonstrates genuine interest in people.

If someone gives you a lead, follow up on it. Send a handwritten thank you card and let them know what happens with the contact. Regularly check in with people; send congratulations notes, holiday cards, copies of articles they'd be interested in, to keep in touch. Sarah keeps in touch with many people by e-mail but when a friend or new acquaintance has gone out of their way to help, she sends cards and when appropriate, small gifts, or CDs.

Tool for Success: Your Business Card

Professionals carry business cards. These simple, inexpensive tools make networking easy. Business cards are a great alternative to giving someone your phone number on a soggy cocktail napkin, and work much better than trying to memorize an e-mail address on the fly. You can exchange business cards with new contacts in order to build your mailing list and network.

What goes on your business card? Your name and what you do (trumpeter, pianist, baritone, etc.), plus your phone number, e-mail, and website if you have one. You can choose a format with an attractive design and font, perhaps matching the letterhead you use on your other promotional materials (more on this in chapter 3). Check for Web sources for inexpensive business cards such as http://www.vistaprint.com and http://www.iprint.com.

Backstage Do's and Don'ts: People Skills for Postperformance Receptions

It's inescapable—at postconcert receptions and backstage after concerts, *all* musicians deal with networking.

Frankly, this is where musicians often behave badly. Some artists hate to go to their own concert receptions because they feel uncomfortable making small talk with strangers, with the audience members who come backstage to meet them.

How musicians view their audiences varies widely. Especially for classical musicians, there can be a cultural gap between performers and non-musician audience members. Classical musicians, perhaps because they spend all those hours alone in practice rooms, may be rusty or unfamiliar with social graces. If you spend all of your free time with other musicians you may feel awkward making small talk with nonmusicians.

At the worst extreme, I've heard musicians when talking among themselves, refer to their audiences with condescension, and a degree of contempt. As though these appreciative yet musically unsophisticated people were unworthy of their performance and of meeting with the musicians after the concert. It's sentiments like these that earn classical music the description "elitist." And though musicians wouldn't act or say these things openly to wellwishers, they think this way, and yes, people can sense their attitude.

A great contrast is the way singer/songwriters and contemporary folk artists interact with audiences. During concerts, the performers invite typically audiences to meet with them and sign CDs after the concert. I've been to showcases where folk singers say to the audience, with open sincerity, "I'd love to talk with you afterward" and explain where the reception will be.

Check your attitude. At the most basic level, music is about communication. Why do you want to perform? Isn't it about sharing something with the audience?

Not every audience is knowledgeable about your music, so not all post-concert wellwishers will use the correct musical jargon when they converse with you. Who cares? These people have made a positive connection with your music and with you. It's part of your job to help people connect to your music, and meeting with them is part of that job. People who attend concerts and love what they hear are naturally curious about the musicians, what they are like as people, what makes them tick. People go to receptions out of curiosity about the performers and to show their appreciation for the concert.

Non-musicians are often fascinated with instruments, with the details of how you trained as a musician, how you rehearse, what a typical day is like for a musician. They may be fascinated with the discipline, memorization, improvisation, or the onstage communication among ensemble members. This is an exotic world to them. Be prepared to entertain a wide gamut of questions.

After your own concerts, you need to accept compliments graciously no matter what you're thinking. You may be obsessing over, "I really screwed up that one section," or "my intonation/tempo/articulation was really #%&* in that movement." Don't share this with your wellwishers, don't dampen their enthusiasm. Don't quash the sense—for both them and you—of the appreciation of the performance as a whole. Remember, perfection only happens on recordings after much editing. Appreciate their congratulations.

If there's a reception, there may be people who'd like to have a conversation, more than simply thanking you for the performance. Show interest in your wellwishers, ask new acquaintances their names, if they play music, what else they do. It's not all about you; it's your job to hold up your end of the conversation. You may find a connection with people beyond the music, whether it's a non-musical interest, literature, theatre, visual arts, sports, and so on. The connections you make with postconcert supporters can lead down the road to developing an advisory board, fund-raising for special projects, and more.

If you are attending other people's concerts, and you'd like to congratulate them, yes, go backstage. It's wonderful for a performer to have people tell them, especially fellow musicians, what specifically they enjoyed about the performance. Don't just say, "Great job! I loved it!" It's very helpful for the performer, especially for an up-and-coming performer, to hear specifics, "I especially the loved the range of tone colors you used in the second movement" or "Your dynamic range is huge! I was so impressed by the effect of that incredible quiet section in the second work, you created such an atmosphere." Think what really struck you about the performance; tell the musician what were the stand-out moments for you, and why. They will appreciate it.

If you go to a concert of someone with whom you'd like to have a subsequent, in-depth conversation, you should go backstage, congratulate them, saying what specifically you found compelling and what specifically you admired in their performance. If you get a receptive response back from them, say, "If you have some time in the next few weeks, [or before you leave town] I would really like to speak with you briefly about . . ." The worst thing that can happen is they'll say they're too busy. They may say instead, you can e-mail me or call me, and here's my card.

Your backstage behavior is part of your professional image. If the performance was booked as part of a concert series, the presenter considers the reception an important part of the artist's engagement. Artists interacting well with the audience members, donors, and board members helps build goodwill and audiences, both for you and for the concert series.

Giving Good Phone ■

A surprising amount of work for musicians is carried on by phone: from booking and negotiating gigs, arranging rehearsals to acquiring students. Your phone technique is part of your professional image. It shows off your communications skills. In many cases, musicians make initial contacts with contractors, conductors, and presenters by phone. To check up on your phone habits, below are tips for phone success.

Your answering machine message should sound professional. What seems fun and cool to your friends may sound embarrassing in a business context. If you use your home number for any professional contacts, your message is part of your professional image. If you have housemates, get a voice-mail system with separate boxes for each of you so that you don't have to worry about missed messages.

Real Life: Craig B., a young musician, had an answering machine message with loud, unidentifiable and distorted music that went on far too long before you heard his voice, shouting, "Wha's up, wha's up!? I'm not here, you know the drill!" I'm quite sure Craig lost work because of his message. People calling him for a possible gig or teaching opportunity most likely wrote him off, assuming his playing and teaching would be as unprofessional as his voice-mail message.

When leaving messages, be concise, speak clearly, identify yourself and state your purpose for the call. If you tend to ramble, jot down a few notes before making the call. Make sure you leave your number and say it slowly: "Hello, this is Jane Smith, I wrote to you last week requesting an informational interview and am calling to follow up. I will try you again but here's my number, just in case: 617-555-1212. Again, it's Jane Smith and I look forward to speaking with you." Even if you are the one returning a call, leave your phone number anyway; it makes it easier for the other person.

Courtesy and respect go a long way. Especially if you are calling someone at home, ask, "Is this a convenient time to talk?" Offer to call back at another time if they sound harried or under pressure. And thank people for returning your calls, for answering your questions, for giving you contacts.

Even if you are frustrated with playing phone tag, don't take it out on the receptionist, and don't be testy in the message you leave. In trying to "cold call" busy people in administrative jobs, it's generally best to avoid calling on Mondays or Fridays and avoid calling first thing in the morning and at the very end of the day.

Check your phone voice—call into your own answering machine and leave a message for yourself. Listen back for volume, pitch and articulation. Ask a colleague for honest feedback.

What Constitutes Rude?

When placing a call, first greet the person, then identify yourself: "Hello, [or Good Afternoon], this is so-and-so. I'm trying to reach Ms. Smith." Telemarketers do the enthusiastic, "Hi Jane! How are you today?" routine before identifying themselves. That's rude.

More common sense reminders: phone use "don'ts" include:

- Don't chew gum while talking on the phone.
- No drinking or eating when you're on the phone.
- Turn your TV, radio, or CD player off.
- Don't use slang, or "colorful" language in business conversations.
- Don't work on the computer while you talk to someone—they can always hear it and it's insulting.
- And especially for you cell phone addicts: never take a phone call when you're in a face-to-face meeting with someone. Turn the phone off in restaurants and when you're in meetings.

Informational Interviewing ■

Let's say you want to meet with someone influential, perhaps someone who works in an administrative position. Perhaps you'd like to meet with someone who administers a grant program for musicians, or who books musicians for a concert series or festival, or who hires music teachers or performers to work in schools. If you don't know anyone who knows these people personally, how can you contact them?

The method to use for cultivating new contacts, people in influential positions, is informational interviewing. A structured form of networking, informational interviews are appointments you set up with a professional contact for the purpose of gaining information about the industry and increasing your contacts. It is *not* to ask for an audition, booking, or a job. But this personal contact may *lead* to a job, an audition, performance, etc. So it can be very worthwhile to invest your time in doing informational interviews.

Why would someone in an influential position want to take the time to meet with an up and coming musician? People like to be asked for their advice; it's flattering. Established professionals like to be asked about their careers and profession and often enjoy sharing their knowledge.

Informational interviews are especially helpful to those just leaving school, changing or contemplating a change of careers, and those moving to a new city. The informational interview is a tool to establish and expand your professional network so that you know the "right" people—the ones who can eventually refer a gig to you, offer you a job, or introduce you to other influential folks.

It's easiest to start your informational interviewing with the people you know: extended family, friends, current and former teachers, and colleagues.

Although you see these people often, you may not have had a real conversation about concrete ideas for advancing your music career. Make an appointment: this can be quite casual, a date for coffee or lunch. Prepare beforehand the particular questions you want to ask each person, tailor your questions to their expertise. Ask for suggestions and advice, and other contacts for networking. Think of this as practice for the meetings you'll do later with people you don't know.

At the very least, the meeting should yield two or three names of *new* contacts. Ask if you can use your initial contact's name when calling the new contact. You'll want to be able to say, for example, "John Doe suggested I contact you . . ." Once you have the referral, your initial contact may be by phone or letter. Ask for a brief appointment, twenty to thirty minutes, in order to ask questions and gather information about your area of interest. If your contact is very busy and has a high-visibility job, you may want to make the initial contact by letter.

Let's say you want to network with someone in the recording industry, maybe at a particular company. You ask everyone you know, your teachers, colleagues and you've checked with your alumni association, and you can't find anyone with a contact at this company. Can you still write a letter requesting an informational interview? Yes! Having a personal contact is great, but yes, professionals meet with people who simply write to them.

When writing an informational interview request letter, and in writing any professional correspondence, it's important to use standard practice business letter format (see example on the next page). Your letterhead goes at the top. Then the date, full name, title, and address of the person you're contacting. Use Ms. for women, since marital status is no concern in a business context (unless you know the woman prefers to be addressed as Miss or Mrs.). Fold your letter in thirds, use a standard business size envelope, and insert it so it opens with the letterhead on top. The envelope should have the mailing address and the return address both typewritten.

Nothing says "unprofessional" louder than letters with spelling or grammatical errors, or the wrong type of envelope, letters folded incorrectly, etc. Your first impression is being made with your envelope and letter. Take the same care with the details of your letter as you do with your music, because your correspondence represents you and your music. People will judge your music and professionalism on the materials you send them.

Here is a sample letter requesting an informational interview, shown with an explanation of the format. Each paragraph accomplishes a specific purpose, as explained in the sentences in bold.

After sending the letter, wait a week and then call. If your call is screened by an administrative assistant you can say, "I wrote to Ms. Borg last week and

Jane Smith, *musician/educator*
1 Main St. Boston, MA 02116 tel/fax (617) 555-1212 name@whatever.com

July 5, 2002

Liz Borg
Program Director
Young Audiences of Mass.
255 Elm Street, Suite 302
Somerville, MA 02144

Dear Ms. Borg:

The first paragraph should establish a connection to the reader through naming your mutual contact, and should establish why you are writing—to set up a brief meeting in order to gain information. Larry Scripp at New England Conservatory suggested I contact you for advice and information regarding arts education performance opportunities in K-12 schools. I would like to arrange a brief informational interview meeting at your convenience to gain from your knowledge and experience in the field. I've read the Young Audiences roster brochure and the information on your website. I'm very impressed with the range of programs and the artists you make available to schools.

The second paragraph should establish your credentials: highlight your most impressive, relevant experience and skills so that the reader will think it worthwhile to spend time speaking with you. I am an oboist and I teach at the Brookline Music School. My quintet has performed for after-school programs in Jamaica Plain and West Roxbury, as well as at two community music schools. I'd love to "pick your brain" to find out what you feel makes a good K-12 program and how you'd recommend we design and improve our school presentations.

The third paragraph should reassure the reader that you are not looking for a job, just feedback, that you will call next week and that you appreciate their help—be enthusiastic. I will call next week to see if we can arrange a brief meeting at your convenience. I would appreciate any advice you have to offer. I look forward to speaking with you.

Sincerely,

[Sign your name above your typed name]

Jane Smith

Sample letter requesting an informational interview

let her know I would be calling to follow up." *Always be polite and friendly to any assistant—they can either help you or hurt you.*

When you *do* reach the person, say, "Hello, this is Jane Smith; I wrote to you last week about an informational interview to get some insights from you about K-12 presentations. I'd really appreciate twenty or thirty minutes of your time. Do you think we might be able to meet in the next two weeks?"

Once you have your informational interview scheduled, some preparation will help you get the most of your appointment.

For in-person meetings, be clean and neat. This doesn't mean wear a suit, but you need to be taken seriously as a professional, so look the part. If you're meeting someone at their office, then wearing jeans and sneakers and a T-shirt is probably inappropriate. Maintain a businesslike posture and demeanor. Be conscious of time. Don't waste your time or theirs; only ask questions that you *really* want to ask. Thank your contact and then keep in touch!

How to Work a Room   ■

Picture this: you are attending a big postconcert reception at someone else's concert, or you're at a professional music conference such as Chamber Music America's annual conference in New York City. Whatever the specifics, you are faced with a room full of strangers and you think, "There may be some people here who would have useful career information or contacts or suggestions." But then you wonder, "How can I talk to strangers when my mother always told me not to?" Read on; here are a dozen tips to working a room.

1. Take time when you arrive to look around, get your bearings, and check who is there. Are there people you know? Where is the food and drink? Are there other people who came by themselves? You might want to strike up a conversation with one of them. Also look for conversation groups of three or more that you might join later. Don't worry about whom to talk with yet, you're just checking out the scene.

2. Notice your self-talk. What you say to yourself determines how you feel. If you're nervous, you may have these kinds of thoughts playing in your head: "This looks awful," "I wore the wrong thing," "No one looks friendly," or "I can't wait to get out of here." Replace these negative messages with positive and realistic statements. You can choose to think: "These are people I have something in common with; they are musicians and music lovers," "Other people here feel just as awkward as I do," "I may feel a little nervous but it doesn't show," or "This is an opportunity to make a new acquaintance, to have an interesting conversation."

   We make our own reality—what we tell ourselves determines how we feel and how we perceive. Do yourself a favor and keep your self-talk positive. This goes for networking as well as for performing!

Real Life: The Anacapa String Quartet, a Santa Barbara-based ensemble, ended up with a sponsor for their first CD through good postconcert schmoozing. It started with someone approaching them at a concert reception and asking if she could buy their CD. The quartet told her they didn't have a CD, that they didn't have the funds yet to record. Well, the woman liked the group so much she ended up eventually helping them finance their recording project!

---

4. Be open and friendly; people can sense your mood and your "approach-ability." Stand tall, and when striking up a conversation, make eye contact, smile. Don't sit—people will not approach you; you need to circulate. Hold your drink in your left hand and shake with your right to avoid soggy handshakes.
5. Don't assume that you are more ill at ease than your neighbor. You'll probably both welcome a bit of friendly ice-breaking conversation. A pleasant or wry comment about the weather, the food, your surroundings, or about the event you are attending may lead to an interesting conversation. For topics, play it safe: stay away from politics, religion, sexual innuendo, and colorful language. It may be easiest to strike up a conversation with someone in the reception line, registration line, or in a buffet/bar line.
6. Ask open-ended questions, like "What do you think about . . . ?" as opposed to yes/no questions. Be interested in the other person, ask questions that show your interest and understanding of the other person's area of expertise. When I'm in a buffet line with strangers, I often find myself asking those nearest, "What did you think about the . . . (performance, speech, workshop, etc.)" If you're in a line just checking in at the event, it's easy to ask the person nearest where they're from and how they heard about this event.
7. Approach only groups of three or more. Don't interrupt a twosome— it's likely to be a very personal conversation. Don't approach groups that appear to be long lost buddies in the midst of a reunion, or groups that appear to be listening intently to an involved anecdote. When you approach a group, stand a little of to the side, make eye contact with one person, and when there's a pause in the conversation, say, "Hi! May I join you?" and introduce myself. People wearing smiles and easy-going

body language are safe bets to approach. If someone doesn't make eye contact as you approach, keep on going. The only way to get good at this is by doing it.

8. Reintroduce yourself to people you've met before. Start with a familiar face. If you can't remember a name, simply say, "Hi, I'm Jane Smith, I think we may have met last week at another concert. And you are . . . ?"

9. If you find yourself talking to someone who seems to have latched on to you permanently and you want to escape, there are tactful exit lines to use. You can say, "Sorry, I need to find . . . [the phone, or the ladies room, or the person my friend told me to find here], it's been so nice to meet you!"

10. Exchange business cards only if there's a reason to follow-up. It's helpful to write a reminder to yourself on the back of the cards you receive, with where and when you met the person and what kind of follow-up is appropriate. I do this because otherwise I'll forget. If someone you've met has given you his or her card and said to call in a week to set up a meeting, then writing a note on the card will help remind you to do it.

11. Be realistic about networking. Don't expect a job lead or a performance opportunity to materialize after one chance meeting. A first meeting may be an opportunity to set up an informational interview, and this may lead to work or to other networking contacts. At a two-hour networking event, you probably should expect to talk to five to seven people and maybe have one or two substantive conversations.

12. Give good follow-up. If you say you'll call or send an article or leave a message for someone, do so. Your promise and your word need to be good. It's the mark of a professional.

Host a Brainstorming Party

There's one other great way to get more out of your network, by harnessing the brainpower of your closest group of supporters, your "success team." The popular author and career counselor Barbara Sher, author of *Wishcraft, Live the Life You Love* and *I Could Do Anything if I Only Knew What It Was*, is the birthmother of the success team approach. This involves forming a career support group that meets regularly, once or twice a month. Members give support, contacts, advice, and hold each other accountable for work they promise to do before the next meeting.

As a version of the success team approach, I recommend hosting a brainstorming dinner party. Invite five or six of your colleagues and friends whose opinions and perspective you value. These should be people who know you well and who are supportive of your goals. It's good if they are not all musicians (you'll get a wider perspective). It's best not to include your spouse or significant other because they often unintentionally inhibit the brainstorming. It can be hard for those closest to you to entertain a range of new ideas, since they have an investment in you, and your plans affect them directly. Most likely, you've discussed your career with your significant other; the point of the brainstorming is to hear *new* ideas. You're going to offer your "team" a nice meal but make it clear that after dinner you're going to put them to work picking their brains.

After clearing the dishes, you want to have people sit in a circle and have someone agree to take notes. The rules are there's no such thing as a bad or crazy idea and all suggestions get written down. You will give the group an issue, such as, "I want to be doing more performing locally, and I need suggestions" or "I want to start a local performance series" or something else you'd like to brainstorm. The trick is to not censor the ideas that will come flying. Suggestions that at first seem impossible or ridiculous often lead to some of the most creative solutions. Don't worry about cost or other issues that squash ideas, the important thing is to get the creative juices going. Don't interrupt with, "Yeah, but . . . " or "I already tried that" or "that won't work." You'll need to be quiet, even if you have to bite your tongue, to let the ideas flow. Afterward, you'll have pages of ideas and you may want to use other members of your network to help you move forward on these plans. You'll want to send thank you cards to your team and regularly update them on your project as you proceed.

In sum, networking is about connecting with people with whom you can share a wealth of ideas, resources, and experiences. Think of the connections with people as a way to build community. If it takes a village to raise a child, it takes a community to build a music career. You are now poised to expand your community through cultivating new contacts, people who may become trusted colleagues, friends, and mentors.

■ Suggestions for Moving Ahead ■

1. Do you have a list of your network? If not, start one. Include name, e-mail, phone, and postal addresses. These folks are your actual and potential supporters, audience following, potential contributors!

2. Do you have a mailing list (both print and e-mail)? This should be a version of your network list used for sending out invitations about upcoming performances. It should include your friends, colleagues, supporters, as well as media contacts. It's best to get your list on your computer, eventually in a database format so you can easily print out mail labels.

3. Who is the most appropriate person from your network list that you could arrange to talk with this week, to ask questions about next steps for your career? How about calling them?

4. Consider your postperformance interactions with people, at your own concerts and when you go to others'. What kind of postperformance impressions are you making? Do you accept compliments graciously? What kind of compliments do you give other musicians? How are you coming across as a person, beyond your performance? What kind of impression do you want to make?

5. Is there someone with whom you'd like to arrange an informational interview? These are often done with people who work in an administrative capacity (perhaps they administer a grant program for musicians, or book musicians on a concert series, or hire music teachers or performers to work in schools).

6. If you were to arrange to have a brainstorming party, who are the five to eight people you'd invite, your core group of supporters? (Include people whose ideas and suggestions you'd welcome, who know you well; include some non-musicians). What question would you pitch to the group?

7. Check out professional development opportunities in your area. Could you attend a conference or workshop that could advance your career and provide networking opportunities? Great places to check this out are: http://www.nyfa.org (the New York Foundation for the Arts Current listings) or your state arts agency or other relevant arts service organizations (see appendix).

8. Do you use a to-do list for the week? Keep it simple; I recommend giving yourself one to three career advancement tasks each week (such as phone calls, compiling a network list, writing letters for informational interviews). Write your list down and tape it to your frig, bathroom mirror, or your phone, any place you can't avoid it. You'll feel great each week when you complete these tasks and cross them off your list.

3

Building Your Image: Creating Promotional Materials That Work

Promotional materials are necessary tools for musicians. These materials are used in building a performer's reputation and for booking performances, attracting audiences, selling CDs, and more. The purpose of promotional materials is to tell the story of who you are and what your music is about. What story you tell and how you tell it matters.

Promotional materials include bios, publicity photos, CDs, and other specialty items to fit the situation such as letters of recommendation, reviews, listings of performances and repertoire, sample programs, and so on. CDs and websites, also promotional tools, are covered in later chapters. Like your career itself, your promotional materials are ever in a state of change. As your career develops, as you gain experience, you will add to and edit your materials. But you do need to start with good quality, usable materials.

Musicians use "promo" materials for a variety of purposes, in seeking bookings and press coverage for performances, and in contacting artist managers, conductors, record labels, as well as in applying for teaching jobs, competitions and grants. Promotional materials are typically sent in a packet referred to as a promo kit (and when sent to the press, as press kits).

The good news is that creating your own promo materials is not rocket science. It takes time and effort but you don't have to be a graphic designer, a publicity expert or spend a fortune to end up with excellent professional-quality materials. Musicians sometimes ask, "Can't I just pay someone to do all this for me?" And my answer is, when you learn how to create and use promo materials you are in the driver's seat with your career. You want to make informed decisions about the story being told about you and your music. Later on in your career, if you work with an artist manager, publicist, or record label, you will want to be an informed and savvy partner in all the decisions about your promotional materials, since after all, it's *your* career. Promotional materials are essential for professional work. It's critical that these materials are in top shape and that they positively highlight your qualifications and experience.

Letterhead ■

On all your promotional materials, you'll need your name, your instrument or voice type, and your contact information. On print materials and correspondence, this is arranged as letterhead, usually across the top of the page. Having a professional-looking letterhead and using it consistently with all your correspondence helps build your image.

Large corporations pay thousands of dollars to advertising companies to design logos for their products and letterheads for their correspondence. You may not have thousands of dollars to hire a top-notch graphic design team, but on your own, you can create a letterhead that looks professional and helps promote your career and your music.

Like a logo, a letterhead helps fix an impression of a company or product—in this case, you—in the reader's mind. Letterheads convey a certain "image" through the choice of font (or typeface, the design style of letters). Typefaces communicate all kinds of personalities and energies. If a picture is worth a thousand words, a font is worth at least seven hundred.

But you're a musician, not a graphic design expert, so how do you choose a letterhead? A good way to find a great look is to type your letterhead text (name, instrument, contact info) and then copy it using a variety of fonts. Computers come with packages of dozens of fonts and you can buy additional packages. Some are available free on the Internet (use a search engine, such as www.Google.com or www.Yahoo.com and type in "fonts" to find various offers). Every font has its own personality. Fonts can be every shade of conservative, elegant, traditional, and modern, quirky, or fun. Think about you and your music and what kind of professional impression you want to promote.

The trick is to see your name as a graphic design element. The particular design features of your name that different fonts will accentuate are: the initial capital letters, any letters that extend above or below the line (k, l, i, and p, g, j, etc.), and any repeating letters. This is why one font may look terrific in one name and not another.

In choosing which letterhead works best, it's not simply a matter of which is the most eye-catching, it's about which one best communicates the image you want to convey. Your letterhead should convey a sense of you as a professional and should be appropriate for all professional correspondence. A font that you might love to use for your wedding or party invitation or for a poster design may not be the best choice for your professional correspondence.

As an example, below are four possible letterheads for the same musician, with different fonts and page layouts. The same name, in four different fonts, reads like four very different musicians. What image is being conveyed in each? What adjectives would you use to describe each version?

For your own letterhead, think about what you want to convey about you and your music. What adjectives would you use? Print out various versions of your letterhead and show them to colleagues, mentors, and friends. Ask them which ones they like best and why. Getting a range of opinions will help you develop your critical eye and help you be more objective.

■

Tip: For your e-mail correspondence, use a signature, an automatic message that appears at the bottom of each message you send. Your signature should include your name, instrument/voice type, phone/fax, postal address, plus e-mail address and website hyperlink. For anyone who prints out an e-mail message from you, this simply makes it easier to get back in touch. People sometimes use attachments for their signature but then there are always those recipients whose computers can't open the attachment and the signature is lost. It's safest to use a plain font for the signature and to have it as an automatic text message at the bottom of your messages. Use color if you like, it will help distinguish your signature from the message, but stick to darker, most easy to read shades.

People sometimes use an inspirational or amusing quote or phrase at the end of their e-mail messages. My only caution is this: choose your quote or phrase very carefully. Is there a signature quote you want people associating with your name for every e-mail message you send? It is a part of your image, it works like an advertising tag line, the way the vacuum cleaner co. Bissell had "Life is messy; clean it up" and Apple used "Think Different." My friend and colleague at Berklee College of Music, Peter Spellman uses a quote from Benjamin Disraeli: "As a general rule, the most successful people in life are those who have the best information." This is a great quote for Peter since his work and passion is about connecting musicians with career information and resources and other people. It's best to steer clear of quotes implying any political, religious leanings or any jokes, since they may not be appropriate for the actual e-mail message you write above your signature.

■

Bios ■

A "bio" is a musician's marketing piece in the guise of a biographical statement, written in paragraph form. A bio is often the first information a club

> # Christine Taylor, soprano
> PO Box 411 • Your Favorite City, State 02222 • (999) 555-1212 email@hotmail.com
>
> ## Christine Taylor, soprano
> PO Box 411 • Your Favorite City, State 02222 • (999) 555-1212 email@hotmail.com
>
> ### Christine Taylor, soprano
> PO Box 411 Your Favorite City, State 02222
> (999) 555-1212 email@hotmail.com
>
> ## Christine Taylor, soprano
> PO Box 411 ◎ Your Favorite City, State 02222 ◎ (999) 555-1212 email@hotmail.com

Sample letterhead designs

owner or concert series presenter will have about a new musician or group. It needs to be compelling enough so that the reader is motivated to listen to the demo CD, or to consider the rest of the promotional materials. Audiences read musicians' bios in concert programs before the performer walks on stage. The bio should help the audience connect personally with the artist. No matter how bios are used, they are descriptive marketing pieces that manipulate the reader's impression of a musician. Like letterhead, bios make strong impressions, so the content, its order and writing style all matter.

John Blanchard, director of the Career Development and Alumni Affairs at Manhattan School of Music, offers this approach for writing bios:

"It's helpful to think of a bio as a 'call to action'—inspiring audiences to become loyal fans and ticket-buyers, inspiring concert presenters to book you for their series, inspiring ensemble leaders to engage you as a soloist, inspiring managers/agents to add you to their roster, inspiring club owners to hire you for their establishment."

Your bio should include your most impressive credentials such as where and with whom you've performed, special repertoire you perform, interesting projects, awards you've won, and where and with whom you've studied. Beyond these dry facts, a bio may include personal information, such as where you grew up and where you live now, and any distinctive information that illuminates what makes you interesting as a person and as a musician. A bio should be informative, descriptive, and engaging.

Your bio should present facts about you in the best possible light. It should create impact by celebrating and describing your accomplishments with specific details. For readers to be impressed, they need to be convinced of the credibility of the information; claims must be substantiated with details. For example, a general statement or description such as ". . . has won top prizes in major US competitions" must be backed up with details, such as ". . . including first prize in the ABC competition and second prize in the XYZ competition." For example, "Ms. Smith has performed recitals in New England and the Mid-West [general], on the ABC concert series in Cambridge, MA and the XYZ series in Chicago" [specific]. Or "John Doe's wide repertoire [general] ranges from Monteverdi to Harbison" [specific]. Without the specifics backing up generalizations, a bio lacks credibility. Without concrete examples, a bio reads like pure advertising or "hype."

Keep in mind that publications and concert programs needing your bio may have strict space requirements. It's helpful to have long and short versions of your bio to fit different situations, including a concise one paragraph version. Besides altering length, musicians often need to tailor versions of their bios to emphasize either ensemble performances, solo performances or teaching experience, depending on how the bio is to be used.

Tip: Musicians seem to have low self-esteem when it comes to working on their bios (no matter where they are in their careers!) They usually feel they don't have enough impressive things to list and find themselves comparing their accomplishments to those of others. We are often our worst critics.

As you read other musicians' bios, don't waste your energy comparing your accomplishments to those of others. Don't fret over not being further along in your career. Professional envy and competitiveness won't help get you where you want to go. Instead, as you read others' bios, focus on the technique used in constructing these.

As you read the examples on the following pages, notice the *order* the factual information appears in, and *how* the accomplishments are described. Ask yourself, where is the most impressive and interesting material? Does it grab me right at the beginning? How is the material organized? How does the piece flow? Is my interest maintained throughout? Is there something that should be cut?

As you become savvier about evaluating the effectiveness of promotional pieces, you'll develop a kind of internal interest-level tracking device, a kind of automatic EKG graph running in your head to track when your interest is piqued, is flat-lining, or taking a nose-dive. As you deepen your awareness of the effects of promotional descriptive writing, you'll become more savvy and effective with all your promotional efforts.

■

How to Write a Better Bio

Start by making a list. Include all the places where you've performed (name the concert halls and concert series, clubs, churches, festivals, etc.). List any awards you've won, degrees you've received, schools you've attended, and people with whom you've studied. List ensembles you've performed with and any impressive or influential people with whom you've performed. Think broadly and inclusively, listing all your experiences and accomplishments. List your recording projects, interesting and unusual repertoire you've performed, and your upcoming projects, such as performances or recordings planned for next season.

List any personal information that might help make your bio distinctive, such as where you were born, interesting places you've lived, unusual hobbies, unusual first musical influences, and so on. If you have good quotes from reviews, add these to the list. You can also use quotes from letters of recommendation as long as you have permission from the person you are quoting. Don't self-censor; don't leave out things you think aren't good enough for a bio. Now is the time to just get everything down; you'll weed out later. Don't worry yet about the order, or about making sentences, paragraphs or grammar—just make your list.

■

Tip: Musicians often leave out some of their best bio material. They either forget about performances and awards from years ago, or they assume that what they did back then is not relevant or impressive enough for their bio. Remember, how you think back on these experiences is not how the reader will view them. For help making the list, look back at concert programs you might have saved, old versions of a résumé, and scrapbooks your parents might have kept. If you can't remember where a particular performance occurred, or the name of an award you won, this is a great excuse to reconnect with friends and contacts who will help you remember.

Enlist your colleagues and friends to help with writing your bio. Musicians often overlook or discount some of their most impressive credentials. Your friends can remind you about your accomplishments and give you perspective on how an "outsider" views your credentials.

■

Tip: Most bios are boring! Your bio should explain what distinguishes you from other musicians of your genre. It should help the reader understand makes you tick, both as a musician and a person. In concert programs, the bio is a way to help the audience connect with you as a person, so look for interesting or quirky elements that you might include.

Next, to choose an opener for your bio, read over your list as though you are an objective "outsider." Circle the top three most impressive or interesting sounding items on the list. Bios should grab the reader's attention immediately. Your lead may be a group of impressive sounding awards you've won, or a quote, or a group of performances at well-known halls. It may be an unusual multi-media project you participated in, premieres of new works, or a research project that led to performances.

Here are sample bio openings, chosen as leads because they are the most compelling items for these musicians:

> Clarinetist John Q. Public has premiered over thirty works by composers such as Elliot Carter, Hans Werner Henze, Marc Anthony Turnage, Ralph Shapey, Michael Finnissy, Sydney Hodkinson, and Eric Mandat. With a repertoire ranging from Mozart, Beethoven, and Brahms to Corigliano, Boulez, and Ferneyhough, Mr. Public's eclectic and innovative programming is redefining the clarinet concert experience.

> Violinist Jennifer Liu made her solo debut at age twelve with the Chi-shien Symphony Orchestra in Kaohsiung, Taiwan, performing Bruch's Violin Concerto in g minor. Four years later she became the youngest soloist ever to appear with the Kaohsiung City Symphony Orchestra (KCSO), performing the Mendelssohn concerto.

> Boston Baked Brass first drew national media attention during the running of the one hundredth Boston Marathon, performing for the mid-race wedding of two runners. Since its inception in 2000, Boston Baked Brass has quickly established itself as a top-flight ensemble. The group has performed at Trinity Church, Longy School of Music, and at many of the area's finest hotels and reception halls for weddings and corporate functions.

Don'ts

- If you are still in school, you should NOT list this first. Your bio should present your performance credentials as a professional. If the reader is very impressed with all that you've done in the first paragraphs and then finds out you're still in school, they'll be that much more impressed.

- Do not write your bio in chronological order; it's boring! A bio is not your biography; it's primarily a marketing tool. If you can't grab the reader's interest right away, you've lost them.
- Avoid using sweeping statements. Don't overstate where you are in your career because people see through this easily. You need to follow up general descriptive statements with concrete details. If you use a phrase like "playing to rave reviews across the United States" the reader expects your bio to include numerous press quotes from well-known music critics from all corners of the country. If you do not deliver these, you've lost the reader's confidence and your credibility. If you write "has performed extensively throughout North America and Europe" you must list a range of venues (concert halls or series), their cities, states/countries where you have in fact performed. Readers are very attuned to advertising hype, and the concrete details assure them that you are indeed every bit as accomplished as you state.
- Avoid sweeping superlatives. You can't credibly rave about yourself, someone else must do it: use of quotes from reviews or letters of recommendation. Without substantiating quotes, do not write such phrases as "the beautiful tone and technical wizardry of this virtuoso flutist sets the standard" or "critically acclaimed trumpeter John Doe." As an emerging artist, stick to detailing what you've actually done, where you've performed, your repertoire, awards, projects, and personal information. In the end, these details are the most interesting and compelling information for the reader, who wants to find out about you, not read a string of adjectives.
- Don't use unattributed comparisons; it's unbecoming. Of course, comparisons are fine if they're from a review or from a respected and well-known mentor. But do not write comparisons yourself, do not use such types of phrases: "The best of his generation" or "The most promising and accomplished guitarist of the decade" or "Judged better than [insert names of your competitors]."
- Oboist Joseph Celli warns: never use the word "unique" in your bio! It's meaningless since *every* human is unique. The challenge of a bio is to specifically describe in what ways you and your music-making are distinctive.

After choosing your opener, see what similar items you can logically group together on your list. Depending on your list, you may group ensemble performances together, or awards and scholarships, or group the community-based performances for children or elders together. These "groupings" are what you'll make into paragraphs.

Next, write a draft that links your grouped list items into sentences and paragraphs. In referring to yourself, vary the writing by alternately using your full name, Ms. or Mr. So-and-So, and she or he. Use transition phrases to link one paragraph logically to the next. If the previous paragraph focused on solo experience, then the next might start with, "Active as a collaborative artist as well, Ms. So-and-So has performed with the ABC Quartet and the XYZ Trio at the 123 festival in Quebec." Other useful phrases: "Her recent [chamber music, jazz club, orchestral, opera, etc.] performances include . . . " and "Ms. XYZ has appeared as a collaborative artist and ensemble musician with [well-known artists so-and-so and you-know-who]."

Once you've edited your draft, proofread it carefully. Give your bio to at least two trusted colleagues and have them critique it. Don't send something off and later find embarrassing grammatical errors or typos when it's too late to correct.

■

Tip: Be careful how you handle dates in a bio. The years of every award, performance, scholarship, or degree you've won is simply not interesting to the reader. *When* things happened is nowhere near as important as *what* happened. Without listing dates you are free to describe your accomplishments in the order that tells the most compelling story about your career, without getting boxed in by chronological sequencing. Also, if you write "this season's engagements include" or "last season, she . . . " you are putting an expiration date on the usefulness of your bio. It's fine to be updating your bio regularly, but if you are planning to use a version of the bio on a more expensive flier, you want to get several seasons of use out of it. ■

What Makes You So Special?

The challenge for every musician's bio is to go beyond a simple listing of performances, awards, recordings, and degrees, to describe the particular qualities of your music-making. What do you actually sound like? What are the remarkable features of your music-making? What have people commented on? Ideally, a bio should paint a compelling word picture of how you sound.

An effective bio contains something distinctive or unusual that sticks in the reader's mind. It may be a degree outside of music that you received or are pursuing, perhaps a special research project, or perhaps a focus on particular and unusual repertoire. For the reader, this kind of feature helps make you distinct from other musicians, memorable and three-dimensional.

John Blanchard, the career guru at Manhattan School of Music, has this to say, "There are occasions when adding information about your hobbies and interests . . . are appropriate and might generate additional interest or press. If you decide to go down this route, here are some guidelines:

(inappropriate)	*(interesting)*
"Avid outdoorsman"	"200m Gold medal winner in the 1996 Mazda Swim Meet in Denver, Colorado"
"Likes to read"	"Has published an article exploring the influences of American 'beat' poets on 1960s jazz"
"Collects antiques"	"Is the proud owner of several vintage guitars from the Big Band era, including a 1939 Gibson L-5 . . ."
"Is married with three children"	". . . as a volunteer soccer coach, has led her son's junior high school team to two District titles"

What's so great about John's examples is that the improved versions include specific interesting details that are memorable. These kinds of quirky details can bring a description of a musician to life as a three-dimensional, multifaceted human being, not just a series of honors and performances.

Bio examples are shown on the following pages, for musicians at various career stages, with whom I've worked. Where can you read even more bios of emerging artists? Check the websites for Young Concert Artists, http://www .yca.org; Concert Artists Guild, http://www.concertartists.org; and the Chamber Music Society of Lincoln Center Two Artists (for emerging artists in two-year residencies) http://www.chambermusicsociety.org/artists/artist_list .php?type=cms2.

Photos ■

If you want to attract media attention and an audience for your concerts, you'll need a good publicity photo to go along with your bio. Photos are powerful communication tools. An effective publicity photo is one that makes a memorable, positive impression, and conveys the image you intend.

Presenters—the people who organize concert series and festivals—expect musicians to have photos ready to be used for posters, concert programs, and to send to newspapers to attract your audience. For singers, publicity photos are required (along with a résumé) at most auditions and for most competitions. For an ensemble, a good group photo accompanying their other promotional materials can make an immediate impact, conveying "we're professional."

Viviane Vocalist, Soprano

123 My Street #6 Our Fair City, MA 02115 (617) 522-9991 vvocalist@hotmail.com

In the Boston area, soprano Viviane Vocalist has appeared as a soloist with the New England Conservatory Chorus, the Boston University Women's Chorus, and the Boston University Collegium Musicum, performing repertoire ranging from Orff's *Carmina Burana* to the Bach *St. Matthew Passion*. Ms. Vocalist has also been featured on WCRB broadcasts as soloist and section leader with St. Paul's Cathedral choir. Her recital performances have included John Harbison's *Mirabai Songs*, the Bach *Coffee Cantata*, and the *Bachianas Brasileiras No. 5* by Villa-Lobos.

As a chorister, Viviane Vocalist has performed with the Choir of Trinity Church, the Boston University Chamber Singers, and the New England Conservatory Chamber Singers. Her choral repertoire includes Libby Larsen's *Billy the Kid* and Daniel Pinkham's *The White Raven*. She has performed in Symphony Hall, Jordan Hall, the Tsai Performing Arts Center, and Marsh Chapel.

Pursuing a strong interest in early music, Ms. Vocalist has studied and performed at the Austro-American Institute in Vienna. Based on her own manuscript research of composer Marianna Martines, a contemporary of Mozart, Viviane Vocalist produced a modern printed edition of a Martines cantata. Upon her return to the United States, Ms. Vocalist performed the Martines cantata at Boston University.

A native of Long Island, Viviane Vocalist is currently pursuing a Master's degree at New England Conservatory in Boston, studying voice with Carole Haber. Ms. Vocalist received her Bachelor's degree in music from Boston University, graduating *summa cum laude* and with departmental honors in Voice.

Ms. Vocalist's upcoming projects include a solo recital at New England Conservatory, solo appearances with the New England Conservatory Extension Division Youth Chorale, and a tour of England with St. Paul's Cathedral Choir. The cathedral choir, with Viviane Vocalist as a soloist, will be releasing a CD later this year.

Example of a biography

Second Wind Recorder Duo

Players Roxanne Layton and Roy Sansom
26 Flett Rd., Belmont, MA 02178
tel (617) 489-3906
dellalsansom@earthlink.net

The Second Wind Recorder Duo is noted for its virtuosity, musical insight, and wit. *American Recorder* praised Roxanne Layton's and Roy Sansom's performance as ". . . evocative, emotional, intense . . . the applause went off the gauge." Lloyd Schwartz of the *Boston Phoenix* described them as "stellar."

The Second Wind Recorder Duo explores repertoire from the Middle Ages to contemporary music, offering imaginative and inventive programming. Their concerts often include works by Chopin, Telemann, Poulenc, Machaut, Bartok, and C.P.E. Bach, as well as the players' original compositions and arrangements.

Since its inception, Second Wind has performed at the early music festivals in Berkeley (Calif.) and in Boston and on the Society for Historically Informed Performance summer concert series. Second Wind has toured the Southeast, performing in Atlanta, Jacksonville, Augusta and Durham, and has traveled to Australia to teach and perform for the Recorder Society of Western Australia and the Recorder Society of Tasmania. As a team, Roy and Roxanne have also appeared with the New World Symphony (in Miami), the Utah Opera, and the Boston Lyric Opera, among others. Both Roxanne and Roy are long-term members of the acclaimed Emmanuel Music, performing in their weekly Bach cantata series and they have both recorded for American Gramophone and Koch International.

Beyond Second Wind engagements, Roxanne Layton has appeared as soloist with the New Orleans Philharmonic and the Handel & Haydn Society Orchestra in Boston. With the *Mannheim Steamroller* she has toured extensively including appearances on both the *Today Show* and the *Tonight Show* on NBC and at two White House Christmas performances. Roy Sansom has performed with the Boston Pops Orchestra and the New York City Opera. His recordings include Bach Brandenburg Concerto No. 4 and Monteverdi's 1610 Vespers with Boston Baroque on Telarc Records. He has taught and coached for many workshops and seminars including Mountain Collegium, Pinewoods, and for the Institute for Historical Dance in Salzburg.

The Second Wind Recorder Duo is available for concert bookings, lecture-demonstrations, masterclasses, and ensemble coachings. For further information and a demo recording, call or write to address above.

Example of a biography

Dan Alias, Jazz Guitarist/Composer

1 Main #2 Boston, MA 02115 (617) 555-1212 dalias@email.com www.hiswebsite.com

A diverse musician, Boston-based guitarist and composer Dan Alias has appeared in a wide range of venues, from New York's CBGB's to Washington DC's Kennedy Center, and Boston's Jordan Hall. Other performances include appearances at the Banff Jazz Festival in Alberta, Canada, and the South by Southwest Independent Music Conference in Austin, TX. In recent years, Mr. Alias has performed as a member of the New England Conservatory Honors Jazz Ensemble, a select group chosen to represent the Conservatory to the public through a series of concerts in the Boston area.

Mr. Alias is also active as a performer and interpreter of contemporary classical music. He worked under the direction of composer Lukas Foss on a performance of his *Paradigm for Five Instruments* at the New England Conservatory. Upcoming projects include an orchestral performance of John Cage's *Cheap Imitation,* under the direction of Stephen Drury, to be premiered locally at Boston's Jordan Hall. A recording of the work is to be released on Mode Records CD series, *The Music of John Cage.*

Dan Alias is currently completing an undergraduate degree in Jazz Studies at New England Conservatory in Boston. He has studied privately with artists such as Mick Goodrick, Danilo Pérez, Jerry Bergonzi, and Charlie Banacos. Dan Alias has been coached in ensembles with George Russell, Cecil McBee, and Allan Chase. He has performed in master classes with guitarist John Abercrombie and bassist William Parker. Dan Alias graduated with a Bachelor's degree in Sociology from the University of Miami, Coral Gables, FL.

Example of a biography

Publicity or "press" photos are also often referred to as "headshots," although instrumentalists need to include more than their heads! Your instrument(s) need to be at least partially included. The standard format is 8x10" black-and-white photo, in a glossy, pearl, or matte finish.

Tip: Newspapers these days are using more and more color, so having both color photos (in slide or print form) and black-and-white photo prints may be advantageous. Sometimes newspaper editors choose which concerts to highlight, in their "pick of the week" calendar sections, on the basis of which artists performing that week have the most unusual or engaging color photos.

What Does a Photo Communicate?

Photos give the viewer an immediate and often lasting impression of a musician, an impression of their personality and their musicianship. An effective publicity photo might communicate that an artist is professional, interesting, intelligent, sensitive and accessible. However, less effective photos can communicate a negative and inaccurate image. We've all seen bad publicity photos that make an artist seem amateurish, hesitant, stiff, vacuous, or just dull.

It's not about looking like a fashion model; it's not about glamour or sex appeal. Although your photo should be appealing, publicity photos for musicians primarily need to communicate to the audience what you actually look like (on a good day), as well as who you are as a musician and what your music-making is like.

The Adjective Exercise

To get savvy about effective photos, try this exercise. When looking at other musicians' photos, ask yourself what you imagine, based on the photo, the performance will be like. What adjectives come to mind? (Intelligent, introspective, fun, engaging, confident, professional, fresh, or honest ? Or on the not so positive side: inexperienced, distant, maybe empty-headed?)

For the prospective audience or artist manager or conductor who first sees the photo, they're making assumptions about your performance based on your photo. An effective photo communicates something distinctive and positive about the performer's musical personality. It's not about glamour; it's about the music.

---

short

On the next pages are samples of musicians' publicity photos, two by the Boston photographer Susan Wilson (http://www.susanwilsonphoto.com), and a photo of Imani Winds by NYC-based Jeffrey Hornstein (http://www .jeffreyhornstein.com). Looking at these photos, what adjectives would you use to describe the sense you get of the musical personalities? What image is being communicated?

Choosing a Photographer

Make sure you choose a photographer whose work you admire. Find someone who specializes in publicity photos, as opposed to one who does yearbook photos, babies, weddings or "glamour" shots. Your photographer needs to know the business—what's current, what's appropriate. Photos for jazz, folk, rock, rap, new age, and classical musicians are not all the same. You may conservatively want to find a photographer who works regularly with musicians in your genre. Or you may, as a string quartet, want to purposefully choose to get the look of a punk rock or avant-garde jazz group. Be clear and go for the photographer who has done the kind of work you want. For referrals, ask your music colleagues or teachers. When you see a musician's publicity photo you like, look for the photo credit to get the name of the photographer.

Once you've gotten some referrals for photographers, check out their work on their websites or visit them to check out their portfolio of work. Make sure you see examples of the type of photo you want. When possible, talk with the photographer to see whether you'd feel at ease working with this person. A good photo reveals your genuine personality and you'll need to feel at home with your photographer to capture this on film.

Do you have to hire a professional photographer? Musicians often ask me this; they want to save money by using an amateur photographer—a relative, friend, or colleague who may be good but is not a pro. If you are planning on using photos for publicity purposes, it needs to be convincing as a professional marketing piece. Good professional publicity photos have a specific look, the result of years of photographers' training and experience. Can people tell the difference between a professional quality publicity photo and something less than? Yes, absolutely. You want to work with a photographer experienced with professional music publicity work. It's a smart investment.

Cost

For a photo shoot in Boston, as of 2004, prices were $250–$700, although so-called photographers of the stars charge over $1,000. Make sure you know

Thula Ngwenyama, violist. Photo by Susan Wilson (www.susanwilsonphoto.com)

Sanford Sylvan, baritone.
Photo by Susan Wilson
(www.susanwilsonphoto.com)

Imani Winds. Photo by Jeffrey Hornstein (www.jeffreyhornstein.com)

what your session fee covers. Items and services included in the "basic fee" vary and hidden costs can add up. Discuss all costs and fees in detail in advance to avoid confusion and misunderstandings. Remember that according to U.S. copyright law, the photographer—not you—owns the negatives and the rights to the images taken.

The photographer should take a minimum of one hundred pictures of you with diverse poses and angles, preferably more for ensemble shots. The more pictures your photographer takes, the more choices you'll have on the contact sheets to find the best shots. Check on how many rolls of film will be shot, film charges, and how many finished 8x10s are included in the fee. Ask if retouching is included in the fee, and for recommendations for help with hair or make-up if needed.

Preparation

A good photographer will begin the session asking you questions to help you get your desired results. Your photographer should know how you plan to use the photos, (for a CD cover, for the media, and for posters), what professional image are you looking to convey, and what kind of music you do. Make sure you've thought all this through and that you communicate it clearly. By talking with you before shooting, the photographer will also be getting a sense of you as a photo subject; this is important in determining how best to photograph you.

After deciding on the types of photographs needed, make decisions about the clothes, hair, make-up and jewelry for the shoot. Come prepared with ideas about lighting, mood and style considerations. Remember that each of these "minor" details will be reflected, good or bad, in the shots you get.

To understand how your photo will be viewed against your competition, it's important to get a sense of what standard publicity shots are like for musicians in your genre. You can find current music publicity shots in *Musical America* (http:\\musicalamerica.com), the music industry annual directory. See the publicity photos printed in your local newspaper's calendar section, and peruse the flyers and brochures of professional concert series. Bring to your shoot the samples of publicity photos or photocopies of photos you like for their mood, composition, lighting, and so on.

Tip: Susan Wilson, one of Boston's top musicians' photographers, recommends bringing to your shoot "reference shots." Bring photos of yourself that you love or hate and be able to explain why. This is so your photographer will know that you hate how your nose looks from a certain angle or that you're self-conscious about your chin. If your photographer knows what you're after, you'll have a much better chance of being satisfied with the results.

She also recommends, before the shoot, making a list of adjectives that describe the YOU that you want to appear in the picture (whether it's fun, accessible, serious, self-assured, whatever). Know how you want to come across. The photographer can't read your mind; you need to communicate the image you want your photo to convey.

Consider shooting for two types of photos, one formal and one less so, with changes of clothing, lighting, and mood. It can be helpful to have several good photographs for multiple uses: with CDs, programs, posters, flyers, and sending to newspapers.

What to Wear

Remember that the bright colors that flatter in color film will photograph as grays when shot in black and white. Bring several changes of clothes—two formal (one all black) and one semi-casual. Make sure your outfit projects the desired impression you want. Get advice on your attire from your photographer and experienced musicians.

Wear clothes that you'd actually wear in performance and for your casual shots, wear clothes that are representative of your casual wear. Stick to solid colors, especially black, which is flattering to most people. Keep it simple; your publicity photo is not a fashion statement. Keep jewelry to a minimum, so that it doesn't distract attention from your face. Take watches off!

The "you" in your photos should be consistent with how you appear when you perform. If you always perform with glasses, you should wear them in your photo. Your photographer will have a much easier time if your glasses are nonglare or if you come to the shoot prepared to pop out the lenses during the shoot. And if your photo is more than five years old, it's time for a new one.

Although many women have a professional do their makeup for a photo shoot, keep in mind that your photo should help you be easily recognizable. So beware of the extreme makeup treatment; people should be able to recognize you if they see you on the street in casual clothes and no make up.

Do's and Don'ts for Your Photo Shoot
- Before your photo shoot, get a good night's sleep.
- Get everything ready the night before (clothes chosen, cleaned and pressed), so that the day of your shoot is a breeze.
- Give yourself plenty of time to get to the shoot and have a stress-free morning before your shoot so that you won't be distracted or tense during the shoot. The camera reads what's on your face and it's usually whatever is on your mind.

The Day of, Bring:
- Comb and brush
- Lip balm (helps to keep your lips from sticking to your teeth while you smile)
- Powder from a compact (handy to cover the shine on your nose; your photographer is going to use a lot of lights on you)
- If it helps in relaxation, ask your photographer if you can bring a friend or CDs to play during the shoot.

During

Make sure your facial expression and pose is consistent with who you are as a performer and person. For example, a sexually alluring expression and pose may look great, but make sure that your photo does not misrepresent you as an artist and the kind of music you make.

Tip: What you are thinking about during the shoot directly effects your facial expression; you need to have something going on behind your eyes. As a performer, your photo needs to convey that you have interesting stories to tell through your music. Janice Papolos, author of the terrific resource, *The Performing Artist's Handbook*, recommends thinking of loved ones, favorite memories, or a juicy secret, to evoke real feeling, enthusiasm, warmth, and humor.

After

Depending on how busy your photographer is, it may take a week or two after the shoot before you can pick up your photo contact sheets. These are sheets with dozens of one-inch sized photo proofs from your shoot. Ask your photographer to mark the shots she or he recommends you consider using, either before or after you've had a chance to look them over. It can be difficult to be objective, so make the most of having expert advice.

Once you've chosen the best from the contact sheets, your photographer will make a "master," a final product, an 8×10″ photo. This is your original that you can take or mail to photo reproduction shops specializing in quantity photos for discounted rates. Look for package deals for less than $2 per 8×10″. Ask your photographer for referrals. Your photographer can also most likely give you electronic versions of your photos for use on your website and for sending by e-mail.

Finishing Touches

At the photo reproduction shop, you'll need to decide on several details. Glossy, matte, and pearl finishes are all fine for use with print media; it's a matter of personal preference. Other choices include whether or not to have border margins on your prints and about having your name, instrument, and or contact info "stripped" into the photo, for immediate identification.

By stripping text into a bottom margin, you make it easy for a viewer to immediately connect name and face and it will not interfere with the photo itself for reproduction in newspapers or other media. To "strip in" text, simply give the photo reproduction shop a copy of your letterhead or simply laser print your name in the font of your choice, so they can copy the font to fit below your photo, for reproduction in all your prints. Your name is the minimum you'd want stripped into the margin; singers of course need to list their voice type, and some musicians choose to include their complete contact info in the margin. When you send out your promotional materials, they will inevitably become separated from each other. If a concert presenter, club manager, or a journalist can't connect a loose photo with the rest of your materials, it won't get used. A photo of an anonymous musician does no one any good. Your photo(s), the same as all your promotional pieces, must also have all your relevant contact information. Beyond your name, additional necessary information can be printed on a sticky label and affixed to the back of the photo (writing directly on the back of the photo will damage it!).

Essential Information to Include on Your Photo
(Either Stripped in on Front or on the Label on the Back)

- Your name and instrument, voice type, or ensemble name (as you describe yourself on your letterhead)
- Contact address (yours or a booking agent or manager's)
- Telephone number / fax
- E-mail and website (if available)
- Other relevant information: publisher or record label, if applicable.
- Photo credit: the name of your photographer (i.e., "Photo: Susan Wilson").
- Just as you would expect to read the names of musicians performing on a CD, and the composer of any piece performed, the photo credit says who did the photographic artwork.

Promo Kits ■

With a bio and photo, you have the beginnings of a promo kit. The other crucial item, a demo CD, will be covered in the next chapter. Beyond these basic items, musicians use a range of other promotional materials in their promo kits according to the particular situation. Promo kits are sent to concert series presenters, conductors, artist managers, record labels, members of the press, and in applying for grants and teaching jobs. Each promo kit you send should be tailored to the specific recipient's interests. And as you gain more experience, you'll acquire and create more items from which to choose for use in your kit. Each piece in your kit should be laser-printed on quality stationery with your letterhead on top.

■
Tip: Get feedback on your materials from your colleagues and acquaintances before sending them out. Don't create your kit in a vacuum. You'll need to compare your materials to others' to gain perspective. If you have not seen musicians' promo

kits, ask your teachers, colleagues and local presenters to view examples. If your music school has a music career center, they probably can show you samples.

Promo Kit Basic Contents

- *Bio*
- *Publicity Photo*
- *CD*, either a full length CD, or a CD demo sampler, burned on your computer

The Extras: Other Promo Kit Item Options ■

In choosing which additional promo kit items to create and use, think of the anticipated recipient. Are you assembling materials for a competition, fellowship application, or for local performance opportunities? What information would be most useful and impressive to provide, given your purpose, background, and existing materials?

> *Letters of Recommendation:* These can be extremely helpful when you're first getting started. Ask your teachers, coaches, conductors, and mentors if they'd feel comfortable writing you a general letter of recommendation. One way to go about this is to ask for feedback on your demo CD. If they're enthusiastic, ask if you might be able to get a quote from them or a letter for your kit. If you've performed on a community concert series or at a festival, and the presenter and the audience response was enthusiastic, ask the presenter for a letter. A strong letter of recommendation from a fellow presenter can be a powerful incentive for other presenters to consider booking you.
>
> *Quote Sheet:* Once you've acquired a number of letters of recommendation from presenters, teachers, or conductors, you may want to use the best portions of these as quotes on one sheet. A few quotes can be used in your bio, but if you have more they can be put together on a separate sheet. I've found that musicians often have difficulty deciding which are the best sound bites to use for a quote sheet. Get advice and suggestions from colleagues who can be more objective. Make sure you get permissions from any individual first before using their letter or quote for your promotional materials.
>
> *Repertoire List:* To give the reader a sense of the breadth of experience and choices for performances, classical musicians use repertoire lists (nonclassical musicians call these "play lists"). This is simply a list of the composers and titles of works you've performed and have avail-

able for future performances. Works are typically listed alphabetically by the composer's last name in the left hand column, with the titles of works to the right. Works can be separated into categories by genre, period, style, and instrumentation.

It may be helpful to have either several categories or separate lists titled "Solo, Chamber, and Concerto Repertoire." Singers may want to use categories such as "Art Songs, Arias, Operatic Roles," or for strictly recital repertoire, to divide the list with categories by language. Composers list their own works, under "Original Compositions," or "Selected Original Compositions" and "Arrangements" if applicable.

Rep lists are also used in applying for competitions, festivals, graduate schools, grants, and teaching jobs. Rep lists are also helpful to musicians themselves, since having an accurate record of past work helps in making plans for future projects and repertoire. Sometimes after making rep lists, musicians will see that they've got some gaps in their repertoire, and this will lead them to exploring new or more diverse repertoire.

A variation of a standard rep list is a version that lists the repertoire available just for the coming season. Such lists can be titled, with the appropriate date: "Repertoire Available: 2005" or some musicians simply detail the full programs available.

Available Concert Programs can be the title of another promo kit item, titled with the appropriate year you are offering them. This is a listing of the concert programs you are offering presenters this season. Interesting programming can be one of the best ways for emerging artists to win over a presenter unfamiliar with their work. Perhaps you have some interesting thematic programming to offer, a premiere of a new work, or you are collaborating with another artist, or are offering programs based on your new CD. If you are including premieres of new works or any unusual repertoire, it may be helpful to include timings.

Recent Engagements can be the title for a list of where a soloist or ensemble has performed. These can be listed without dates, and placed in order of what's most impressive, detailing where the performances took place, the name of the concert hall, concert series, festival or other venue, with the city, state, as well as country, if outside the United States. A variation of this list is upcoming engagements already booked for this season. Such a list can be titled with the appropriate date: "Engagements: 2005" Or, for another twist, provide a listing of the previous season's bookings. The idea is for the presenter to be able to quickly get a sense of the artist's track record and level of experience.

When you're just getting started, you may not want to use these lists. That's fine, just keep it in mind for later, as your career progresses.

Concert Programs or flyers from past performances: A group of these can be especially impressive if they are from performances that were presented in several different states or countries.

Press Reviews and articles written about you or your ensemble. If you have had any favorable print media attention, it's impressive to include photocopies of these pieces in your kit. People who book concerts want to know whether or not you can draw the attention of the media. Reviews can be hard to come by but there are other types of newspaper pieces you can include. Consider including any preview articles that were printed in advance of concerts you gave, or any congratulatory notices of a scholarship, grant, or competition you have won. Include any human interest pieces where you were interviewed or quoted, whether it's for your work as a musician or for other community work (an unusual hobby, or anything else interesting and positive). Any positive press clipping is worth considering for your promo kit.

To present these pieces well in your kit, you need to carefully cut out the original article and the masthead of the newspaper, which identifies the name of the newspaper, its location, and the date the piece was printed. You can then separately enlarge or reduce the masthead and the news piece to create a balanced presentation on an 8 1/2×11″ sheet of paper to make your "master" copy. Newsprint fades, so make a great master copy from which you can make additional copies for your kit. If the piece mentions several performers, you will want to direct the reader to the most relevant portions. Use a light-colored highlighter sparingly on each photocopy (not on your master) to direct the reader to the most impressive and relevant parts.

Press Quotes or Review Excerpts can be the heading for a list of the most impressive things that have been written *in the media* about you. You must list the publication's name and you should also include the reviewer's name if they're well known. If the dates are impressive, because they are recent or because they show a consistent track record, include them; otherwise, leave the dates out. If you are mixing review quotes with quotes from recommendations (described earlier under "quote sheet"), do not label the sheet "Press Quotes." Instead, label it simply, "Quotes" or "What People are Saying."

Workshop topics and descriptions can also be included in your kit. Concert presenters may view workshops and master classes as bonus items in addition to a formal performance. These days, presenters are particularly interested in booking artists who will offer lecture-demonstrations, pre- or postconcert talks, master classes or other community engagement activities. Presenters are in the audience development business. It's in your interest to offer ways to help them attract an audience to your performance.

Extras Beyond the Kit

Ensembles may want to think of other promotional items for giveaways or sales at performances or for sale on the group's website. The Zephyros Woodwind Quintet's website (http://www.zephyrosquintet.com) offers mugs and t-shirts with an attractive logo to their fans. Other groups sell or giveaway their logo-bearing memo pads, refrigerator magnets, bumper stickers, and baseball caps. The purpose of these items is to build name recognition and to strengthen fans' connection to your group, while at least breaking even if not making a small profit. Rock groups do this. Why not you?

Putting It All Together

After you've created your individual promotional pieces, you will need to assemble these as a kit for mailing or giving to various contacts. You can organize your materials in a two-pocket folder, available at most office supply stores. On the front, you can design a label with your name and instrument or voice type, use your business card as a label, or glue a copy of your flyer on as a label. If the folder has slots for it, you can insert your business card inside on one of the pockets.

These folders are bulky, so if at this point you have only a few items for your kit, it can work better to create an inexpensive flyer using a great photo and your (or your group's) name, and simply staple on your supplemental materials: your full bio, quote sheet, rep or performances list, letter(s) of recommendation, and so on.

Flyers

As an additional promotional tool, flyers or brochures can be produced in a variety of ways for a range of costs. Most artist management companies use 7×10″ glossy flyers to advertise their artists. Generally, flyer fronts have an interesting and inviting photo of the artist(s) with the name of the group or voice type, and a few of the artist's best quotes. On the reverse, flyers often include a brief bio, more quotes and possibly another photo—less formal than the one on the front. The costs for such a flyer depends on how many you print, the number of colors used, number of photos, type of paper, and the costs for graphic design. The terrific book *Making Music in Looking Glass Land* by Ellen Highstein, published by Concert Artists Guild, includes a ballpark budget for the costs of producing flyers. For 2,500 four-color flyers, the cost breakdowns shown are $1,500 for photography, $400 for design, and $1,200 for printing, for a rough total of $3,100. Less expensive flyers can be created using desktop publishing programs, scanning in your photos, and using a color copier. Using a graphic artist friend or perhaps a graphic art student from a local school can also save you money.

For mailing your press materials, if you are not using a folder, you'll need to place rigid cardboard in an envelope with your photo or CD to ensure they aren't damaged in the mail.

The following pages show sample additional promo kit items: rep lists, recent engagement lists, as well as a quote sheet, sample programs, a workshop topics list. You may not have or need all these items. Remember, your promo kit should be tailored to your specific purposes and to the recipient's interests. Don't worry if you don't have press quotes, or other items yet, because you can get these in the future. The point is to make the most of what you have now and to present yourself professionally.

Summary

How you present yourself matters! Invest the time and effort it takes to make your promotional materials reflect your professionalism and artistry. In many cases your promotional materials will precede an audition, a meeting, a phone call, an opportunity. Make a great first impression, so that your total presentation—your artistry, interpersonal skills, materials, and professionalism—are all consistently attractive.

■ Suggestions for Moving Ahead ■

1. Do you have a letterhead? If yes, what kind of impression does it make? Ask friends, colleagues. If no, design several versions on your computer and print these out. Ask friends for feedback.
2. Do you have a bio? If yes, who is the intended reader? Is it geared toward concert programs, club managers, presenters, or CD liner notes? If you have a bio, you may want to work on several different versions for various situations. If you do not have a bio or would like to improve yours, follow the easy directions and then show your draft to colleagues and mentors for feedback.
3. Compare and contrast two or more bios of professional musicians, soloists or ensembles. This can be helpful especially if you choose

Carl Troubadour, Trumpeter

1 Main St. • Boston, MA 02116 • (617) 555-1212 • name@whatever.com

Trumpet & Piano Repertoire

Damase, J.M.	Hymne
Enesco	Legend
Hindemith	Sonata
Honegger	Intrada
Kennan, K.	Sonata
Peeters, F.	Sonata

Trumpet & Organ Repertoire

Damase, J.M.	Trois Pièces Sans Paroles
De La Lande, M.R.	Suite
Hovhaness	Prayer of Saint Gregory
Pinkham	Psalms
Sampson, D.	The Mysteries Remain

Trumpet & Soprano Repertoire

Aldrovandini	De Torrente
Bach	Cantata 51
Bassani, G.B.	Quel Che Dice
Conrad, L.	The Chariot
	The Path
Handel	Eternal Source of Light Divine
	Let the Bright Seraphim (Samson)
	Revenge
	The Trumpet's Loud Clangor
Melani, A.	"All'Armi, Pensieri"
Plog, A.	Two Scenes
Purcell	Thus the Gloomy World
	Trumpet Song From Messaniello
Scarlatti	Seven Arias
	Su Le Sponde Del Tebro
	Vaga Cintia

Example of a repertoire list

Sarah Songster, singer/songwriter

Recent Engagements, New England

Clubs, Massachusetts
Club Passim, Cambridge
Colonial Inn, Concord
Kendall Café, Cambridge
Kevin's Café, Pepperall
Old Vienna Kaffeehaus, Westborough
Plantation Club, Worcester

Bars / Restaurants / Coffeehouses (New England)
Café Pierrot, Milford, NH
The Courtyard, Manchester, NH
Coyote's, Framingham, MA
Dolphin Striker, Portsmouth, NH
Hermanos, Concord, ME
Jerky's Café, Providence, RI
The Pickle Barrel, Killington, VT
The Rock, Newport, RI
Sugarloaf Lodge, Sugarloaf, ME
Wellesley Inn, Wellesley, MA

Theaters
The State Theater, Portland, ME
The Ioaka Theater, Exeter, NH
The Strand Theater, Providence, RI
The Music Hall, Portsmouth, NH

ABC Artist Management, 1 Main St. Boston, MA 02116
contact John Doe: tel/fax (617) 555-1212
jdoe@whatever.com

Example of a recent engagements list

Second Wind Recorder Duo

Players Roxanne Layton and Roy Sansom
26 Flett Rd., Belmont, MA 02178
tel (617) 489-3906
dellalsansom@earthlink.ne

"The applause meter went off the gauge . . . their personalities also helped set in relief the lines of a duo by Telemann and shaped the evocative, emotional, intense Xylophobia . . ."
– American Recorder

"Roy Sansom and Roxanne Layton, recorders, made the piece [Bach Brandenburg Concerto #4] sound much easier than it is and negotiated the high tessitura without a hint of shrillness."
– Boston Globe

"The recorder players [in the Boston Early Music Festival Orchestra] were particularly fine."
– Wall Street Journal

". . . stellar . . . sexy recorders (yes, recorders, especially in their undulating introduction to the duet of the two sirens . . .)"
– Lloyd Schwartz, Boston Phoenix

"What Second Wind has, in fact, is a rich blend of exquisite technique and diverse repertoire stretching from 14th century dances to Sansom's own compositions and arrangements."
– Middlesex News

Example of a quotes list

Reinmar Seidler, cellist

P.O. Box 548, Boston, MA 02130 • (617) 524-2736 • reinmar.seidler@umb.edu

Program 1

Solo Cello Spanning 3 Centuries

2 Ricercari, for cello solo (1689)	D. Gabrielli
Ricercar in C Major	
Ricercar in d minor	
Suite No. 5 in c minor, for cello solo (ca. 1720)	J.S. Bach

intermission

Suite No. 1 for Solo Cello (1964)	Britten

Program 2

Fables and Fantasies for Cello and Piano

Fantasiestücke	Schumann
5 Stücke im Volkston	
A Fairy Tale	Janacek
Capriccio	Foss

intermission

Variations on *"Frog He Went a' Courting"*	Hindemith
Serenade	Henze
Tango, Boogie, and Grand Tarantella	S. Hodkinson
Sonata	Britten

Example of sample programs

Reinmar Seidler, cellist

P.O. Box 548, Boston, MA 02130 • (617) 524-2736 • reinmar.seidler@umb.edu

Selected Workshop Topics

Baroque Performance Practices for the Modern String Instrumentalist

An introduction to the various musical tastes and styles of the Baroque era, designed specifically for players of "modern" instruments. Includes the art of Rhetoric—music as "text"—the functions of music in Baroque society, Baroque musical architecture, contrasting national styles, ideals of sonority, and an introduction to 18th century ornamentation.

The Healthy, Happy Cellist—Techniques for Healthier Playing

Discover how physical "tension" differs from energetic expression. Explore ways of integrating rhythm more deeply into the whole body, and how to let musical shapes guide physical response patterns. Clarifies the false dichotomy of "technique" versus "musicality." Specific practice methods are shared for changing habits that can make players uncomfortable.

The Compleat "Basso Continuist"—Baroque ensemble playing for cellists

Explore the musical architecture of 17th and 18th century repertoire and its special demands on the continuo player. Develop a sensitivity to harmonic progression and tonal function in order to shape bass lines powerfully and expressively. Examine both ensemble and solo repertoires.

Music, Politics, and the Visual Arts in Postrevolutionary Mexico

Multimedia presentation relates the "social-realist" painting, architecture and mural work of Diego Rivera, Jose Clement Orozco, and David Alfaro Siqueiros to the symphonic and chamber music of Silvestre Revueltas and Carlos Chavez. Together they forged a vivid and politically-charged artistic identity for the new Republic in the 1920s and 1930s, using folk elements and consciously non-European techniques.

Example of workshop list

up-and-coming musicians, people maybe just a bit further along in their careers than you are at this point. You can find musician bios on their websites. In reading these bios, ask yourself what works well about the way the information is put together. Which bio do you think is more effective, more compelling, and why? What do you imagine a non-musician audience would find most interesting in each? What do you imagine a concert series presenter would find most compelling in each?

4. Compare and contrast two or more musician photos. Use ones you find in your local or regional newspaper, announcing upcoming performances. Which do you like best and why? What does each communicate about the soloist or ensemble and their music?

5. Do you have a photo? If so, ask your colleagues and mentors if they think it works well for you. Ask them what they think the photo conveys about you and your music or what adjectives they'd use in describing the impression it makes. And for your next publicity photo shoot, what qualities would you like your photo to communicate about you and your music? Use four specific adjectives.

6. Are you keeping track of the repertoire you've performed and where you've performed it? If not, make a draft of your rep list using categories for various types of music (solo, concerti, ensemble performances, and for nonclassical this might be standards and originals or a variety of subgenres.)

7. Do you have letters of recommendation from former teachers, mentors, coaches, conductors, or from people who've booked your concerts? If not, start asking people for these! If they haven't heard you perform in a while, invite them to an upcoming concert or send them your latest demo recording, and ask for their feedback. If they're enthusiastic, you may get a full letter or a descriptive blurb for general use in your bio, website, or flyer.

4

Expanding Your Impact:
Demos and CDs

Jenny, a talented pianist and master's degree candidate, visits me to ask a question. She's in the process of recording a few pieces to submit with her application for a major competition. She also has a degree recital this spring that she will have professionally recorded. Jenny asks, "How can I get the most out of these recordings? Should I make just a few copies for demos or what?"

Jenny's housemate is Amy, an excellent jazz vocalist with her own band. Amy has been gigging steadily throughout her student years and uses a demo with her promo kit when contacting club managers and festival presenters. Amy wants to do a full-length CD and shop it around to labels. Amy asks, "How do I get a record contract?"

Bob stops by and proudly hands me a copy of his new CD, asking me to listen to it when I have the time. With his brass quintet he plays about twenty regional concerts a year plus lots of K-12 in-school performances and mini-residencies. Bob asks, "Now that the CD is done, I want to know how to promote it; how do I get it into stores and get it reviewed?"

These are composites, scenarios and conversations I've had with musicians over the years. For many musicians, lacking perspective on the recording industry and on the music business side of their careers, the path to a successful CD project can be strewn with roadblocks. After all, if you can't see the forest for the trees, and you want to find the best career path through the terrain, it can be tough going. This chapter is intended to help you see the forest, the trees, and the path you choose to create. We'll discuss the Why, the What, the How, and the How Much.

Performing and recording go hand in hand. CDs are used in seeking performance dates, and then sold at concerts, in stores and on the Web, to help build a musician's following for future performances. Debut CDs and demos are often viewed as a kind of business card, a necessity for professional introductions. For most emerging musicians, CDs are an investment in the future, not a source of income. And just like any investment you might consider, it's important to get all the crucial information before putting any money down.

Context: Record Industry Basics (and What It All Means for You) ■

Because there are so many misconceptions about the recording industry and the role of recordings in a musician's career, let's start with an overview of the recording industry and the myths about getting signed to a label.

■

Record Label Overview
Major Labels

The major labels dominating the recording industry (and further mergers are pending as of this writing) are BMG, EMI, Sony, Universal Music Group, and AOL Time Warner (Warner Brothers group), huge multi-national media conglomerates. Recordings make up just a portion of their business dealings. These companies put significant amounts of money into marketing a handful of superstar musicians, the ones with immediate name recognition. In the classical arena, it's people like Yo-Yo Ma, Anne-Sophie Mutter, Itzhak Perlman, and, in the jazz arena, it's people like Wynton Marsalis, Diana Krall, and Josh Redman. A recording project for one of these celebrity artists can cost hundreds of thousands of dollars. The promotional campaigns for such CD projects can include full-page newspaper ads and for use in retail chain stores, promotional posters and cardboard life-size artist likenesses as floor displays. This is the blockbuster model, how the music industry and the major labels handle recordings for a handful of superstar artists.

Indie Labels

Beyond the major labels, there are several thousand independent ("indie") record labels. These vary in size and operation. Unlike the majors, most indie labels specialize in one or more specific musical genre (classical, folk, jazz, world). Indie labels vary in size from one-person operations run by performers marketing their own music, to large, competitive companies. Some of the more well-known classical indie labels are Naxos, Harmonia Mundi, Koch, New World, Albany, Channel, and

Bridge. Well-known jazz indie labels include Thirsty Ear, Concord Jazz, the Hat, and Palmetto. The promotional campaigns for indie label CD releases are far more modest. There is no mass marketing here because the recording artists—though they may be well known to other musicians and to their fans—are not "household names" to average Americans. Indie labels market CDs to specific segments of the population, to classical, jazz, or world music enthusiasts. This is the model of niche marketing.

■

Record Industry "Secret"

Here's the dirty little secret about the recording industry: the vast majority of records released, by both the majors and the indies, do NOT make money. So how and why do labels stay in business? They are basically gambling. They're betting that of the CDs they release in any season, there will be one or more that will pay off big—that will make back enough money to subsidize the cost of the other releases.

I've heard it described this way: labels throw new releases against a wall, like spaghetti, to see what sticks. It is, to some extent, a crapshoot. For example, who would have figured that a few years ago a recording of medieval chant by monks would go platinum? To hedge their bets, the major labels put the big money on acts they know will sell, the superstar musicians. And all labels try to gamble smart by choosing to record artists and projects they believe have a chance to make a profit.

State of the Biz

In recent years, because of the ease of file sharing and the rampant downloading of music, the recording industry has been in great flux. Average consumers think, why pay $18–20 for a CD when you can download it for free? Some labels have gone out of business, the rest have had layoffs and retrenchments. Many CD retail stores have closed, and retail chains have declared bankruptcy. People are predicting the end of the traditional CD retail store and a new system of distribution for music. Perhaps we'll be able to buy anything ever recorded, finding it on the net in a handy search engine, and then pay for only the tracks we want, downloading it in our media of choice. Perhaps we'll subscribe to a monthly service for unlimited music access. At any rate, the issues to be resolved are distribution and compensation.

According to the Recording Industry Association of America, of the total recordings sold nationwide, classical music and jazz each make up about 3 percent. The numbers have fluctuated somewhat in the past few years, but 3 percent is a good ballpark reference point. It wasn't always like this. The *New*

York Times reports that in the early 1960s, classical music still counted for one-third of all record sales in the United States. Now classical and jazz are very small segments of the industry, very specialized audiences. New recordings compete with historic re-releases for a relatively small segment of consumers. A typical classical music consumer, even an aficionado, doesn't want to own twelve CDs of the same Beethoven sonata, no matter how wonderful each interpretation may be.

What does all this mean for recording artists? Many symphony orchestras no longer have recording contracts. To compensate, some are re-releasing their own historic performances and are experimenting with streaming concerts over the net. There are very few multirecord label contracts anymore, because labels need to show immediate profits; they're not investing in musicians' long-term careers, but in media-grabbing projects. For major labels with large distribution networks designed for blockbuster sales, emerging artists—unless they have already developed a large following—are just not on the radar screen.

Getting Signed

But how *does* one get a recording contract? To get a contract with *any* label, a musician needs a solid performance track record and reputation, and a "saleable" project—a proposal for a recording that people will want to buy. Labels look for musicians with large local and regional "fan bases." This translates to a label as good potential CD sales, good ticket sales for a concert tour to promote the CD, and the ability to generate radio airplay to promote the CD.

Before approaching a label with a project, a musician needs to do some homework. To determine whether or not your project would be an appropriate match, check label websites. Find out what a label has released, what kinds of repertoire projects they pursue, and at what career stage the recording artists seem to be—read their bios.

Where can you find listings of indie labels and contact information? *Musical America: The International Directory of the Performing Arts,* comes out annually; it's the "Bible" of the professional music world, and includes listings of classical labels and their contact info. *Musical America* is fairly expensive but you can most likely find a print copy or read the online version at your nearest music school library or perhaps at larger public or university libraries.

How to Cultivate a Contact at a Record Label

Start with your network. Ask all of your colleagues, mentors, and contacts if they know anyone working in the recording industry. Check with the alumni office of your college or conservatory. If you find a contact whose label is not appropriate for your music, chances are that person has contacts at other labels that may be the right fit.

Check other emerging artists doing similar work to yours. With which labels are they recording? If you know any of these musicians or meet them at performances, ask if you could send them your demo to get some feedback. If they are enthusiastic, they might be willing to help you make a contact at their label.

If an indie label representative decides that you have a marketable product and project, you may be offered a contract. Note the "marketable." You may not be used to thinking of your artistry, your music, as a product. But a record contract is a business deal; the label has to determine if there's an audience for your CD project—if it has a chance at making decent sales. Signing a musician to a contract is a business investment; the record label is a business and it needs to make a profit in order to *stay* in business.

Do you Really Want a Recording Contract?

Not all recording contracts are created equal. "Getting signed" with an indie label often means the musician fronts thousands of dollars for the recording costs and then the label handles the manufacturing, promotion, and distribution. How much effort and money a label puts into marketing your CD depends on the contract, the project and the label. Before signing any contract, have it checked out by an experienced entertainment lawyer or a veteran artist manager. For help finding an entertainment lawyer, consult the Volunteer Lawyers for the Arts (VLA); they have local chapters nationwide (http://www .vlany.org).

Here's how the contracts work. Until the entire budget (the cost of making the CD) is made back in sales (recouped), you do not make a cent in profit. If sales are good, you may recoup the money you invested, and break even—otherwise you'll take a loss. Again, most people, and most labels, do not recoup the money they invest in making a CD, unless they are very creative and informed about how to market their CD.

How a Label Evaluates a Project

Picture this: an emerging artist with no name recognition has a project to record standard repertoire. There are ten recordings of the same repertoire available with well-known artists. Is there any reason for a label to be interested in this artist's project? If the artist has just won an international competition, maybe. But otherwise, unfortunately, no.

However, if an artist has a CD project of unusual repertoire, such as a CD of premieres of works by composers of a particular nationality, or a project to record rarely heard works—undiscovered gems by a lesser-known historic composer—then the project may be of interest to an indie label. For instance, the indie label Naxos, well known for its extensive catalog of standard works and rarities, has frequently signed emerging artists to record lesser-known works. Started as a budget line of high quality CDs, Naxos's catalog now comprises many series, including ones dedicated specifically to guitar, organ, opera, historic performances, and jazz; check their website at http://www.naxos.com.

And for new music, New World Records is dedicated to the proliferation of both new and neglected treasures of American music. The label's website, http://newworldrecords.org, has proposal guidelines for submitting potential recording projects.

In general, labels look for CD projects with a compelling "hook" or "concept." This simply means that the choice of repertoire has to make sense as an attractive program (such as "Flute Concertos by CPE Bach," "The Mozart Effect: Smart Baby Lullabies," "New American Works for Solo Clarinet" or "Louis the XIV's French Court Music"). The choice of repertoire and the CD title/idea are especially important if the recording artist is not well known. If the idea behind the CD is interesting enough to consumers, they may take a chance on an unknown artist.

In stores, the majority of CDs are organized in bins by composer names, to help shoppers find what they're looking for. Compilation CDs, of works by various composers, usually end up in the no-man's land of "miscellaneous." Because of this, labels most often prefer CD projects with works by one composer.

The Entrepreneurial Solution

Here's the good news: emerging artists without record contracts or prospects for such can take matters into their own hands. For artists wanting to record a CD of standard repertoire or a set of unrelated works, going the independent route and releasing their own CD makes the most sense. Marketing and selling your CD to audiences at performances and on various websites means you can be free of a label's priorities and restrictions. It means you can record what you want and what you think your specific niche audience will want.

Many musicians have started their own labels or formed cooperatives with a group of musicians to start a label. Violinist Gil Shaham's contract with Deutsche Grammophon was cancelled after ten years and more than fifteen albums, so he started his own label, Canary. Cellist David Finckel, of the Emerson Quartet, and his wife, pianist Wu Han, started their own label, Artist-Led, in 1997 and they market their critically acclaimed CDs exclusively on the Internet (http://www.artistled.com). Flutist Ransom Wilson's label, Image

Recordings, http://www.imagerecordings.com, has released CDs by violinist Joseph Silverstein and the Borromeo String Quartet. GM Recordings, founded in 1981, is composer Gunther Schuller's company, focusing on jazz and classical and multigenre works. Other artist-run labels include composer John Zorn's Tzadik label, Bang on a Can's Cantaloupe Music, violinist Paul Zukofsky's CP2, pianist Santiago Rodriguez's Elan Records, cellist Matt Haimovitz's Oxingale Records.

Musicians who release their own CDs and start their own labels have some specific advantages. They control the projects, artistically and financially; they choose the repertoire, and are in charge of the recording process, marketing and promotion. The musicians determine the budget, and so when there is profit, it's all theirs, they don't share it with a label. You may not want or need to start your own label at this point, but the do-it-yourself, entrepreneurial model is a good general approach to take with your career. Recording a demo and using it strategically to jumpstart your career is a smart move.

A demo is a short, ten- to twenty-minute *demonstration* recording, a kind of aural business card. A demo should showcase the range of a musician's abilities with a range of contrasting works (periods, styles, and genres). Demos are often required for grants, competitions, festivals, orchestral auditions, and college-level teaching jobs. Demos are also necessary for booking concerts. They are used in contacts with conductors, composers, prospective teachers, and freelance "gig" clients.

Your Recording Project Worksheet (in progress)
✓ Why: Reasons to record?

Why Record? ■

What *specifically* do you want to achieve? Be clear about your purpose and your expectations. Do you want to:

- ❑ Use your recording as a demo, for contacts with festivals, concert producers, conductors, managers or booking agents?
- ❑ Use your CD as a demo to interest a record label in signing you?
- ❑ Document your original compositions?
- ❑ Sell your recording at your performances?
- ❑ Sell your CD on your website? On other websites?

❑ Sell your recording on consignment at local shops and retail chains?
❑ Have a distributor market your CD to record stores?

Clarifying your purpose and goals is one of the most important first steps in any large project. No matter how you'd like to use your CD, you'll make smarter decisions if you have an understanding of the recording industry and of the procedures to record, package, and promote CDs.

Recording Project Worksheet (in progress)
✓ Why: Reasons to record
❑ What: Repertoire decisions

Repertoire Decisions ■

Musicians need recordings for different purposes at various career stages, but the most basic recording a musician usually needs is a demo. The choice and variety of the material you use on a demo is critical. It's good to have three or four contrasting short works or movements that highlight your strengths and range of technical and interpretive skills. The order of your selections should make an interesting contrast of keys, tempos, styles, periods, and genres.

The first work on the demo should be your best. Decision makers, such as competition judges and concert series presenters, don't have the time to listen to everything. You really only have the first ninety seconds of a recording to grab the listener's attention, so that they'll want to hear more.

Think carefully about what your intended listeners would want to hear. You may need several different demos for different purposes: one demo for applying for competitions, another for applying for festivals or residencies, and another for securing concert dates. You may want to record a full-length CD and use parts of it as a demo and package the full-length version for selling at performances.

In considering what to record, there are three basic questions:

1. What repertoire do you have ready to record, that is polished and professional quality (i.e. you've already performed it several times in public and can convey it convincingly)?
2. Does this repertoire demonstrate your own unique "voice"? You should *not* sound like an imitation of a teacher, mentor, or idol.
3. Is the repertoire appropriate for your demo needs? If it's intended for a competition, does your repertoire meet the requirements? If your demo

is to be used in concert bookings, is the repertoire representative of the music you are planning to perform in the next few seasons?

These can be tough questions. Ask your mentor, former teachers, and experienced colleagues about your repertoire recording plan and get some honest feedback. Don't make all these decisions on your own; think of your trusted network as your advisory committee.

Recordings of live performances, excerpted or edited, can be used as demos. And a good live performance may have an adrenalin edge, an electricity absent from studio recordings. Live performance recordings are often a requirement for competitions and grant programs. And concert series presenters prefer live recordings to edited studio recordings—especially when considering booking an emerging artist.

For musicians still in school, the most economical way to make either a demo or a full-length CD is to use recorded material from a degree recital (if the school records these professionally). Chicago-based clarinetist and composer James Falzone made his first full-length CD in Boston in 2001 from the edited recording of his 2000 Master's degree recital, a program of his own works. His music combines elements of jazz, world, and classical, some is notated and some improvised. Although he sells the CD at his performances, his goal in making the CD was not about financial gain. Making the CD was an investment in his future, in his career.

The cost? For a professional quality CD, James got off easy; there was no studio time involved, since it was an edited recording of a live performance. He did not pay his collaborating musicians (as friends, they did his recital as a favor, and he gave them gifts and a great dinner). James paid $80 per hour for the editing. The bulk of his budget went to professional artwork and printing, manufacturing and packaging.

What did James spend? His budget was about $3,500. If this seems high, keep in mind that for a *professional quality* CD project, musicians often spend $6,000-10,000. (Budget issues are covered later in this chapter.) Can CDs, especially demos, be made for much less? Yes, but if you want *professional quality*, from the recorded sound, to the artwork, liner notes, packaging, through to promotion and marketing, you should expect to invest real money.

What was the payoff for his career, from the investment of $3,500? James initially sent out about one hundred CDs as promos, and after that, has sent one or two out every month. He sells the CDs at various performances, five to twenty per gig. What work opportunities and connections did he gain as a result of the CD? James says, "Many. So many people have heard my music—people who would not otherwise. The CD got radio play in Massachusetts, Vermont, and Illinois, and this led to more gigs. I also sent the CD when I applied for several teaching jobs *[he landed them!]* and it gave me a degree of prestige at gigs that I had a product to sell."

■

Note: to plan what specific repertoire to record, you'll need to know whether you can do so legally. If the works you plan to record are in the public domain, there's no issue, but if not, you must obtain permission (the mechanical license) to record the works, from either the composers in question, their publishers, or their estates (more on this later).

■

Recording Project Worksheet (in progress)
✓ Why: Reasons to record
✓ What: Repertoire decisions
❑ How: Recording options

■

Recording Options ■

Once you've determined what you plan to record and why, next comes *how*. Whether it's for a twenty-minute demo or a full-length CD you plan to release and promote, you have three options:

1. Record in a professional studio
2. Hire an engineer to record "on location"
3. Rent or borrow the equipment and do it yourself

These are all good ways to make a recording. What matters is determining which option will best fit your budget, timeline, and project.

■

Learn the Lingo: Recording Terminology
CDr: Recordable CD, engineers can record directly onto these, then download and then edit on computer.
DAT: Digital audio tape. DAT recorders work by translating sound digitally, into a language of numbers: zeros and ones.
Distributor: Company that gets recordings into retail outlets. Major labels have their own distribution companies. There are independent distributors as well, some large national ones and other smaller regional companies. You can find listings of indie distributors in the annual directory, the *Recording Industry*

Sourcebook or in the directory put out by AFIM, the Association for Independent Musicians, or in *The Billboard Buyer's Guide Directory.*

Engineer: The person who gets your live performance onto a recorded format, chooses equipment, places mics, checks levels, and may do mixing and editing.

Manufacturer: Companies that produce CDs from your master; they may also print and assemble the graphics, package and polywrap your CDs and ship them to you (or to a distributor). Of course you can burn your own CDs, but if you're looking for a large number, you'll want to use a manufacturer. Besides the well-known U.S. CD manufacturers like Discmakers and CD Baby, there are Canadian CD manufacturers that may offer lower prices. To find a list of manufacturers, see the annual directory, the *Recording Industry Sourcebook,* or *Mix Magazine,* or *Billboard International Buyers' Guide*. If there's a music school near you, their library probably has these or you can do an online search.

Master: The first generation of your recording, the "original" from which duplications are made. Only send out copies, never send out your master!

Mastering: Final process after editing to complete a professional-quality recording. Mastering should be done only by an experienced professional, usually someone hired specifically just for this step. The mastering engineer runs the tape through multiple processors to compress or expand the dynamic range, equalize or add reverberation so that it's consistent from one cut to the next and so that it conforms to the standards used for radio broadcasts and professional labels.

Mixing: The blending of recorded tracks, to perfect balance, volume, and blend, for multi-track recording sessions (where there are more than two stereo mics being used).

Producer: Person who oversees the recording session, listening carefully to catch whatever the performers may miss; marks scores, helps decide what "takes" can be used, and what needs to be rerecorded. A producer can save you precious and expensive studio and engineer time if you do not have to both play and then listen back to every take. The producer should be someone who knows the performers and their abilities well, a trusted colleague, teacher, or mentor.

Retailers: Stores, including large chains as well as small independent shops. Major CD retailers include HMV, Tower, Virgin Records, and Borders. The online CD retailers include Amazon, http://www.CD-kiosk.com, and http://www.cdbaby.com.

Choosing an Engineer

If you want a professional quality recording, and are opting for either recording option 1 or 2 above, hire an experienced professional engineer. Make sure you get recommendations—ask your colleagues, mentors, and teachers for referrals. Music schools have engineers on staff who may do freelance projects or who can at least make recommendations. You want someone experienced and knowledgeable about the music you are recording, whether it's chamber music, vocal or jazz. Ask to hear samples of demos your prospective engineer has recorded. Find out exactly what is included with the engineer's hourly rate, how they handle editing time, costs of DATs, duplications, and so on. Make sure you discuss with your engineer the type of sound you want *before* you get to the recording session. You might even provide your engineer with one or two examples of CDs with recorded sound you like.

More Tips

From Discmakers, a CD manufacturing company: www.discmakers.com/music/request.html
Order your free copies of:
   "Guide to Making a Great Master"
   "Musician's Guide to the Web"
   "Independent Musician's Survival Guide"
And check out the tips, articles and advice at http://www.CDBaby.com.

Recording in a Studio

The costs for studio recording may vary depending on the equipment, space, and local competition. Keep in mind, most studios do not provide concert-quality grand pianos. If you need one, you will have fewer studio choices and you will run into higher fees.

In choosing a studio, get references from trusted colleagues. Listen to samples of the work done by the recommended studios. You also may want to visit or tour a prospective studio to make sure you'd be comfortable recording there.

Make sure you understand everything included in the rates you are quoted. Studios may offer various package deals with a certain number of studio hours, an engineer, editing of a master tape, a certain number of duplications, and so on. Make sure you compare studio offerings carefully before making a decision. Sometimes studios offer reduced rates for sessions done after midnight; this can be a big savings for night owls.

Recording on Location

Most classical recordings are done on location, because of the acoustics of a particular concert hall or for the use of a specific piano. The acoustics of the hall or venue are crucial to getting a good recording. Explore inexpensive potential sites in your community. Churches, temples, ballrooms, libraries, community centers, and schools may be some of your best options.

Be careful about the reverberation—look for a hall sound that's not "boomy" but warm and cushioned. Halls that are great to perform in aren't always the best for recording. When you're "shopping" for a recording site, you can bring along your own personal recorder and get at least a sense of what the recorded acoustics might be like.

A hall may have great acoustics, be available at little or no cost, and still be impractical. I've heard of churches with superb acoustics where the recording sessions had to be scheduled for spring or summer to avoid the heating system noise. And to avoid the traffic sounds, sessions had to be done between midnight and 4:00 A.M.

Location, location, location. It's all about the sound of the space where you record, the ambient sound. In Boston, New England Conservatory's Jordan Hall is used extensively for solo and chamber music recordings (Yo-Yo Ma has recorded there often). There's no way to simulate the acoustics of a great hall. Do some research to find where musicians in your area record. If you have a church job or a teaching gig, you may be able to get the use of a recording space for free or at a discounted price.

Do-It-Yourself

This is option three, best for producing a low budget demo. You can either do it on your own or enlist a friend with recording experience and equipment. If you have access to a school's concert hall or another space with good acoustics, you might be able to record with rented or borrowed equipment at minimal cost. As a graduate student, I recorded demos in my school's concert hall and hired a fellow student as engineer. In considering where to record, find a place fairly isolated (no traffic, bathroom, or neighbor noises), with a moderate temperature so that you and your instrument(s) are comfortable.

How to Avoid "Studio Shock"

Musicians who are recording session "virgins" can be thrown off by the playback they hear in a session, whether it's on location or at a studio. They may be surprised or shocked by their recorded sound. There's often a difference between what we hear (or don't hear) as we perform and what the recording equipment picks up and our audience perceives. To avoid this shock, record yourself regularly. My best advice is to purchase a decent personal recording system and use it every day in the practice room. Many musicians use mini-disc recorders for this purpose.

Professional percussionist Mike K. says that it was only when he started recording himself regularly as a grad student at Juilliard, that his progress dramatically improved. He thinks recording practice sessions should be required of all music students. The playback doesn't lie. Recording yourself educates your ear. When you hear more accurately, you can make the minute corrections necessary to better align your actual performance with your ideal one. In this way, recording trains a musician to be her or his own teacher.

Preparation for the Recording Session

Be completely prepared; you don't want to waste expensive recording time with rehearsing. Many people find it helps to have the repertoire they plan to record memorized, that this allows them to concentrate better and listen more carefully. If you plan to read from music, rearrange any page turns so that they can be done as silently as possible, or if necessary, bring a page-turner.

Do several practice recording sessions before the real thing, using your own recording equipment. Make yourself play through entire movements and then listen to the playbacks so you'll know what to expect of yourself in the actual recording session. Beyond listening for technical or interpretive points, listen for extraneous noises. If you have a habit of tapping your foot or humming to yourself as you perform, you'll need to curtail this so as not to ruin the recording. Glenn Gould and Pablo Casals aside, no one wants to hear musicians hum and groan. Be careful of your breathing and any noisy body movements before and after each take—clean beginnings and endings are important.

If you are planning to record in a studio, your practice recording sessions are best done in a dry or "dead" space (such as a heavily carpeted, low-ceilinged room). You want to be accustomed to how you sound without the feedback from a hall.

If you are doing your own recording with borrowed or rented equipment, it's smart to practice using the equipment. Try recording selections off the radio or a CD to make sure you can properly set levels (recording volume) and use the play back. Making a few mistakes in advance of the session will help you avoid mistakes when it counts.

What to Bring to Your Recording Session

❑ Two extra copies of the music (piano score if you are using accompaniment), for your producer and engineer to make notes; the scores should be marked in sections and measure numbers to save expensive recording session time referencing retakes

❑ Tuning fork or tuner
❑ Metronome—to check tempi for any repeated takes
❑ Extra strings, reeds, basic instrument repair equipment—expect the unexpected
❑ Folding wire stand(s)—these don't block sound the way the solid metal ones do
❑ Stand lights (depending on the space, extra lighting may be necessary, check this out in advance)
❑ Quick snack food in case your energy sags (energy bars or bananas are good for this)
❑ Water to keep yourself hydrated
❑ Wear layers so you can adjust your comfort to the recording location temperature
❑ Your producer
❑ Your patience and sense of humor; you'll need both

Tips for Making the Session Run Smoothly

Warm up carefully before your session, but don't overdo it. Discuss (again) with your engineer the type of sound you want in the recording. Check for that sound, balance, and level at the start of the session and periodically throughout the session.

Plan out the order you want to record pieces, with an estimated time allotment for each, and keep to your schedule. Record the most difficult pieces first, when you are fresh and have the most energy. In general, if you haven't nailed a passage, section, or movement after three takes, you're probably not going to get it in that session. If you've recorded something twice and haven't gotten it, you may want to take a short break or record something else first and come back to it later.

How much recording time should you book? The ratio of recording time to finished product is at least four to one, and then there's time needed for listening to playbacks. So to make a fifteen-minute demo, it can take two to three hours of recording.

During the session, you'll need to "slate" all takes, announcing into the mic the specific work or movement before performing it, that is, "Schubert Trio, 1st movement, take 2," so that your engineer can easily edit afterward. Your producer can help by taking notes on the order of the takes, noting the better ones.

For more in-depth technical assistance, I highly recommend Diane Sward Rapaport's *How to Make and Sell Your Own Recording*. It's thorough and detailed. I also recommend Tim Sweeney's *Guide to Releasing Independent Records*, an excellent, down-to-earth, practical guide to the entire process. Both of these resources are geared more toward pop/rock music but all of the principles apply.

And for a grassroots approach to marketing and selling your CD, with lots of creative ideas and examples from the singer-songwriter world, I highly recommend Jana Stanfield's *Making and Selling Your Own CDs & Cassettes*. There are more recommended resources in the appendix.

Once you've completed your recording sessions, then next comes mixing and editing. It's smart to wait a day or two before listening to all the takes. Give yourself and your internal critic a breather so that you can listen more objectively. When you do listen to the takes, you'll decide which ones to use whole and which need massaging. Depending on the equipment and expertise of your engineer, some slight performance glitches can be fixed in the editing, others cannot. Ask your engineer. If you are planning to use the recording as more than a demo, the final step for the recording itself is the mastering. This is necessary for a polished professional quality sound and for broadcast on radio.

Whether you are making a quick demo for a grant or competition, or a full-length CD to sell at performances and on your website, you should be informed about a range of issues. These include CD artwork, liner notes, licensing, copyright, bar code, marketing, and sales.

CD Artwork and Graphics ■

The first impression your CD makes is *visual*. Do NOT underestimate the importance of CD artwork. Your cover design should attract attention and draw people to your CD. If they don't feel compelled to pick it up and read about you and your music, why would they listen to it? Your cover design should pique the viewer's interest and graphically communicate a sense of your music, its energy, mood, period, or genre.

How Graphic-Savvy Are You?

Take a look at the CDs in your collection. You probably have a wide range of music of various genres. Most likely you have CDs released by major labels, indie labels and some CDs released by friends. Take a random sampling of your CDs, at least thirty, and spread them out flat on the floor so you can sit back and take a look at the covers as a group. Imagine this is a display in your local record store where you are browsing. Which CDs, based on the cover alone, most attract your attention? Which CD covers are you most drawn to? Why? Is it the colors, the artwork, an interesting photo, the font or logo design? Noticing what works and why is great preparation for making smart choices about your own CD artwork.

You want your finished CD to compare well with those released by record labels. Think about it. Madison Avenue advertising firms make millions designing packaging to promote products. Major labels spend big bucks using top photographers and graphic artists to create CD covers. They do this because it matters. The picky details of color choice, fonts, layout, photos, and liner notes are as much a part of the experience of the recorded music as a performer's stage presence, choice of clothing, and program notes are a part of the live performance experience. So it isn't merely a question of commercial packaging. CD graphics are an artistic statement about you, your professionalism, *and* your music.

If you're making a CD purely for your own satisfaction, as a vanity project, then sure, choose your favorite colors, type of art, or typography for your CD artwork—you're pleasing an audience of one. But if you plan to use the CD to advance your career, then you need to use more than your personal preferences to determine artwork choices. Just because it looks good to you doesn't mean it will work well as the marketing package for your music. And you get what you pay for; if you use artwork by your cousin who is not a professional graphic designer, chances are your CD may look "nice" but it won't convey the crisp professionalism of many of the CDs in your own collection.

Under-Cover Work: Playing Detective at Your Local Record Store

Do your research. Make a reconnaissance trip to your local CD retailer. Check out the CD covers for similar artists and repertoire. What do you notice about the use of photos, colors, and period artwork? Early music CD covers tend to use reproductions of beautifully detailed oil paintings and tapestries of the period in rich colors, suggesting the detail and opulence of the music. Likewise, CDs of early-twentieth-century music, for instance, sport designs and typography suggestive of the artwork of the period.

Notice what is being emphasized on covers. For less well-known musicians, cover art tends to emphasize the CD title and repertoire more than the artists' names. The "concept" of the CD, the idea linking the works, is usually played up graphically as the strongest selling point, whether it's a title such as "New American Works for Solo Marimba," "Romantic Gypsy Accordion Music," "Jazz for Lovers," or "Brahms for Reading." So the title of your CD matters. If you use an obscure or cryptic phrase for a title, you hurt your marketing efforts.

Covers with photos of the performers work best when the performer is either:

- well-known, with immediate face/name recognition, or
- very photogenic, or
- a child prodigy

In cases in which all three conditions exist, an artist and her or his label hit the jackpot. After all, fame, glamour, and sex make for good sales, as does extreme youth.

Use a professional graphic designer with CD cover experience. If you live near an art school, you may be able to find a student with the necessary training and experience for much less money. For graphic designer referrals ask everyone in your network—chances are you'll get some great recommendations. Ask at any recording studios or smaller indie labels in your area. Make sure you see examples of several artists' previous CD covers before hiring anyone.

Why do you need a pro? Professional designers have years of experience using specific design programs such as Freehand, Illustrator, QuarkXpress, and Photoshop. They use these to create the proper composites, format and specifications necessary for printing CD covers. An experienced graphic designer will save you headaches and dollars when dealing with printers and your CD manufacturing company.

CD manufacturing companies offer various packages that often include design, layout, jewel boxes, bar code, assembly, and shrink wrapping. Be a savvy consumer; get recommendations, and compare package deals at several companies. The graphic design services included in these package deals are usually a limited set of formulaic design templates. My best advice is get a professional so that you can have a CD you'll be proud to look at five or ten years from now.

CD Cover Quiz

	Answers
• Do people judge a CD by its cover?	(yes!)
• Do musicians, sound-oriented people, tend *not* to be sensitive to graphics?	(yes)

- And so do musicians tend to underestimate the importance of the visuals, the graphic design issues involved in producing CDs?   (yes)
- On CD covers, should the copy (printed word text) be easy to read?   (yes)
  [Pay attention to point size, choice of fonts, choice of background and foreground colors.]
- On covers, where should the CD title and names of performers be?   (top third of cover)
  [The title and performers need to be readable in CD store bins.]
- Should you and your designer pay attention to color issues, i.e., warm vs. cool colors, as studies show there are predictable human reactions to particular colors and color combinations?   (yes)
  [Reds, oranges and yellows are warmer; blues, greens, and purple are cooler. Certain colors have cultural associations, too: deep reds and golds read as sumptuous and rich; purple suggests royalty; pastels read as gentle, sentimental; and green suggests springtime and fertility. A trained graphic designer is acutely aware of the power of color as well as the print costs involved in using multiple colors, and ways to get the most graphic punch on a budget.]
- Does your cover art itself need to suggest the genre and period of your music?   (yes)
- Should the graphic design of a CD booklet and disc complement the cover art?   (yes)

Conclusion: This is not obvious stuff—which is all the more reason to hire a pro! ∎

What Info Should Be Included in a CD Booklet Insert?

❑ Composer names
❑ Titles, movements (include year of composition if work is new or obscure)
❑ Timings of each work or movement in minutes and seconds, plus the total timing of the CD
❑ Names of all performers and their instruments/voice types
❑ Bios of performers

❑ Program notes about the works and composers
❑ Texts and translations, if applicable
❑ Name of label (if you have signed with a label, or if you create your own)
❑ Contact information for either you, your label, or your manager, with website, e-mail, phone, and address. For booking performances, this info is essential
❑ Photos or graphics to help break up solid text pages
❑ Copyright notices

Credits:

❑ Recording engineer
❑ Recording location or studio
❑ Photographer
❑ Graphic designer
❑ Include the title, artist, and permission notice for any reproduced artwork

❑ Thank you's and acknowledgements to contributors, funders, supporters.

Note: Program notes and bios should be well written: engaging, imaginative and informative. They should be appropriate for a non-musician reader; leave out the technical info and musician jargon. Once you've written your draft text, have a professional writer edit it. A music publicist is best. Ask any public relations staff at your local arts organizations for referrals. For ideas on how to engage a non-musician audience, see chapter 8; for ideas on bios, see chapter 3.

Pianist Catherine T. made her first CD using an edited version of one of her degree recitals. She wrote about this fact in her liner notes and later regretted it. She found that some people, when they read the liner notes, prejudged the performance as "student" level, and viewed the CD as less than professional quality. Catherine's advice: "If you use a degree recital recording to make a CD, keep the circumstances of the performance to yourself! Simply state the performance occurred at XYZ University or Conservatory and never mind the why."

What Info Goes on Both CD Spines (the Sides)?

❑ Title of CD
❑ Name of ensemble or soloist
❑ Label name and catalog number (if you have these)

What Info Needs to Be on the Tray Card (the Back Cover)?

❑ Name of ensemble or soloist
❑ Titles and movements of all works, track numbers, individual timings, PLUS total recording time
❑ Label name and catalog number
❑ Contact information
❑ Bar code, necessary to sell the CD in a retail store or on the Web, more later
❑ Copyright notices
❑ Production credits: engineer, recording studio, artwork, graphics, and photo credits
❑ Possible brief description of music, performance, or musicians (a quote from a review or mentor), or an impressive notice such as "winner of the XYZ international competition"

On the Disc Itself

Because discs and jewel boxes inevitably become separated, labels and savvy artists repeat the most crucial identifying information on the disc itself, including:

❑ Title of CD
❑ Name of ensemble or soloist
❑ Contact info
❑ Titles of works and track numbers
❑ Copyright notices
❑ Name of label (if a label is involved, or if you create your own)

Bar Codes

If you want to have the option to sell your CD in a retail store or through an online retailer, you must obtain a bar code, a universal product code (UPC), so that the sales transaction can be scanned and digitally recorded. UPCs are assigned by the Uniform Code Council, Inc., and as of this writing, they cost $750. The bar code is a series of vertical lines representing a unique twelve-digit number. This number identifies the company offering the product (for CDs, this can be a label or a CD manufacturer) and then the particular product (the specific CD). Manufacturers such as CD Baby and Discmakers offer various packages that include the barcode; check out carefully what you're getting with any package deal. And yes, after the fact you can also affix bar code stickers (CD manufacturers offer these) on top of the CD polywrap, in case you originally did the graphic design and printing without a bar code.

But the best way is to incorporate the bar cord into your printed CD art-work—do it right the first time.

To get a Universal Product Code (UPC) number, a bar code, contact:

Uniform Code Council, Inc.
7887 Washington Village Dr., Suite 300
Dayton, OH 45459
tel. (937) 435-3870
http://www.uc-council.org

Harpist John T. regrets he did not put a bar code on his first CD. He sells the CD at gigs and uses it as a demo, but he's found that some people unfortunately consider the CD as less serious because they don't see it as a commercial product. John T.'s advice: "Don't forget the bar code!"

Copyright Issues ■

Once you've recorded your CD, you will want protection against the unau-thorized use of it by others, say as background sound on a website, or in a TV commercial or film. Copyright is for protection. Technically, copyright is es-tablished automatically when a work is created, when it is established in a *tangible* form, either in a recording or in a score or lead sheet format. This means simply that a person owns the work he or she makes, and the rights to repro-duce, publish and sell this work. However, *proof* of copyright is established through registering with the Library of Congress Copyright Office. The pro-cess to secure your copyright registration is simple. You'll need to get a form from the U.S. Copyright Office, fill it out, and send it in with a check. Form SR is used for sound recordings. If you are recording your original composi-tions, you'll also need form PA.

To download copyright forms, see the Library of Congress Copyright Of-fice site:

http://www.loc.gov/copyright

or call:

(202) 707-5000 (for general information)
(202) 707-3000 (for copyright forms and questions about them)
(202) 707-9100 ("Forms Hotline," for ordering forms if their name and number are known)

You may have heard of the "Poor Man's" copyright protection method: sending yourself a copy of your CD or your original score by registered mail through the postal service, and keeping the sealed postmarked envelope as proof of authorship. This method is NOT recommended. In a case in which copyright is being contested and legal action is being pursued, you want to be the one who established your copyright by registering it properly.

Licensing Issues ■

Just as you want to have your recording protected from unlawful use, if you plan to record works composed by other people, you need to make sure you're not infringing on their rights. If you plan to record a work that has never been recorded before, you need written permission from the copyright holder— the composer, or his or her publisher or estate. Permission is fixed in contract form with whatever terms of the agreement you negotiate with the composer. If you are not already in contact with the composer, most likely you can find her or him through one of the composer rights organizations listed below, ASCAP, BMI, or SESAC. These organizations license and distribute royalties for public performances of their composer members' copyrighted works.

Once a copyrighted work has been recorded and distributed, however, anyone else may record it without permission *as long as they obtain a compulsory mechanical license.* A mechanical license is a written authorization from the publisher to manufacture and distribute a recording of a specific copyrighted musical composition. The rates for mechanical licenses are set by Congress and these rates increase every two years. For current rates, see the Harry Fox Agency site: http://www.nmpa.org/hfa.html. Musicians are charged the rate times the number of CDs they manufacture. If you are planning to make 2,500 CDs or fewer, you can apply for an HFA mechanical license online at http://www.songfile.com. HFA arranges for the clearances, calculates the costs, handles the reporting and payment obligations, and adds a small administration fee. Keep in mind that CD manufacturers require proof of mechanical licenses before beginning a client's CD project, so the best thing to do is obtain mechanicals before recording.

How long does copyright protection last? As of this writing, copyright protection is good for the life of the composer plus seventy years if the work was composed on or after January 1, 1978, and for works composed before that date, it's the life of the composer plus renewable terms totaling ninety-five years. If the copyright on a work has expired, then the work falls into the "public domain" and can be recorded and performed without a mechanical license. If you're not certain of the copyright status of a particular work, you can request a clearance check from the Copyright Office. They will research the work and tell you whether or not it is in the public domain.

To obtain Mechanical Licenses

Harry Fox Agency, Inc.
Mechanical Licensing Dept.
711 Third Ave., 8th Floor
New York, NY 10017
(212) 370-5330
licensing@harryfox.com
http://www.songfile.com
See FAQ at www.nmpa.org

Composer Rights Organizations (these license performance rights)

ASCAP: American Society of Composers, Authors & Publishers
One Lincoln Center Plaza
New York, NY 10023
(800) 95-ASCAP
info@ascap.com
http://www.ascap.com

BMI: Broadcast Music, Inc.
320 West 57th St.
New York, NY 10019-3790
(212) 586-2000
classical@bmi.com; jazz@bmi.com
http://www.bmi.com

SESAC, Inc.
152 West 57th ST
57th Floor
New York, NY 10019
(212) 586-3450
http://www.sesac.com

After you've registered the copyright for your CD, make sure you include the copyright notices in the text and design of your booklet/insert, tray card, and disc. There are two different copyright notices to indicate. One covers the sound, the performances on the recording, indicated by ℗ (stands for phonorecord) followed by the year the copyright was established and the name of the copyright owner (usually the label). The other copyright notice covers the text and artwork on your CD, indicated by a ©, followed by the year the copyright was established. In addition, some standard but somewhat flexible legal language usually follows, such as a variation of "All rights reserved. Unauthorized duplication is a violation of applicable laws" or "All rights reserved. Unauthorized copying, reproduction, hiring, lending, public performance and broadcasting prohibited." See the CDs in your collection for examples of this language.

With these basic recording issues mapped out, the next big topic to consider is money. How will you finance your CD project?

Recording Project Worksheet (in progress)

✓ Why: Reasons to record
✓ What: Repertoire decisions
✓ How: Recording options
❑ How Much? Finance issues

Finance Issues ■

If you know you'll need to raise part or all of the money to make your recording, the first step is to know how much money you need. You'll need to write a budget: a plan that accounts for all the expenses involved as well as the assets you have to cover these expenses. A budget is a plan to help you use your resources well.

What does it cost to make a CD? There's no easy way to answer this, because it can cost anywhere from practically nothing (you do your own recording on your own equipment, burn copies on your computer, and photocopy or laser-print a CD cover) to hundreds of thousands (what major labels spend in the production and promotion of a CD). But to produce a *professional quality* CD, musicians often spend $6,000 to $10,000 (and up) to record, edit, master, manufacture, and promote a CD.

Your costs will depend on where and how you do the recording, how much you pay people to assist you, how "fancy" you want to get with the artwork, and then how you plan to promote the recording. To make these decisions wisely, think carefully about how you want to use the CD before you start recording or spending money.

Start by writing a list of *all* anticipated costs. Don't leave anything out— you want no surprises. If you aren't certain about costs, do your homework. You'll need referrals and price quotes for photographers, graphic designers, engineers, recording studios, mastering, and manufacturing companies. Ask your friends, colleagues, and mentors; call local recording studios for prices and call music schools for recommended freelance engineers. Be a savvy consumer. Get several price quotes from recommended professionals for each item on your budget.

A working budget has two separate parts. There's a list of specific, itemized costs, your expenses, and another list of resources, your itemized assets. Use the budget plan below as a template, adding in all the costs you've researched as well as the resources you plan to commit to the project. With expenses itemized in the left-hand column, and resources in the right, the goal is to get the two sides to balance each other. This is where the term "bottom line" comes from; the bottom line totals should match. If your current resources will not cover your anticipated expenses, then read on. The next section covers creative ways to finance your CD project.

Write Your Budget

Expenses, production costs:	*Resources:*
Collaborating musicians:	Savings:
Studio costs:	Loans:
Hall rental:	Grants:
Recording Engineer:	Gifts:
Producer:	Other:
Editing:	
Mastering:	
Piano Tuning:	
Graphic design:	
Photography:	
CD Booklet Editor:	
Copyright registration:	
Licensing Fees:	
Bar code registration:	
CD Press:	
Artwork printing:	
Expenses, production costs:	
Promo material printing/assembly:	
Mailing to radio/media:	
Follow-up phone costs:	
CD Release Concert/Party:	
Online retail sales arrangements:	
Total:	Total:

What kinds of numbers do musicians actually end up with? Here is a sample budget, a composite of projects from emerging artists.

Sample Production Budget

Collaborating Musicians	FREE
Hall rental	FREE
Producer	FREE
Recording/Editing	$1,250
($50 per hr. @25 hours)	
Mastering	$ 500
Piano tuning	$ 60
Bar Code	included with manufacturing
Copyright	$ 30
Thank you dinner for musicians	
& producer	$ 200
Photos	$1,000
Graphic design	$ 500
Booklet editing	FREE
Printing	$1,000
Initial Pressing of 1,000 CDs	$1,200
Subtotal	$5,740

Promotion Costs:	
Promo material printing/assembly	$ 500
Mailing to radio/media	$ 400
Follow-up phone calls	$ 50
Postcard invites to CD release	
concert	$ 700
Posters for concert	$ 50
CD Release Concert/Party	$1,000
Subtotal	$2,700

Total CD project, production and promotion: $8,440

Your costs may be quite different from these, based on your specific situation, your location, help from friends, and so on. The important thing is to do your research, get accurate numbers for the costs of your own CD project. There's nothing worse than running out of funds mid-stream, completing your recording sessions only to find you've nothing left for manufacturing, let alone promoting, your CD.

Options for Financing: Fund-raising Projects and Personal Loans

Some musicians borrow money to make their CDs; others raise the money with contributions from their network: their extended family, friends, and supporters. And still others use a combination of fund-raising and loans. Your best asset for either raising or borrowing money for a CD project is your network—the people who are already invested in your career advancement, who know you well and are interested in seeing you succeed.

To make her first CD, vocalist Linda B. needed to raise $5,000. She came up with a short list of five fairly wealthy people among her supporters. These five came to her concerts regularly, and knew her well. Linda asked each for a personal loan of $1,000, knowing that this amount of money was fairly small change for them. All five said yes and Linda made out loan agreements for each, including pay back schedules. With the $5,000, Linda was able to make her CD and afterward she paid every penny back on time. She has since gone on to make several more CDs. But in looking back, Linda realized, as she got to know her five supporters even better, that they would have been happy to simply *give* her the money, because they wanted to contribute to Linda's success and her career advancement. What's the moral of the story? You too may be able to raise the money for your CD project with the help of your friends, family, and supporters, and you may be able to do it without even going into debt!

Start by making a detailed list of the people who know you or your family well and who have shown interest in your career: your former teachers, extended family, friends, family doctors, dentists, and so on. Use your address books (old and new) and ask your family for leads and contact information. These people are potential contributors to your CD project fund. I guarantee you that you know people now who would contribute to your project—it's a matter of how you ask them, how much you ask them for, and how much discretionary money they have to give.

Most people would sooner undergo surgery than ask someone for money. Fortunately, there are ways to approach fund-raising to minimize the discomfort and maximize the likelihood for success. With the right advice and a little coaching, musicians do fundraise successfully. Chapter 11 covers fund-raising in more detail and provides the outline for organizing a small-scale fund-raising campaign, such as one appropriate for a CD project. So don't rule out the possibility of raising the money to make your CD!

And as for loans, be careful. Don't attempt to finance your CD project by juggling credit card payments or by taking out a high interest rate loan. Personal loans, like the ones Linda B. arranged, can be made for a mutually agreeable interest rate (or better yet, no interest) and a reasonable payback schedule. You should base a payback schedule on income *other* than CD sales. Again, for most musicians, a CD—especially a first CD—is primarily a promotional tool, not a profitable income source.

Grants

A grant is a sum of money given by an organization for a specified purpose, such as education, research, or career advancement. Grants are awarded by national and local foundations, community, civic, and religious organizations, federal and state governments, and by corporations.

According to myth, there's plenty of grant money out there and it's easy to get. Not true. The majority of grants are given to nonprofit organizations, not to individuals. Grant programs in general are highly competitive and researching grants and writing proposals takes time, skill, and effort. Frankly, musicians have a much better chance of raising money for a CD through their own fund-raising efforts, within their circle of extended family, friends, and supporters.

However, you may have affiliations with local community organizations that make various grants and scholarships available. Sometimes church groups, community clubs, and local businesses have small-scale grant programs or will make one-time special contributions to deserving projects. In smaller cities and towns, it may be easier to apply for and be awarded such funds. So, if your hometown is a close-knit community in the Midwest but you're currently living in Manhattan, do your community grant research when you're visiting back home. To research possible funding sources, ask the reference librarians at your hometown library and inquire at your local chamber of commerce, social service agencies, and religious organizations. Your best connections to local funding, of course, are through the people who know you and your family and are interested in your career advancement.

The Aaron Copland Fund, administered through the American Music Center, offers a grant program for CD projects. This fund supports recording projects of contemporary American classical music. Applications are accepted from professional performing ensembles, presenting institutions, and either nonprofit or commercial recording companies. For example, an ensemble with an idea for a CD project of new American music might "shop" their project to an indie label. If the label is interested, the label may apply to the Copland Fund. The program covers the production, promotion, and distribution of CDs.

> *Aaron Copland Fund for Music*
> Recording Program
> c/o American Music Center
> 30 West 26th St., Suite 1001
> New York, NY 10010-2011
> (212) 366-5260
> http://www.amc.net

See chapter 11 for a full discussion of fund-raising and grants. Note: there are also some music competitions that offer prizes of CD production or contracts (see the appendix).

CD Sales ■

You may be able to finance at least a part of your CD project by selling advance copies of your CD to your network of supporters at your performances, by mail order, and over the Internet. For this to work, you need to have a healthy-sized network. If you've raised a portion of your budget and need to come up with the last $2,000 you could raise this amount by selling one hundred advance copies of your CD for $20 a piece. It's your supporters and fans who are most likely to pay $20 for an as yet unheard future CD; strangers would not.

How Are Advance Copies Sold?

Evan Harlan, an active jazz musician in the Boston area, has financed several CDs using this method. Because he performs so often, he has a good-sized and constantly growing mailing list of enthusiasts. His method? Evan mailed fliers to his network, announcing the upcoming CD. These were simple yet well-designed, done on $8 \frac{1}{2} \times 11''$ paper, folded in thirds. On the flier was an engaging description of the music on the new CD, the expected release date, testimonials and quotes about his live performances and previous CDs, and an order form to purchase the CD by mail. The selling point to the reader was to "Be the first on your block to get the new Evan Harlan CD." With this method, an added incentive can be for advance CD purchasers to get a special invitation to a CD release party, performance, or reception. Excellent planning is essential. Obviously, you would want the CD release to be no more than a few months from the time of the mailing (people don't want to wait indefinitely and they will understandably feel cheated unless you deliver as promised!) This method makes sense to consider if you've paid for and completed the recording and editing, and need money to fund the insert printing, CD pressing, and promotion. ∎

In creating a flyer for selling advance copies, be strategic. Because people get so much unsolicited mail, and most of it gets trashed, your invitation needs to stand out from the crowd. To be effective, your CD flier must be attractive, well designed, and well written. Again, get help from someone with graphic design training and experience, and get help with writing the text. If you've created a draft of the mailing, you may be able to get a busy professional to spend twenty minutes with you and get concrete suggestions for improvements. If you don't already have a good graphic designer within your network, consider the public relations, marketing, or graphic design staff and faculty at your local university.

Keep in mind most musicians finance CDs with a combination of savings, assistance from family and friends, and then loans, grants, or by selling advance copies. Musicians are creative and resourceful people, and those same qualities are necessary in handling the business and budget issues of careers. If you're still stuck on the money thing, start by talking to people in your network and asking for advice.

How Can a Self-released CD Make a Profit?

In general, a first CD is made for promotional purposes, not for making a profit. However, it may be possible to recoup, through CD sales, some or all of the money you invest. So, yes, although you'll need to front the money to produce the CD, with work you may be able to make back part or all of your expenses by selling the CD. It's also possible, with even more effort, to make a profit.

How well a musician does selling a CD depends on a number of factors. Of course, there's the obvious, the quality of the CD, of the performance and of the recording itself. Beyond this, it matters how many performances the musician books, if their promotional efforts are effective, if the CD is reviewed (and favorably), and how large a support network the musician has.

To illustrate two different CD sales outcomes for the same budget scenario, read on. The first one (Mike D.'s) details how you might recoup your expenses; the second (Samantha K.'s) shows how you might do even better, and make a profit.

Situation

Imagine: you've completed your CD and have spent, as you planned, $6,000 total on the project. You had one thousand CDs pressed. Of these, you'll use three hundred for promotional purposes, mailing these to radio stations, critics, and to concert and festival presenters for potential bookings. That leaves seven hundred CDs to sell in order to recoup your expenses. You plan to sell these at your performances, by mail order to your network, by consignment at record stores and specialty boutiques, from your own site, and on CD retail sites such as Amazon.com and CDBaby.com. Here's how two different musicians handled this.

Scenario 1

Mike D. performs twenty concerts the year the CD is released, selling an average of ten CDs at each performance (two hundred total). Mike sells two hundred more CDs from a mailing to his network and from having his CD available through Amazon.com. He sells a final one hundred CDs at several local retail stores on consignment. All this takes time and effort. In this scenario, 450 CDs are sold the first year after the release, leaving an additional 250 for possible future sales. Mike recoups his initial investment of $6,000.

CDs sold at performances: 200 at $15.00 = $3,000
CDs sold through mailing and on Web: 150 at $15.00 = $2,250
CDs sold by consignment in stores: 100 at $7.50 = $ 750
Profit from CD sales total − $6,000
Less expenses − $6,000
Mike D.'s initial investment is recovered: Net Profit = $ 0

Scenario 2

Samantha K. also spends $6,000, and has the same plan to press one thousand CDs, using three hundred as promos, leaving seven hundred to be sold. Samantha performs more, sells more at each concert, has a larger network, and uses a more aggressive sales campaign. She also has her own website and e-newsletter. Her situation and hard work yield bigger profits. On average, Samantha sells fifteen CDs at each concert, and performs twenty-five concerts the year the CD is released (375 CDs sold). Samantha sells 225 more to her supporters via mailings and her website. Like Mike, Samantha sells a final one hundred by consignment in local shops. In this scenario, Samantha sells all seven hundred CDs the first year after the release. She makes a profit of over $3,000, a very successful outcome for a first CD.

CDs sold at performances: 375 at $15.00 = $5,625
CDs sold through mailing and off websites: 225 at $15.00 = $3,375
CDs sold by consignment in stores: 100 at $7.50 = $750
Profit from CD sales total = $9,750
Less expenses − $6,000
Net Profit = $3,750

Why don't these scenarios reflect what happens to most musicians? Why is it that most musicians fail to recoup the money they invest, let alone make a profit? There are two reasons: musicians tend to overestimate the number of CDs they can realistically sell and they underestimate the work involved in selling them. If you aren't performing regularly, and don't have a large support network, it's unlikely you'll recoup your investment. Think carefully about the appropriate number of CDs to make, and how many of these you can realistically sell.

Some CDs are more profitable than others. Projects with commercial value include ones with a "hook," or an immediate or timely appeal, such as CDs that tie into an idea of current popular interest. Some musicians have used more commercially successful CD projects to finance other, less lucrative projects. The recording industry itself does this each year, releasing and rereleasing Christmas albums in time for the annual holiday shopping bonanza. The profits from holiday albums in turn finance other label projects. You might consider doing a holiday album in order to raise money for more adventuresome repertoire projects. Holiday music is an "evergreen" project: there's a fresh market for it every fall.

Online Distributors: Selling CDs Online

A number of online retailers/distributors carry independently released CDs. Below are listed a few of the major players as of this writing. The typical arrangement is for the retailer to take a portion of each CD sale in exchange for managing the transaction, exactly the way any distributor works. Prices vary. Check out their current arrangements/offerings:

CDBaby: http://www.CDBaby.com
The Orchard: http://www.theorchard.com
Amazon.com: http://www.amazon.com (through their Advantage program)
Barnes and Noble: http://www.bn.com

Selling CDs at Performances

The absolute, number one best way to sell CDs is at your live performances. There's no other method that works as well. Why? Because on a good night, your audience connects with you and your music, they're enthusiastic, and therefore most likely to make an impulse purchase, wanting to take a bit of the evening's "magic" home with them.

For many musicians, the CDs they sell at performances substantially enhance the fee they are paid for the performance. As a clarinetist friend says, the sales of her CDs at her performances can often turn a not-so-well-paying gig into a very good one. Chapter 6 covers booking performances in detail but, in the meantime, here are ways to promote your CD at performances. You'll need to make appropriate choices among these options, according to your audiences, programming, and performance venues.

Tips for Good Sales at Gigs

· Consider programming your concerts with at least some of the repertoire on your CD. At your concert, verbally introduce this repertoire and explain that you recently recorded it on your latest CD.
· At some point during the concert, announce—or have someone do it for you—that your CD is available tonight and explain where the sales table will be. Announce that you'll be on hand to meet with the audience and sign CDs after the performance; it will boost sales.
· Arrange to have a friend sell your CDs at a table during intermission and at the end of the concert. Bring an attractive nonwrinkling fabric table covering so that the CD sales table is noticeable and welcoming. Make it easy on your customers; it's best if you can arrange to accept credit cards, issue receipts, and offer a special concert discounted price, less than the regular retail price, but that includes the sales tax built into the price.

Note: for tax and financial management purposes you'll need to keep excellent records of your CD sales. Knowing how many CDs you've sold at what price and where will help you fine-tune your promotion and marketing plan. Avoid financial mismanagement. Find a qualified accountant (perhaps a friend of the family) to help you organize a basic bookkeeping method and make sure your friends at the CD sales table follow through with it. See chapter 10 for detailed finance and tax issues.

· Have a mailing list sign-up for everyone who visits the CD sales table (capture names and e-mail addresses). Make sure each CD buyer gets added to your network mailing list so you can send them invitations to your next concerts. And they can forward your e-mail to their friends, "Jane, I *love* this pianist, you've got to hear her next concert!"
· For ensembles, consider having giveaways at the CD sales table, inexpensive promotional items printed with your group's name, logo,

and website. Promotional postcards, decals, refrigerator magnets, pencils, and pads of paper with your logo are all fine, or anything else that is both cost-effective and creative. Some ensembles also have promotional t-shirts, mugs, or caps to sell at their performances and on their websites.

You may be thinking something like, "This is getting way too commercial. I'm not a businessperson, I'm a musician! If people hear me and like my music—and they will—my career will take off, I won't have to worry about all this #&@%." If so, you're not alone. I've had many clients express a version of these sentiments.

Of course we'd all love to spend more time and energy on the artistic side of our careers, in rehearsing and giving performances. But the truth is, developing a performance career takes more than practice. If you make a CD and would like to use it to help advance your career, it takes work. If you would like to recoup your investment by selling a portion of the CDs, this also takes work. Booking your own performances, building your mailing list and audience, all this takes even more work. It's not impossible, but it takes time, effort, and planning. Whether you're investing time or money, the trick is to think strategically. Think long-term outcome as you make what look like short-term decisions.

Mail Order Sales Tips
- Add a shipping and handling fee to the price of the CD
- Provide a choice of shipping methods (first class, UPS, FedEx)
- Include a business reply card or return postage paid envelope (make it easy for fans to buy your CD)
- People like a menu of choices. Include extra items to order: your ensemble's t-shirt or mug.
- Consider doing a cooperative mailing with your colleagues, with other musicians with CDs. Use a combined mailing list, pool your resources, and increase your profits.

Consignment Sales at Stores

In the two scenarios described earlier, both musicians sold CDs on consignment at local stores. If you consign your CD at chain record stores, your CD is competing for attention with those being hyped by the powerhouse publicity of the major labels. What can you do? Ask the stores in your area if they have, or might set up, a special CD bin section for local artists. Placement of your CD in such a section would help draw attention to it. Also, depending on a store's space and layout, there may be opportunities for local musicians to present live in-store performances. Check out the possibilities in your area.

Think beyond record stores. Depending on your repertoire, there may be particular local specialty shops—boutiques, jewelry, health food, or craft stores—interested in playing and selling your CD. Go to these stores, introduce yourself to the manager, bring a portable CD player and your CD and invite the store manager to listen. She or he might agree to regularly play your CD in the store and keep a small display for sales at the register. You can purchase small display stands through many CD manufacturers.

If a store agrees to sell your CD, you'll need to provide the manager with a consignment agreement, stipulating the terms of your arrangement. You provide the CDs. The store only pays you for what they sell, minus their commission. A simple consignment agreement between you and the store can serve as an order form or receipt for the CDs you provide. Below is an example of a basic consignment agreement. The amount the CD sells for and the amount the store keeps is something you'll negotiate with the store manager.

Promoting Your CD ■

The way to kick off all these sales efforts is by celebrating your CD release with a well-publicized event, inviting your network, and creating a "buzz" in the local media. The object is to have people reading and talking about you, your music, and the CD. A well-publicized CD release concert and party is just the ticket.

Staging Your CD Release Concert/Party

To make the most of your CD release, make it an event. Plan a performance and a party and invite everyone on your mailing list. Get friends to invite their friends. Use a guest book sign-in to get everyone's contact info for your database to expand and update your network.

Where to hold the event? To keep costs down, consider venues where you have connections, perhaps a church, temple, school, community center, a supporter's home, or any workable setting you might be able to use for little or no cost. For further savings, you may have friends, family, or other supporters who'd sponsor the event or cater the reception.

How do you announce the event? Below is the text from a postcard invitation from a few years back. The invite was to a CD release event for an excellent Boston-area chamber ensemble. Analyze the invitation; look for

Consignment Agreement

Date _____

Consigned to _____
                                              (name of store)

Address _____   Phone _____

_____ copies of the recording titled _____,

_____
(label name)   *(catalog number)*

Suggested Retail Price: $ _____
Price to Consignee: $ _____

Payment is due when additional recordings are consigned or
_____ days after the receipt of an invoice for records
sold. Full returns accepted.

Recordings are the property of _____ and
                                              (you or your label)
may be removed at their discretion.
Thank you,

_____
(signature of consignor, you)

_____
(signature of consignee, the store)

Consignment agreement example

the "selling points" to give you ideas on how to describe and promote your
own event.

This is an effective marketing piece. The invitation has specific selling
points that help make it compelling:

- Special occasion value (not just a CD release, concert and party, but the
  group's tenth anniversary)
- Quality of the venue (historic inn)

CD RELEASE CONCERT & PARTY

The Tenth Anniversary Season will mark the release
of Musicians of the Old Post Road's second CD
Trios and Scottish Song Settings of J.N. Hummel.
For this special event at the historic Wayside Inn, the ensemble
will perform selections from the new CD and will offer rare
period instrument performances of chamber music and songs by
Felix and Fanny Mendelssohn. The Inn's ballroom will provide an
intimate setting for this lively evening, which will conclude
with a champagne and dessert reception.

Suzanne Stumpf, flute; Julia McKenzie, violin; Daniel Ryan, cello;
Michael Bahmann, fortepiano;
with guest artist Pamela Dellal, mezzo-soprano

Saturday, March 20, 8:00 P.M. • Wayside Inn, Sudbury
Seating is limited! Subscribe early!

For reservations, please call the office at (781) 466-6694, or
send e-mail to musicians@oldpostroad.org, or check our website
at http://www.oldpostroad.org

Wayside Inn • Sudbury: Located just off of Route 20 in Sudbury.
From Route 128 take exit 26 west; from Route 495 take exit 24 east.

"[The performers] bring grace and elegance to their
period instruments"
– *The Strad, London*

Release party invitation

- Specific repertoire (the CD selections plus rarely heard works on rare instruments)
- Fancy extras (champagne and dessert reception in a ballroom)
- Exclusivity ("seating is limited; subscribe early!")
- Easy directions to get there
- An impressive endorsement of the quality of the group (the quote from *The Strad*)

This example is for a well-established group's posh event. What about invitations for more modest CD releases? Below is a hypothetical e-mail invitation for a lower profile CD release event (there's no actual Boston Baked Brass).

Greetings!

I'm writing to invite you to Boston Baked Brass Quintet's First CD release Performance and Party Sat. Mar. 5 at 7 pm at the French Library in Boston.

We'll be performing excerpts from our new CD plus other surprise repertoire from this season's touring. The CD, titled, "Boston Baked Baroque" features seldom-heard works by Couperin, Purcell, Corelli, and Marcello, plus new transcriptions of works by Bach and Vivaldi arranged by our own trombonist, Jane Zeller.

And after the performance, please join us for the party, great conversation and special baked treats from Michaela's Gourmet Pastries. Your ticket price (just $35) includes a terrific concert, a catered party, and signed CD!

We'd love to have you join us for this special event!

Yours,

The Boston Baked Brass
www.BostonBakedBrass.org

Directions: the French Library is located in Boston's Back Bay, at 53 Marlborough St. (at the corner of Berkeley and Marlborough, near the Public Garden). By public transportation, take the MBTA green line to either the Arlington stop, or on the orange line, the Back Bay stop.

For driving directions, see http://www.frenchlibrary.org or call (617) 912-0400.

E-mail invitation for CD release

Subject line: "You're invited to a CD Release Performance and Party!"

E-mailings are perfect for sending out invitations to CD release events. Your e-mail invite should be short and friendly, yet provide all the critical selling points and details. Avoid using attachments that your recipients might have trouble opening. Make sure your message includes hyperlinks to all relevant websites.

And for life beyond your CD release, follow up with your network at regular intervals with invitations for other performances and career updates.

Publicizing Your CD Release

You'll want to announce the event to a wider group than your own network. Check relevant music organizations for listservs or newsletters where you could include an announcement about the event. For example, Chamber Music America, the service organization for ensembles, has an excellent listserv for its members. People post CD release announcements and other news about their groups regularly. CMA also offers terrific grant programs, so check out the member benefits at http://www.chamber-music.org.

There are many other music organizations for specific member interests, such as the American Choral Directors Association, the American String Teachers Association, the Double Bass Society, the Beethoven Society, and so on. To find local and national music organizations listed by specific interest area, see the *Encyclopedia of Associations* at your local library. A relevant organization, interested in the kind of music you perform, might list your CD release information in their newsletter, or even do an interview and feature story about you and your music. And if your music or your group itself has a particular ethnic or national orientation, you may find relevant cultural associations and newsletters to help you reach a target audience.

Fiddler Lissa Schneckenburger (http://www.lissafiddle.com) plays a range of traditional repertoire from Irish, Scottish, French Canadian, and contemporary folk music. When releasing her CD, *Different Game*, Lissa planned three CD release concerts. She had done quite a bit of performing in three New England cities, and had sufficient support and contacts to organize a mini CD release tour. Lissa researched the press contacts for each city and sent out invitations to her mailing list plus announcements to appropriate folk music oriented organizations and businesses in her three target areas. Her work paid off; the turn-out at all of the performances was great and she was able to make a "buzz" in not one but three communities!

Media Coverage, Getting a Buzz

To create media attention for your CD release, you could spend a small fortune on advertising in your daily newspaper or you could get a range of media attention for free. Free is good. The way people get their stories and events into the news is by sending out press releases to contacts in the media. A press release is simply an account of your newsworthy event or story, written in a concise news format. Releases are sent to the journalists and editors for consideration as material for potential articles, calendar listings, interview pieces, and so on. To get printed, the story, the event and angle, has to be interesting to the public, to the newspapers' readers.

Releasing a CD in and of itself does not make for an interesting news story. But if the release includes a premiere of a new work, or works seldom heard, or if the funding of the project or the recording process itself was unusual or noteworthy, then these specifics might be the "hook" for a newspaper or music magazine article.

To write an effective press release, consider what is interesting about your music, your ensemble, and you. Think of human-interest angles: does your group have an improbable story about how you first got together, or do you have interests beyond music that a general reader might find compelling? Beyond the CD release, has your group contributed in a large-scale charitable cause, a marathon, an opening of a new arts or community center? Look for news angles that help the media turn a simple CD release event listing, of narrow community appeal, into a compelling profile piece that would engage a broad readership. Press releases and media relations are covered in detail in chapter 7.

Radio Play

In order to get airplay for your CD, you'll need to compile a media list of appropriate radio stations and particular program directors at these stations. The process is to send each radio program director a personalized "pitch" letter, your CD, plus your bio. To find a list of appropriate radio stations, see *Musical America*. Radio stations are most interested in playing CDs of groups or soloists with upcoming local performances, so timing is critical. Indicate in your letter that you are available and interested in a radio interview before the performance. Check if your local station broadcasts interviews and studio performances. In order for a radio station to consider playing your CD, it must be easily available for purchase. If your CD is not readily available in retail record stores, you at least need a website where fans can buy the CD, either your own site or a CD retailer's.

CD Reviews ■

To get your CD reviewed, you need a media list of critics who review CDs in newspapers, magazines, and on the Web. A listing of print and Internet publications with CD reviews is in the appendix. For more information, see *Musical America* and check the Indiana University School of Music library's site: Worldwide Internet Music resources: http://www.music.indiana.edu/music_resources/journals.html#C.

To get your CD reviewed, you'll need to send it out to music journalists at appropriate publications with a personalized letter, no generic "To whom it may concern." The letter should describe the repertoire on the CD and include engaging and relevant information on the background of the performers. The purpose of the letter is to personalize the interaction, to invite the recipient to listen to the CD and consider reviewing it.

Like radio stations, publications are only interested in reviewing CDs that are readily available for purchase. Some of the larger publications will only review CDs that have been released by a label with national distribution. Other publications may review self-released CDs if they are accessible for purchase on the artist's website, or on a well-known online retailer, such as Amazon or CDBaby. Research carefully to find all the publications, big and small, where you might be reviewed (start with the list in the appendix).

If you are just getting started building your career, it may be easier to get a CD review in smaller, local publications. Browse your local newspapers, magazines for local musicians' CD news. Ask your local librarian how to research this further. And if your instrument has a membership organization with a print or web-based newsletter, this might be another source for a possible review. A good review can be very helpful, even if it's from a smaller, or local source. And a testimonial or endorsement from a well-known artist can also be useful in marketing your CD. See chapter 7 for more information on contacting the media and writing press releases and an example of a publicist's letter submitting a CD for review.

To wrap up, for a recording project or any other, advance planning can help minimize frustrations and maximize success. It's possible to scale recording projects to fit almost any budget but not every aspiration. Clarify your purpose, plans, and expectations.

Recording Project Worksheet (complete)

✓ Why: Reasons to record
✓ What: Repertoire decisions
✓ How: Recording on location?
       In a studio?
       Do-it-yourself?
✓ How Much:

Expenses, production costs:	*Resources:*
Collaborating musicians:	Savings:
Studio costs:	Loans:
Hall rental:	Grants:

Recording Engineer: Gifts:

Producer: Other:

Editing:

Mastering:

Piano Tuning:

Graphic design:

Photography:

CD Booklet Editor:

Copyright registration:

Licensing Fees:

Bar code registration:

CD Press:

Artwork printing:

Expenses, promotion costs:

Promo material printing/assembly:

Mailing to radio/media:

Follow-up phone costs:

CD Release Concert/Party:

Online retail sales arrangements:

Total: **Total:**

■ Suggestions for Moving Ahead ■

After filling out the worksheet above, here are a few more questions to help you advance your recording project.

1. Describe the audience(s) for your recording. Be specific.
2. Once your recording is completed, what do you plan to do with it? What is your marketing and promotion plan? Be specific.
3. If you need to raise part of the money needed for the project, how do you plan to do this?
4. How many CDs do you plan to send out for promotional purposes? Where do you plan to send these?
5. How many CDs are you expecting to sell? How?
6. What organizations and individuals can you contact for referrals and suggestions about your recording project?

Online Promotion:
Using the Internet to
Advance Your Career

Note: Because technology and Web addresses can change so quickly, this chapter keeps the specialized technical information to a minimum. Instead, the focus is on how to make the most of the Internet, issues to consider in developing websites, types of website features that have proved useful and popular with musicians and Web browsers, and the planning that will help you develop the best website for your particular situation.

What the full impact of Internet technology will be on the music industry and on individual musicians is not yet known. In the coming years, as Internet sound quality improves, as broadband, high speed Internet access proliferates, as streaming of live concerts becomes more practical, and issues of copyright are sorted out, musicians will have unforeseen opportunities. How the technological developments will affect record labels, distribution companies, and traditional concert series remains to be seen. Be that as it may, the perennial question is this: how can musicians best use the Web to advance their careers?

What's So Special about Web Technology in Relation to Musicians' Careers? ■

The beauty of the Internet is that it makes it simple to make personal contacts with people around the world. The Web is all about personal interests, networks of friends, and ways of exploring interests. The Web is about grassroots, word of mouth campaigns, and people to people connections. The technology can seem impersonal, but what it allows is very much about personal connections, about making community.

The Internet allows musicians to connect with others and to over time create a worldwide network of supporters, colleagues, and collaborators. That's how you build a community. It's how many indie rock groups create followings and how political activists organize campaigns and protests. It can work the same for you, to help in building an audience and group of supporters. If we think about music as communication, as a way for humans to create community, then it's terrific that the Internet, another medium, can be such a perfect tool to assist us in music.

There are many ways you can use the Internet to advance your career. You can find all kinds of music career information, resources, and advice on the Web. You can join relevant e-mail newsgroups to connect with a wider group of professionals. You can send e-mail announcements and performance invitations to your mailing list, and "publish" your own e-newsletter to grow your fan base. And you can create your own website where supporters and browsers can find information about you, your upcoming performances, and more.

The Web as Information Source ■

There's an incredible amount of online information useful for music career building. For finding performance opportunities, the Web makes it easy to find information on concert series, festivals, and other performance venues. For help in developing promotional materials, it's easy to tour other musicians' websites to find sample photos, bios, and demos. There's also general career advice and specific music career advice available online. With so much information, the issue is separating out the good stuff and knowing how to use it.

For help finding what you want, use a search engine such as http://www.google.com, or http://www.excite.com, http://www.lycos.com, or http://www.altavista.com. A search engine combs the Internet for you, and then produces a list of results, sites in which the words you entered appear prominently. Keep in mind that on the Internet, everything is not equally good, accurate, or current. So be a savvy Web sleuth: when researching information, check for notice of when the site was last updated. When sleuthing for career advice, check the source of the info, the organization, or the bio and credentials of the author. Below are sites I've found useful for musicians. Note that by the time this goes to print and is read, some of the websites listed in this chapter may not be in operation, or may have drastically changed.

■
───

Recommended Websites for Musicians

For Staying Current

Find out what's happening locally, nationally, and internationally in your field (see the appendix for more resources). These websites cull the most relevant articles from major news outlets in the United States and the United Kingdom and with most of these you can subscribe to get the news direct by e-mail.

http://www.NYFA.org: NYFA Current is a free weekly e-mail arts news service
http://www.ArtsJournal.com: weekly or daily update option
http://www.MusicalAmerica.com: the music industry bible online also includes current arts news
http://www.newmusicbox.org: Web magazine from the American Music Center; emphasis on new music
http://www.ClassicsToday.com: includes extensive CD review coverage

Opportunities: Grants, Fellowships, Commissions, and More

http://www.MusicalAmerica.com: extensive opportunity listings, see calendar; also reference listings of recordings, compositions, labels, concert notes, and more
http://www.nyfa.org: New York Foundation for the Arts; sign up for free weekly NYFA currents, e-mail listing of grants and fellowships
http://www.amc.net: American Music Center; for composers and performers of new music
http://www.composersforum.org: American Composers Forum; for composers and performers of new music.
http://www.chamber-music.org: Chamber Music America, for grants, listerv
http://www.operaamerica.org: Opera America offers publications, professional development, workshops
http://www.music.indiana.edu/music_resources: Indiana University Worldwide Internet Music Resources; includes links to organizations, competitions, festivals, more

Audition Listings and Music Jobs

http://www.afm.org: the American Federation of Musicians, the Musicians' Union, for auditions, U.S. and abroad
http://www.rochester.edu/Eastman/careerservices/joblinks.htm: Eastman School of Music Office of Career Services, for links to music job listing websites
http://www.classicalsinger.com: subscription magazine with audition listings and several online directories
http://www.newenglandconservatory.edu/career: NEC Career Services Center, for subscription information on e-mail Job Bulletin and career info
http://www.peabody.jhu.edu: Peabody Conservatory's Office of Career Counseling and Placement job listings
http://www.utexas.edu/cofa/career/musiclinks.html: University of Texas at Austin's links page for musicians
Note: Many other music school websites offer job listings as well

Music Career Advice/Info

http://www.MusicBizAcademy.com: for straight-talking advice about online self-promotion, recording, and more.

http://www.knab.com: from music business consultant Chris Knab, great info on self-promotion, CDs, radioplay, and more.

http://www.mbsolutions.com: Music Business Solutions for resources, links, articles, newsletter, advice

http://www.menc.org: MENC the National Association for Music Education for careers in music: basic descriptive information on a wide range of professional options, plus job openings for music educators.

Promotion on the Internet ■

Posting Announcements to Web Calendars

To publicize upcoming performances and announce CD releases, you can e-mail announcements to sites that post calendars of events. Many newspapers, radio stations, and city or state tourism organizations run sites with Web calendars. These are designed to help people find out what's happening where and when. To find the Web calendars covering your local area, do a Web search for your local newspapers, radio stations, and tourism departments and then look on these sites to check for their calendars and e-mail addresses for sending your listings. Most likely, you'll find instructions for submissions right on the site. Chapter 7 covers tips on contacting the media and writing press releases in detail.

Connecting with Networks of Like-minded Professionals

If you have an e-mail account, you can join relevant newsgroups to receive info and participate in discussions geared toward your career interests. Many organizations offer newsgroups to their members, to post notices to all subscribers. Chamber Music America's newsgroup is great for finding out who is performing what and where, and great for posting your own information on upcoming concerts, CD releases, etc. To find newsgroups of interest to you, see http://www.groups.yahoo.com or http://www.topica.com.

Create Your Own E-newsletter

E-mail is great for sending out invitations to your performances and sending occasional career updates (news of winning a competition, releasing a new CD or going on tour) to your mailing list. If you do this periodically, your mail messages can be your "e-newsletter," always sent with a link back to your website. Be careful about how often you do this. Four to six times per year is plenty, and only send messages when you have real news. Don't be a "spammer"! Make sure that people signing up on your website or at your performances know they'll be receiving periodic news about upcoming performances.

Your e-newsletter messages should be consistent in format and style: short, friendly, and informative. In the text, insert hyperlinks to your website, to the performance site, and to MapQuest for directions.

Below is a good example of a musician's performance invitation. It's short, friendly, with complete details, links for more info, and engaging descriptions of the concerts. Reading this, would you be interested in going to either performance? Very often, musicians simply list their upcoming performances, without describing the repertoire, guest artists, or anything that would distinguish one performance from the next. Here, it's the descriptions, the website

---

Greetings!

I wish to invite you to a couple of upcoming concerts:

The Spirit of Spain: Saturday, Sept. 21 from 3:15-4 PM in the Boston Common. Brief History of Spain with Classical and Flamenco compositions. I'll be joined by special guest flamenco dancer La Chana! This is FREE. The Boston Lyric Opera will be presenting Carmen that evening. This concert is sponsored by Young Audiences of Massachusetts (www.yamass.org).

A Tribute to Ned Rorem as he enters his 79th year. Thursday, Oct. 10 at 7 PM, FREE at the Community Music Center of Boston (www.cmcb.org). On Warren in between Clarendon and Berkley St.'s in the South End, next to the Boston Ballet. I'll be performing *Romeo and Juliet* with flutist John Ranck as a part of a concert devoted to Rorem's works. This is one of the masterpieces in the flute/guitar literature.

I hope to see you at one or both of the concerts!

Aaron Larget-Caplan

http://www.alarget-caplan.org

Performance invitation

links, and the personal invitation that work so well. What makes this personal? It's the simple, right up front, "I wish to invite *you* . . ."

E-newsletter subscribers appreciate having the option to unsubscribe. It's good to include a short note at the bottom of each message on how to unsubscribe or have "unsubscribe" as a hyperlink with instructions.

When is the right time to send e-mail notices for an upcoming performance? A week to ten days beforehand is good for an initial e-mail invitation. If I get an invitation more than ten days before a local performance, it can seem too far in advance, not quite "on my radar screen." But then it's good to follow up with a short reminder e-mail the day before or the day of the performance. Many people make last minute decisions about their social plans, so sending the friendly reminder e-mail may just tip the balance in favor of your performance. If you're combining mailing a printed postcard invite with an e-mail invitation, I'd send the printed postcard first a week to ten days before, and follow it up with the e-mail reminder the day before the performance (see chapter 7 for more details).

■

When's the best time of the week to send e-mails? Marketers have found that e-mail gets the most attention when sent Wed.–Fri., noon to 1:30 P.M. (Of course, they're thinking of folks who work a Mon.–Fri. 9–5 job.) People are more likely to read and respond to e-mails when they're on a break, or just returned from lunch and more relaxed.

■

The focus of this chapter so far has been on ways you can use the Web for career advancement without having your own site. With your own website, there are many more opportunities. As with a CD project, the first step is to clarify your purpose. *Why do you want a website? What do you want out of a website?* The answers will help focus your design and budget decisions.

Creating Your Own Website ■

How Can a Website Benefit a Musician's Career?

What's in it for you? With your own website, you can extend your networking. A website is an economical, noninvasive publicity tool that can work for you 24/7 and across the globe. You can connect with people and then refer them to your website, or hand them your business card with your website address on it. This allows them to, at their convenience, check you out, and reconnect. With your own site, you can give the media instant access to your online promo kit, perfect for journalists and presenters on deadline, who need your up-to-date information and photos for publications. Online promo kits typically include multiple length bios, press quotes, list of past performances and upcoming dates in PDF file format, as well as a range of high resolution photos in jpeg files, for easy downloading.

With your site, you can also

- Provide opportunities to interact directly with fans, closing the distance between performers and audiences.
- Offer visitors a more complete impression of you—through sound clips, photos, writings—than is possible with print promotional materials (it's cheaper too!).
- Build your network by providing a mailing list sign-up on the site, so fans can receive newsletter updates, concert invitations, CD release announcements, fund-raising appeals, and so on.
- List upcoming performances, provide directions and details, sell tickets.
- Sell CDs directly to fans, without a label or distributor.
- Sell other promotional merchandise, t-shirts, mugs, baseball caps, or bumper stickers.
- Help create community by sharing links and e-mail contacts, with supporters, colleagues, collaborators, and organizations.

Creating a website to promote your career is a smart move. But much depends on how you go about it. Developing a website is an investment of time, energy and money. Musicians without the technical know-how and design skills can experience a website project as a big drain on their resources without much immediate payoff. Keep in mind that a website is basically another promotional tool, an electronic version of your promo kit and your business card. A website, by itself, will not get you "discovered," will not get you bookings, create audiences, and will not sell your CDs. A website is not a magic bullet, but as part of a musician's strategic plan it can be tremendously useful. Having a clear sense of what you'd like to get out of your website and how you plan to use it will help you in all the decisions you make along the way.

Karl S., a young jazz musician, was developing his own website with help from a group of his "techie" friends. Karl's "prelaunch" website was visually appealing, uncluttered, well organized, with great photos on each page. The menu let you easily find his bio, info on how to order his CDs (with a photo of each cover and a description of the contents), a calendar of upcoming performances, and info on his teaching.

As he was developing the website, Karl asked me for feedback and suggestions for improvement. There were several things I noticed.

1. First, his bio was long for Web reading. If a prose piece is more than one screen-length, either shorten it, or break it into pages with links. Reading on the Web, people have shorter attention spans than when reading hard copy. Offer both short and longer versions of bios, to fit visitors' needs.
2. The page with Karl's calendar of upcoming performances was arranged clearly by date but only listed the venues. Readers want ticket or cover price information and written directions and a map, if possible, for each venue. It's good to include a hyperlink to each venue or to written directions and a link to http://www.mapquest.com or a similar mapping site.
3. On Karl's CD page, he had no audio clips to preview his music. Few people would purchase a CD unheard.
4. Karl needed to add an e-mail list sign-up, perhaps for his own e-newsletter about upcoming performances.
5. Karl's page on his teaching included his fees for private lessons and just a bit about where he was currently teaching. I suggested he add more information, describe his teaching philosophy, and perhaps add some testimonial quotes from students, parents, and colleagues. Instead of the price per lesson, he might instead include a teaching studio policy statement, such as, "Private lessons are arranged and paid for in advance in scheduled six week installments. Lessons are generally taught either at the ABC Community Center in Brookline or at the XYZ United Universalist Church in Boston. Ensemble coaching is also available."

I asked Karl if he'd found the website worth all the effort so far. He said he was surprised at how impressed people were with the fact that he had a website. He said it was as if they were now seeing him at a new level of professionalism. He said it was easier to network with people, now that he was able to direct them to the detailed information on his site. But he also said that arranging for gigs remained the same: plenty of cold calls, a lot of work.

Karl was at the right point in his career to make good use of a website; he had plenty of interesting content for his site. He already had two self-released CDs to sell, he had a decent set of gigs to list on his performance calendar, and had the teaching going, as well. There were reasons for people to visit his site and reasons to return to it.

Is Now the Best Time for You to Develop a Website?

Beware: it's easy to fall in love with the idea of a website, with the technological bells and whistles, the animation possibilities, and all the great gizmos.

However, it's a website's *content* that visitors care about. What do you have to offer readers? If it's basically a bio at this point and a list of past performances, you might want to put your efforts toward performance opportunities and recordings first, before developing your website.

What about Costs?

Website development can cost anywhere from nothing to thousands of dollars. If you have a friend or fan with website design experience, or if you can find an art school student or graphic design student, you can save big bucks. Professional designers in the Boston area charge $50–$75 per hour, and most projects would be at least $300. For the do-it-yourselfer, many local adult education programs and community colleges offer low-cost courses and short-term seminars on Web page design. In addition, there are software programs you can buy (about $300) for do-it-yourself Web page construction, such as Macromedia Dreamweaver (http://www.macromedia.com), Adobe GoLive CyberStudio (http://www.adobe.com/golive), and Microsoft FrontPage (http://www.microsoft.com/frontpage).

Tips from an Expert Web Designer

From Kathy Canfield Shepard, President, Canfield Design Studios, Inc., Web Design & Development (http://www.canfielddesignstudios.com). If you choose to work with a web designer, Kathy recommends:

- Use a contract. It should spell out exactly what the designer/developer will deliver to you, as well as the process they will follow, costs, time frame, and payment schedule. It will also detail what the designer will need from you, the client, and by when, including content, feedback, and approvals. The contract should also specify who owns what (domain name, graphic design, and so on) Having a signed contract will prevent misunderstandings once your website project is underway.
- Work with someone who understands your vision! Find a designer who will collaborate with you, who will learn about you and your music, and who will work to represent you well in graphic form. Your website should be a reflection of you and your music, not your designer."

As you browse musicians' websites with a critical eye, you will find that there are many unattractive, cluttered, and boring musician websites. Great looking sites don't just happen. Website design is a profession; people have specific talents and get years of training to do this work. While it's great to save money, my advice is always to get the best assistance you can afford. In the end, finding a talented graphic art student wanting to build their portfolio may be the best way to go. Working with a designer, professional or not, won't take you off the hot seat, though. If it's your website, you are the one who must describe the image you want to convey, write the text, approve the photos, menu items, color schemes, and so forth. So, again, get savvy.

Do-it-yourself Website Necessities

· A computer and a modem: powerful enough for website development; check your manual!
· An HTML editor, and you don't have to take a course to learn HTML code because there are inexpensive software packages that let you simply drag and place to design a website.
· A Web browser, such as Microsoft Explorer or Netscape Navigator, to allow you to view files on your hard drive before adding them to your website.
· Graphics software: so that you can add photos and design elements.
· Domain name: to get your own (i.e., http://www.yournamehere.com), it's $35 per year; there are many companies such as http://www.register .com and http://www.networksolutions.com, that offer registration with various packages, easily found on the Web.
· Site Host: check if your ISP provides free hosting. If you want your own domain name, though, you'll need to pay a provider. To find inexpensive providers, check http://www.budgetweb.com.

For more detailed info on getting the most out of the web, see the highly recommended book *The Musician's Internet: On-line Strategies for Success in the Music Industry* by Peter Spellman. Chock full of resources, tips, and great examples. See his other resources online at his site Music Business Solutions: http://www .mbsolutions.com.

Your Site: A Work in Progress

Websites should be fluid, current and flexible documents. They are works in progress and they should document your career as it progresses. Every few months you should review all parts completely, with a critical eye toward revising. The best websites are most often the result of many revisions over time. The one you put together first is just your starting point. In fact, asking for reader comments and feedback on your site is a great way to gather suggestions for later revisions. And by including tracking features to your pages, you can find out which pages of your site get the most hits, so you can make adjustments accordingly.

Investigate Other Sites

Before planning your own website, research a wide range of musicians' sites. Some of the best ideas may come from musicians working in other genres. Some of the best sites I've seen are from singer-songwriters and avant-garde ensembles, maybe because these folks are more accustomed to entrepreneurial thinking. It doesn't matter where the ideas come from, as long as they help you develop a site that conveys your intended image. And check out this site, to learn what *not* to do: http://www.Websitesthatsuck.com!

Website Savvy 101

To develop your critical eye, visit other up and coming musicians' sites and ask yourself the following questions about each:

- Does the site give you a real sense of the individual's (or the group's) music? Is this conveyed in the written descriptions? Photos? Sound clips?
- Do you find the information on the site relevant? Interesting?
- Is the site easy to navigate?
- Is there anything fun or unusual on the site? Any surprises?
- What do you think of the use of graphics and photos on the site?
- Does the site offer opportunities to contact the artist(s)? Are you motivated to do so?
- Is there an opportunity for readers to become more involved in the music, either by purchasing a mug or t-shirt, joining an advisory board, or volunteering to help at concerts?
- How is the site helping the artist(s) build an audience and reputation?
- In what ways is the site helpful to someone considering booking the artist(s)?
- What do you like on the site? Why?
- What don't you like? Why?
- How could the site be improved?
- What ideas does the site give you for your own?

Visual Impact

We are all bombarded with an overload of visual advertising each day, so much stimuli competing for our attention. People need a visual hook to engage with a website; otherwise, we continue to browse, staying only for a few seconds. This makes the choice of photos and graphic design extremely important. You want a site that makes people want to stop and read.

Classical musicians' websites tend to be somewhat conservative and uninventive, so it can be helpful to look for pointers and inspiration outside the classical realm. The contemporary folk-roots singer-songwriter Patty Larkin's site (http://www.pattylarkin.com) uses an arresting color photo on the home page to draw you in. It's a full-screen enlargement of the cover from her CD *Regrooving the Dream*. Only a portion of her face is visible in the frame, and the extreme close up, the direction of her gaze, the odd unfocused background image, all make the photo mesmerizing. Throughout her site, the use of unusual photos and fragments of photos to offset text is inventive and aesthetically interesting (one page includes a cropped photo of feet in cowboy boots).

Make It Personal

Patty Larkin's site also includes a "Dear Diary" section with Patty's short writings from the road over the past few years. While many musicians include a tour diary portion on their sites, Ms. Larkin's entries are not of the usual ilk; hers are short, introspective, almost poetic narratives. The writings are an intriguing glimpse at her life on the road and how she experiences the world, and they offer a clue to her creative process. Ms. Larkin's website is not simply a marketing tool. It's a form of artistic expression. As such, it does what a hardcopy press kit cannot; it tells a three-dimensional story about her music and the creative personality behind it.

The Hook

For instance, the alternative soul singer-songwriter Titilayo Ngwenya's site (http://www.titilayongwenya.com) has an unusual menu item: modern riddles. She regularly posts unusual riddles and visitors can e-mail her for the answers. A riddle is a fun thing to run across on someone's website, in the midst of the usual promotional materials. A riddle is all about engaging the imagination. The fact that she has these on her site conveys an impression of her music and her sensibility—fun, creative, imaginative. On the practical side, anyone asking for the answer to the riddle has the opportunity to sign up for her mailing list.

Keep It Simple

Your homepage is your website's front door. It should be attractive and easily maneuverable, with a clear menu of all your site's options. For sites with a Flash introduction (animation and music), it's a good idea to provide an option to "skip intro," so that returning visitors or those in a hurry can get to your site's content immediately. A great example of a simple, elegant layout is the cello/piano duo of David Finckel and Wu Han, as found on the website of the duo's public relations firm Milina Barry PR (http://www.milinabarrypr .com/clients/dfwh.html). The duo's photo communicates an edginess, the strength of their personalities, and something of their chemistry. For the layout, the small but arresting photo is surrounded by a plain white background and a clean modern-looking menu allows for clicking through to the duo's bios, tours, links, press, more photos, and recording information, or else clicking on to Milina's other clients or back to the home site. The layout, with all the white space, emphasizes the photo and the simplicity in finding what you want on the site. The openness of the layout makes the visitor curious to explore all the menu items (a desired effect).

Well-designed websites have a consistency to each page: the relative amount of text, graphics, and open screen should stay the same, as well as the fonts and design sense. A website should promote a consistent image of the musician or ensemble. There should be a unifying element used on each page, so that no matter what the page's content, it is easily identifiable as belonging to that website.

Keep It Current

Visitors look for a "last updated" date and appreciate a website that has today's date listed. Your performance schedule should be current, so that visitors can either search by month and date. If it's a simple list, present the most recent first. A tour diary should be changed at least once a month. People hate returning to a website and reading the same old thing. It sends the message that there's nothing new going on for you, that your career is stalled.

One of the best-designed musician websites I've seen is for the New York City–based contemporary chamber ensemble Sospeso: http://www.sospeso.com. The front page is simply the group's name laid out attractively and each letter alternates with a photo of a member of the ensemble. The site has a black background with text in light tones of greens and blues and peach. Despite the reverse color contrast, it's easy to read. The graphic design is terrific: there's a logo motive that's used consistently as hyperlink buttons, a small square with horizontal stripes of the contrasting shades. There are black-and-white photos of the ensemble, some of them distorted for an interesting art photo effect. Although there's a lot of text on the site, it's well laid out with barred sections on the pages, sidebar quotes, and background graphics that suggest movement and music. One way the pages are made more attractive and easy to read is by subtle variations in the shades of the text, with hyperlinks in a rose color and plain text in a greenish hue.

One of the site's best qualities is its wit; a sidebar on the press page has this quote by Eleanor Roosevelt: "Do what you feel in your heart to be right, for you'll be criticized anyway." Next to it is a small black and white photo of a newspaper with alternating historic dramatic front page headlines, including the headline of Muhammad Ali regaining his title from George Foreman.

Planning

In planning your website, *think what your visitors might want.* Place the most useful and most sought after information at the top of the menu. More complex websites are designed with multiple layers. Start by making a map of your layout, your home page with offshoot pages for the items on your menu, and label these. Think of ideas for a unifying element you want to appear on each page.

More Tips from a Pro

From Kathy Canfield Shepard, President, Canfield Design Studios, Inc., Web Design & Development (http://*www.canfielddesignstudios.com*). Whether you're working with a pro or doing it yourself, Kathy recommends:

- *Keep your audience in mind.* Will your audience be using a dial-up connection or have cable access? A cable connection will allow you to use Flash or other high-bandwidth options. Will they need to print out your content, such as a concert schedule? Then Flash could be a real problem.
- *Have a professional writer edit your content.* People surfing the Web are usually looking for information quickly—just using your existing brochure or print media copy may be too involved to hold their attention. Also, grammar is extremely important—even a poorly worded sentence can drive people away.
- *Be consistent.* Your site, printed materials and all promotional materials should be unified and consistent in their design and message. If you do not have printed materials before you begin your website design you might want to consider having them created before or at the same time as your site.
- *Your contact information should be easily accessible.* Include an e-mail address, phone, fax if you have it, and a mailing address. This seems obvious, but based on the number of sites I visit where I cannot find a simple phone number, people are not paying attention to this!
- *Respond promptly.* Be responsive when people contact you through your site. This includes answering e-mail requests and fulfillment of merchandise orders in an appropriately timely fashion."

Items on the Menu

Musicians' websites typically include some or all of these elements:

Bio: if the website is for an ensemble, you'll want both a group bio and individual bios. Web bios should be brief, fit easily on one screen with plenty of margin, and have room for a photo. But it can be great to provide options, a concise one-paragraph opener bio and a link to the rest, or else menu buttons for both short and long versions. Web bios, meant for fans and potential performance bookings, should be informative and intriguing. The visitor wants to get a sense of what makes the musician "tick." Additional pages can be linked from the bio, for use by prospective concert presenters, with items related to bookings, such as repertoire lists, sample programs, descriptions of educational presentation offerings, press releases, and so on.

Performance listings with where, when, and what you'll be performing. Include ticket and program information and either a hyperlink to the venue's website or written directions and perhaps a link to http://www.mapquest.com. Depending on the music you perform, you may want to include well-written and brief program notes, information on the composers, and intriguing aspects of the piece written for a non-musician audience. You may find colleagues who are especially good at this. Remember, these days people have so many leisure activity options, you need to provide compelling descriptions of the works, performers, and the concert experience itself to help draw audiences.

CD page: include photos of your CD covers, and list titles and descriptions of the music. Include reviews or testimonial quotes from mentors, colleagues or fans. This page needs to link to your . . .

Purchase page: for selling your CD and other items. The simplest way is to have a printable order form on your website that people can use to mail a check. Although this is the simplest, note that without credit card purchase power, you may lose impulse buyers. You can also link to a CD retailer, such as Amazon.com, CD-kiosk.com, or cdbaby.com. You can also set up a merchant account for taking orders by credit card, with companies such as clickbank.com and paypal.com. For a fee, they process the purchase transactions on your site with a secure server.

Sound clips: either via downloadable files, such as an MP3 file or via streaming your audio by using software such as RealAudio. Pros and con: the sound quality is better with downloadable files but streaming is much quicker for the visitor. The good news is that technology is changing fast, and the expectation is that sound quality will improve further in coming years. Note: the point of the sound clips is to give the visitor a preview of your recordings or live performances. For ease of downloading and because you may not want to give your recordings away, keep your sound clips brief; thirty- to forty-five-second excerpts are typical.

Photos: If your website is for an ensemble, use group shots on most pages, but if you're planning on having individual bios, having accompanying individual photos is great. It works well to use a variety of photos, but these should have a coherent connected "look" so that they recognizably belong together on the same site. Your website needs to work as a continuous narrative, so the photos should complement each other.

Press or testimonial page: If you have reviews, you can use quotes from these, making sure you include the newspaper, city, and state; if the critic is well-known, include their name too. If you don't yet have reviews, it's fine to use quotes from conductors, mentors, and concert presenters, as long as you have their permission.

Electronic press kit: This can be a specialized portion of your website offering versions of your promo materials geared toward booking and media purposes. For presenters and the media, you can provide several lengths of your bio as well as programming materials in ready-to-print downloadable PDF format. It's good to include a series of high-resolution photos for downloading for use in the print media.

Links page: you want to have fun, interesting, and relevant links to other websites. Think what your visitors might be interested in, other groups you've collaborated with, resource sites for musicians and music lovers, and more. Don't over-do it; keep the number of links to ten or fewer. You can update or rotate these links as you find new sites; you could offer your top ten websites each month, for instance.

Personal or fun pages: some musicians include a tour diary, with casual photos from their performances, backstage or on the road, with commentary. Audiences are fascinated with the creative process, with what goes on in rehearsals, and with the "glamorous" and unconventional lives of musicians. Your anecdotes of interesting experiences can make your website memorable and worthy of return visits.

FAQ page: Many websites have a Frequently Asked Questions page. For musicians and ensembles, this can be a fun page with quirky personal information interspersed with factual, interesting tidbits about your group, your repertoire, and your upcoming projects.

Contact page: Include an e-mail link to contact you and a sign up for your e-newsletter, and upcoming performance notices. This is essential; if you can't connect with your visitors, you can't let them know about future performances. It's about cultivating your mailing list, audience, and potential supporters. Some ensembles list opportunities for fans to get further involved by becoming volunteers, joining an advisory board, or helping with fund-raising projects.

The new music group eighth blackbird (http://www.eighthblackbird.com) had a fund-raising appeal on their site, describing their project to raise the money for a rehearsal piano for their studio. The group eventually raised $7,000, enough to purchase (through a friend), a refurbished 1930s Mason and Hamlin with a beautiful sound.

To connect even more with your visitors and supporters, think of ways to involve them with the music. One group reserves the last concert of their home season as an audience choice program. People vote on the group's website for the repertoire for the final concert, choosing encore performances from the pieces played earlier in the season.

Interactive elements: the most successful and popular web pages are those that are interactive. If you can, include a music trivia quiz, questionnaire, raffles for free CDs or tickets. At the least, on the page with your e-mail contact information, indicate that you welcome questions and correspondence.

Educational pages: If you also teach, you may want to use your website to offer teaching information for potential students and their parents. Include a version of your bio emphasizing your teaching skills and experience, and a teaching philosophy statement. A photo of you working with a student or coaching an ensemble will help bring the text to life. If you play a somewhat unusual instrument, including pages on the mechanism of the instrument can be interesting and appreciated by readers. Marimbist Nancy Zeltsman's site—http://www.nancy-zeltsman.com—is terrific and includes an introduction to the marimba and a memo to composers on writing for the instrument.

Trombonist Mark K. has a brass quintet and a teaching studio. On his website, the front page easily allows you to choose the area of first interest, the quintet or the teaching. This simplifies what might otherwise be a confusing menu if the two areas were combined. The quintet does lots of gigs, weddings, and corporate events. Its pages include an ensemble bio and separate bios for each performer, a repertoire list, sample programs, descriptions of workshops and booking information.

More remarkable is the teaching studio portion of the site. The menu has separate areas for kids, for advanced students, and for parents. For parents, Mark includes his teaching philosophy statement, a short bio about his teaching experience, and his studio policy. There are resource and method books listed, as well as advice on how to encourage children to practice. For students, there are recommended CDs, an "expectations" section, audio files, fingering charts, and music theory worksheets. In addition, there is a student news section, featuring accomplishments, photos, hobbies and news about his students and a special set of links for kids. The site is engaging, impressive, and helpful for both students and parents.

Keep in mind, the particulars on any musician's website should be tailored specifically to the musician's goals and accomplishments. What works well for one person won't work for the next.

Elizabeth W. started her own ensemble with its own concert series. The group's website is quite sophisticated. It has:

- ticket order and secure credit card transaction capabilities
- a group bio and group photo, plus individual bios and photos
- the mission statement for the ensemble
- an e-list sign-up
- reviews from previous concerts
- descriptions of preconcert talks with the musicians
- photos of postconcert receptions
- the listing of the full season of concerts, with hyperlinks to . . .
- program notes: well written, engaging descriptions of each piece and its composer, along with photos and drawings relevant to the work. There are also recommended recordings of these works (by other artists) with links to Amazon for purchase.

The value of this website lies in how well it serves the mission of the organization. The ensemble strives to attract a diverse audience, to take the "snob factor" out of the classical concert scenario. The site describes the programs in an engaging way, the photos and reviews add to the positive impression, the preconcert talks and post concert receptions (catered by a local bakery), and the ease of purchasing a ticket, all help to create a welcoming, compelling invitation to the concerts.

What to Avoid: The "Don'ts"

What annoys you in websites you visit? Avoid the mistakes you've seen others make. Here are some universal faults website visitors dislike:

- ✓ Having no photos or poor quality photos. Browsers want to connect to YOU, they want to see you.
- ✓ Slow sites: if the site takes too long to load, people move on. Remember, not all your visitors have fast computers with lots of memory. If your site has a video sequence, music that plays automatically, or a large set of photos, beware; make sure these files are small enough sizes to load quickly.
- ✓ Too much text per page; no one like to read too much on screen. Less is more; big margins are good.
- ✓ Poor balance of graphic interest vs. text. There should be an appealing visual element (photo or graphic design) to each page.
- ✓ Unattractive color choices (such as pink or purple text on a black background).
- ✓ Color scheme difficult to read or print. If people want to print out any page on your site, make it easy. White print on a black background can be a hurdle for some, or if the text and background colors are not high contrast (blue text on a green background is not a good idea).
- ✓ Unattractive or hard to read fonts.
- ✓ Point size too small to read easily. If you use a PC, keep in mind that Macs display smaller print. A small size font on a PC will translate as minuscule on a Mac. Make sure you check your site in both platforms.
- ✓ Spelling and grammatical errors; proofread carefully and have someone edit your text.
- ✓ Not easy to navigate: make sure that the menu choices are logical and help visitors to easily find everything. If the menu appears on every page, it's simple for the visitor to hit everything they want in the order they choose.
- ✓ Links that no longer work. You'll need to check often and regularly update your site.

Attracting Traffic to Your Website

To connect with potential site visitors and CD buyers, you'll want to register your site with all the major search engines, including http://www.google.com, http://www.excite.com, http://www.lycos.com, and http://www.altavista.com. There is no charge for this, so be wary of search engine signup services with fees! Beyond the search engines, you should exchange links with other sites that will drive traffic to yours. Think about fans of your type of music and which websites would make sense to link with yours.

Whatever your genre of music, join the appropriate newsgroups and post information about your site, your music, and your CD. Join in worldwide conversations among folks as passionate about your kind of music as you are. It's about making connections with individuals.

The number one way to drive interested visitors to your website is through your e-mail list, by sending e-mail invitations to your performances, by sending occasional newsletters. Always include a link to your website in your e-mail signature. Make sure your website is on your business card, performance posters, and all your print promotional pieces.

Calculating a Website's Effectiveness ■

How will you know if your website is paying off for you? How will you determine if it was worth all the work? You can add web page counters to your site to track the number of visitors. Make these hidden from the public; there's nothing worse than having people see your site has only had a few hits so far. And most ISPs allow clients access to their online account to view accounts of the traffic patterns on their site. Knowing which of your web pages are the most popular helps as you continually improve your site.

To further assess the effectiveness of your site, you'll want to track how many people sign up for the e-mail list, how many people buy your CD off the web, and how many people coming to your performance found out about the event via your site. Always ask people how they heard about you, your CD, and your performances.

■

Websites for the Do-it-Yourselfer

Indie Centre
http://www.indiecentre.com
Site is focused on do-it-yourselfers, with articles on CD distribution, promotion, tour booking, and more.

Music Business Solutions
http://www.mbsolutions.com
Articles, links, resources for successful music careers, focus on do-it-yourself recording, gigging

Internet Service Providers, where to find them
http://www.thelist.com

■

■ Suggestions for Moving Ahead ■

1. What do you want from a website? What do you want your website to do for your career? Be specific.
2. What can you include on your website to convey a sense of you as a person, as an interesting individual?
3. What would you like visitors to be able to find on your website? List the menu items.
4. What interactive elements are you planning for your site?
5. Whom can you contact for referrals and suggestions about your website project? Think about anyone in your network who is web-savvy or who has already developed a website you like.
6. A great website won't help if people can't find it. How are you planning to drive traffic to your site? Which search engines will you register with? Which websites will you be linked with? What organizations' websites will list you as a member with links to your site? What newsgroups do you or will you participate in?
7. If you do not have a website, or have one that needs improving, what is preventing you from moving forward with the project?

Interlude:
Fundamental Questions

Clearing the Runway: Removing
Obstacles to Your Success ■

Before venturing further with the practicalities of your music career, there are some larger conceptual issues that need attention. The four questions that follow speak to essentials: motivation, success, community, and meaning. These core issues often go unexamined by musicians. Unfortunately, when left unexamined, these issues can be stumbling blocks on the path to success. Asking yourself these essential questions will help you identify obstacles and clear the path to your future.

1. Why Are You in Music?

Musicians rarely grapple with this crucial question of their motivation. If you take the time to reflect, most likely you will identify a range of reasons why you're involved in music. And your motivations have probably shifted and changed over the years. Re-examining your motivations regularly over the course of your career will help you assess if you're on track, if your investment of time and energy is satisfying. It's good to keep in mind that we're all "works in progress."

■

The Motivation Quiz

Check off the reasons why you're in music. Add more as needed. Note: there are no right or wrong answers here, only the value of examining your motivations.

- ☑ Sheer love of music itself, whether as a listener or as a performer
- ☑ Passion for *making* music: the physical, intellectual, and emotional experience

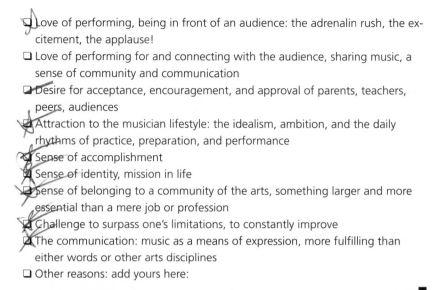

❑ Love of performing, being in front of an audience: the adrenalin rush, the excitement, the applause!

❑ Love of performing for and connecting with the audience, sharing music, a sense of community and communication

❑ Desire for acceptance, encouragement, and approval of parents, teachers, peers, audiences

❑ Attraction to the musician lifestyle: the idealism, ambition, and the daily rhythms of practice, preparation, and performance

❑ Sense of accomplishment

❑ Sense of identity, mission in life

❑ Sense of belonging to a community of the arts, something larger and more essential than a mere job or profession

❑ Challenge to surpass one's limitations, to constantly improve

❑ The communication: music as a means of expression, more fulfilling than either words or other arts disciplines

❑ Other reasons: add yours here:

What is driving your ambition? What is fueling your desire to become a successful musician? What aspects of a musician's life and work are real priorities for you? It's easy to get bogged down with everyday life and lose sight of why you first got involved with music and what you most value in your musical activities. There are many ways to be involved with music, so knowing what you want out of your involvement is essential to making your best choices. Understanding your motivations should help you in making the daily decisions that shape a career.

2. How Do You Define Success?

Musicians can be so focused on improving their abilities as performers, that they avoid defining the version of success they are seeking. How do you picture success? What does creating a satisfying life in music mean to you?

In advising musicians, I generally run into two extreme camps. On the one hand, there are the complete idealists, interested only in *artistic* success, not financial success. They don't care what they have to do to make a living as long as they have time and freedom. These people proudly wear the starving artist badge. Dealing with any aspect of the business side of music is selling out. This extreme position is difficult to maintain without a trust fund or second income.

On the other hand, there are those musicians who define success as having a major international career, worldwide acclaim, and the appropriate financial reward for such stature. For these people, success is the rarefied atmosphere of superstardom.

Both positions are limiting. An all-or-nothing mentality doesn't allow for the variety of lifestyles and satisfactions that musicians actually enjoy. Outside the "entertainment" arena, other highly skilled, accomplished professionals are considered successful even if they are not famous. It reminds me of a riddle I heard recently: Question: What do you call a person who graduates from an Ivy League medical school at the bottom of his class? Answer: A doctor.

There are musicians, highly skilled and accomplished, who do not consider themselves successful because they have not attained national or international recognition. They perform locally and regionally, and they have created wonderful lives for themselves, combining performing and teaching with recording and freelancing, working with a wide range of artists. Their lives, viewed from the outside, seem interesting, varied, and satisfying. But they do not consider themselves successful because they have not achieved wider recognition. It's not unusual to hear older, quite accomplished musicians lament the fact that they never got that lucky break or the major label contract of their dreams. And they may express some version of, "I could have made it big if only . . ."

The problem in all this is how narrowly musicians define success, how they discount their own value and accomplishments. How you define success for yourself determines how you will assess your life's work. How either content and satisfied, or bitter and resentful you may find yourself in the future. So when you take the measure of your life, what kind of yardstick will you use? As you advance in your career, will you be able to notice and appreciate the everyday triumphs, the series of small successes along the way? Will you be realistic and patient about the process of building a career? Will you be able to separate the fantasy of media-hyped fame from your own values and goals? Will you value those aspects of your life that give you the greatest satisfaction, so that you can define success for yourself?

It's typical to have goals and priorities change over the years. Your goals at age twenty are different from what they are at thirty or at forty. Look at how the priorities of Astrid Schween, the cellist of the Lark quartet, have shifted more than once over the years. Early in the quartet's history, the Larks played one hundred concerts a season, a grueling tour schedule. Later on, as several members were starting families, they focused more on New York City–based residency work and asked their manager to limit the touring schedule. These days, Astrid is excited to be adding concerto and recital work to her quartet schedule, something she didn't have room for earlier on.

It's important to acknowledge that career success and happiness don't necessarily go hand in hand. Life is just more complex. Talk to people whom you consider successful, people in any profession. Ask them about their sense of happiness. I find that most often people speak of a balance in life, of having meaningful and challenging work balanced with a rich personal life. That in the balance is where they find satisfaction, joy, and contentment.

3. What Kind of Partnerships Are You Creating through Your Performances?

There's a kind of thinking that musicians often fall into: I call it us/them thinking. Sometimes it's musicians (us) versus the rest of the world (them) or else it's art (us) versus the crass business side of a career (them). This us/them thinking can keep musicians isolated and disconnected from others, even from potential supporters and collaborators. But careers don't happen in a vacuum. A practical alternative to the us/them dichotomy is to think in terms of partnerships.

Consider the live performance experience itself. In terms of arranging for a concert, there's plenty of work involved, from securing a hall, to publicity, writing and printing program notes, press releases, invitations, and organizing a reception. To be successful, performances usually need a team of people, all working together for one goal: a successful musical experience for both the performer and the audience. To get beyond the us/them trap in thinking, it's helpful to acknowledge that performers work in partnership with others to create the live performance experience. The diagram below shows the process and the collaborators. The performer, whether or not she or he works with a manager, works with the presenter to arrange for the performance date and negotiate details. In order to attract an audience to help create the live musical experience, a performer needs to connect with the media, newspapers, radio, and more. Everyone in the circle is a partner in the process. They are all contributing to the desired outcome, a successful live musical experience. If you view the people working "behind the scenes" for a performance as collaborators, it changes the quality of your interactions—making it easier on all.

It may seem strange that I've included the audience in the circle of collaborators. What is the audience's role? What does an audience contribute? For the musician, the successful performance may mean a high standard of technical accuracy and a close approximation to her or his ideal interpretation. For the presenter, the successful performance may mean a full house, a good post-concert reception with artists and donors, lots of media attention, and names and addresses of potential new season subscribers. But what does the audience want?

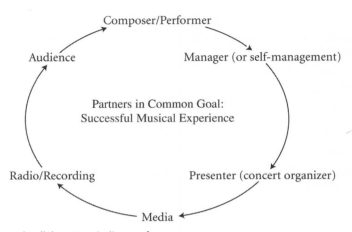

Process and collaborators in live performance

Several years ago I heard the Borromeo quartet perform Schoenberg's String Quartet Op. 7, a dense and difficult forty-five-minute, single-movement work I'd never before heard. The performance was spectacular. But what I found most memorable was my experience during the performance. For once, I wasn't analyzing the work or the performance (this is the curse of a trained musician's experience as an audience member). Instead, I noticed the effect of the hall, the acoustics, and my pleasure in watching expressive, passionate performers, and the communal sense of the audience's intent listening making a kind of electricity palpable in the hall. At times my thoughts were racing, trying to keep abreast of my own sensory overload, making connections, associations, and trying to take in the total experience of the performance. Because it was in one long movement, a sustained experience, I was even more conscious of my continuous thought process. At some point after the quartet finished, during the applause and cheers, it dawned on me that each person in the audience had experienced something individual, perhaps nothing like what I had experienced. But, as a communal experience, we'd all shared in something powerful.

I used to think of performances as fairly one-way transactions. The musician gives the performance and an anonymous audience receives it. At the end, the audience signals its pleasure or disapproval. But now I think of the performance as the real transaction going on, not as the actual sounds the performer produces, but the *experience* that each audience member and performer create in partnership. The performance experience occurs in the listener's mind, the non-verbal dance of ideas, emotions, reminiscences, and associations. The performance experience is creative, associative, individual, and communal. In the best situations, a performance creates a sense of community between musicians and audience.

What do you imagine your audience to be getting from a live performance? What do you imagine runs through their minds as they listen? It can be difficult for trained musicians to imagine what a non-musician experiences, someone not listening critically. They may be there for entertainment or escape, as a break from their hectic lives. Or a concert may be a special social occasion with family and friends. They may come for inspiration, emotional and intellectual challenge, or a spiritual experience. What would you like your audiences to experience?

"I believe that musical talent is a gift given and that it is inextricably bound to social responsibility. . . . I believe that musicians are agents for positive change in the world."

> —Pianist Kwang-Wu Kim, former Administrative Director of El Paso Pro-Musica, an innovative community music program in El Paso, TX at his inaugural address as President of the Longy School of Music in Cambridge, Mass.

---

4. How Meaningful Is Your Work?

In a culture obsessed with materialism, money, and status, it can be easy for musicians to feel marginalized. To feel disconnected from their community and from people working outside the arts. It's important to step back from our everyday concerns to take in the bigger picture, to gain a broader perspective of how music functions in our culture, and to examine the larger purpose of our work.

After the terrorist attacks of September 11, 2001, there were many memorial concerts, many examples of how music can serve to help people frame powerful emotions. A year after the attacks, on September 11, 2002, there was a memorial "Rolling Requiem" project presented worldwide. It was a continuous series of performances of the Mozart Requiem, crossing all the time zones circling the earth, each beginning at 8:47 A.M. (marking the time the first plane crashed). I went to a Boston-area performance of the Requiem, held at one of the churches in my neighborhood. The building was packed beyond capacity, with people listening outside on the front lawn. It was so crowded, they piped the performance into the basement and set up another auditorium space with chairs for people to sit and listen. There'd been few rehearsals and the orchestra and chorus was made up of community volunteers, so it was not a very polished performance. But sitting in that crowded basement, listening to a heartfelt but spotty performance of a masterpiece, listening intently surrounded by neighbors and strangers, as part of a large community grieving together, I have rarely been so moved by any performance. For me, this was an important reminder of how music, in the most basic sense, serves to create ritual and meaning. It helps create community.

There are many ways for people to experience the value of their work. Have there been moments in your life that crystallized for you the meaningfulness of the work you do in music? What do you see as the function of music in our culture? If you're going to devote your life to music, it's good to know that the work you do serves a purpose, that it's a part of some larger mission beyond your own particular career goals.

These four questions are worth revisiting periodically throughout your career. Core issues deserve your attention. Your stance, conscious or not, on these issues will resonate throughout your career. Articulating your responses to these questions will help you clarify your values, and this, in the long run, will help you make better decisions—big and small—on your career path.

Here is a terrific article with still more questions to consider, these concerning the creative process, performance, and practice. This article is by trombonist Abbie Conant and her husband, composer William Osborne, reprinted by permission. This piece is one of several articles found on their website: http://www.osborne-conant.org.

Abbie Conant was formerly solo trombonist of the Munich Philharmonic. The International Trombone Association Journal has featured Conant in a cover article and described her as "in the first rank of world class trombonists." She performs as a soloist and performance artist internationally and is professor of Trombone at the Staatliche Hochschule für Musik in Trossingen.

Composer William Osborne has received two ASCAP awards, a Doctoral Fellowship to Columbia University, alternate to the American Rome Prize, and a major prize from the Theater Commission of the City of Munich for his Beckett productions. He founded The Wasteland Company in 1984 along with his wife as the main performer to explore women's roles in music theater. In recent years they have toured over 115 cities in America and Europe to great critical acclaim with his compositions.

21 Questions for Young Performers   ■
By Abbie Conant and William Osborne

Many of these questions for musicians stem from our work in music theater, and suggest how interdisciplinary endeavors might enhance one's understanding as a performer.

1. Are you practicing and performing with a sense of authenticity and commitment, or working as if you had a musical factory job?
2. Some stage directors are interested in the "performer's personality and process." Are you working with such people, or preparing to simply be a cultural institution's "personnel"?
3. Do you try to discover the musicality of a piece for yourself?
4. A performance is a sort of response to the public. The ability to respond begins with silence, stillness and neutrality. Receptivity. Can you respond when performing, or are you too buried in routine or fear?
5. Are you trying to discover your own identity as an artist? Find it, feed it, fatten it. Think of the stage personality of Maurice Andre, Jean-Pierre Rampal, Maria Callas, or Louis Armstrong. Every person has the potential to express his or her own identity. Who are you? How will you find your artistic identity?
6. A stage director uses responsiveness, receptivity, and intuition. Do you direct the music when you play?
7. Have you thought of working together with a composer or performer to develop a music that fully expresses your identity? Is there a music that is really yours? If not, why not? What would such a music be?
8. To explore yourself without performing (just practicing) leads to excessive introspection and inaudible music. With a little practice and encouragement you can evolve as a performer who projects his or her ideas. Are you learning by doing? How often do you perform?
9. Do you practice to be aware of and remove habits and clichés? Do you practice mechanically?
10. There are three steps to "recreating" a composition. The first is the existential, which is considering what the piece means to you. The second step is the psychological, which is considering the composer's motives for writing it. The third is the semiological, which is determining how you will perform the work so that others can perceive its meaning. Have you considered these steps? How will your performance make vivid the composer's motives, and your inner relation to the composition?
11. We communicate when we perform. Have you considered that everything has a meaning, including your presence on the stage?
12. Do you realize that humans think with their whole bodies, and not just the brain? Do you realize that performing is essentially an act of the body? Do you consider it presumptuous to consider performance as poetry in space made possible by intense physical preparation?
13. Art is the creation of symbolic forms. How do you highlight and detail your performance to create an iconic vividness?
14. The antics do not make the clown, it is when he or she reveals some

truth about him or herself. Authenticity. Is it the technique or acrobatic perfection that makes the musician? Do you reveal the truth about your inner identity when you perform? How can you learn to?

15. Have you noticed how instantly and unthinkingly you catch yourself when you slip on the ice? It's not instinct. When you were born you couldn't even walk. When you play do you make active the knowledge that resides in the body? When you practice are you adding the right knowledge to it?

16. Music and theater were given birth by the same muse. Do you realize that every concept, idea, or method in theater has its corollary in music, and vice-versa? Do you realize how this understanding can enrich your music?

17. Have you considered your internal repertoire of physical, imaginative, and emotional skills? Are you trying to increase them? What are you calling upon when you perform? What do you have to offer as a human being?

18. When you practice and perform do you confront yourself in a state of perpetual discovery?

19. Do you practice with the goal of making things so natural and spontaneous that you no longer feel your body? You must divest your body, it must in effect cease to exist. Ironically, only then does it really begin to exist. Do you "subdue the flesh" by removing its blockages?

20. What are you doing to learn to come before a public and not be afraid?

21. Perhaps music isn't sound. Perhaps it doesn't exist outside of our heads, because nothing in the world is a perfect realization or performance of our abstract ideals. Are you learning to operate with your mistakes? Every performer must. It is part of the human condition to constantly proceed from failure. Is there not a certain frailty and miraculousness to creation?

6

Booking Performances
Like a Pro

Jenny makes an appointment to discuss performance opportunities. She's in her late twenties, a talented and ambitious pianist, who's won a few competitions. Since getting her master's degree two years ago, she's been teaching at a community music school. She also has a few private students, accompanies for a voice teacher's studio, and has performed with several new music ensembles in the area.

At the appointment, I ask how things are going. Jenny tells me, "The teaching is OK, I like working with kids, but this isn't what I had in mind for life after graduation. I really want to be making a living as a performer, playing solo recitals. I was hoping you could give me the names of a few artist managers so that I can get representation."

I'm asked a version of this question about once a week: "How do I get a manager?" And it's similar to the question in chapter 4, "How do I get a record contract?" in that the answer takes some deconstructing.

Myths about Artist Management ■

Musicians tend to perpetuate myths about management, because they often are uninformed about the realities of the way artist management works. Fantasies are passed along from teachers to students, to colleagues, in a loop of misinformation. Circulated fairy tales often contain kernels of truth about how management either worked in the past or how it has worked in a few exceptional cases. The problem lies in accepting these myths as reality, as general rules for all.

Myth #1: Careers happen like this: if you're talented, practice hard, and win big competitions, you will be rewarded with a manager who will make you a success. Your manager will provide enough well-paid performances that you won't need to have a day job.

Myth #2: Finding a manager is a straightforward process. You simply send in your publicity materials with a letter requesting management, and, eventually, someone will sign you on and then you'll be a success.

Myth #3: Once you have a manager, your career will take off. Your manager will handle *all* of the business aspects of your career, the details of publicity, contracts, and finances, leaving you free to practice and perform.

Myth #4: In order to get bookings and have a successful career, you need a manager.

Reality: What Do Managers Actually Do?

The main work of artist managers is booking concerts for their artists. An experienced, successful manager is someone who has built solid relationships with presenters, the people who organize concert series, festivals, and residencies. Managers use their connections and skills to convince presenters to book their artists. Managers do their "sales" work with presenters by phone, fax, e-mail, in-person visits, and by attending regional and national booking conferences. Unfortunately, there are far more talented and deserving artists than there are ready-made performance opportunities. Because of this competition, it can take an enormous amount of time and energy to get bookings for an emerging artist on the higher-profile concert series.

Beyond getting bookings, artist managers also create or oversee the development of their artists' promotional materials, negotiate fees and contracts, arrange for their artists to audition for conductors, and sometimes make connections and contracts with record labels. Ideally, managers work in partnership with their artists in strategizing long-term career development.

Who's Who?

Booking Agent: Books artists to perform at a variety of venues in exchange for a commission of the artist's fee. Generally does not get involved in promoting artists' long-term career, or in their recording or commissioning projects, as managers often do.

Manager: Books performances nationally and internationally for those artists she or he has agreed to represent, creates or oversees promotional materials, and promotes their careers. Managers must develop and maintain good relationships with presenters. Faces stiff competition in trying to book artists for a shrinking number of prestigious series.

Personal representative: An individual who works on behalf of one artist or a small list of artists, booking concerts and managing some parts of their careers, generally on a retainer basis.

Presenter: Administrator in charge of organizing and running a performance series, festival, or residency. Oversees bookings, contracts, publicity for the series, and the financial health of the series. Generally, ticket sales cover only a fraction of the costs of presenting a series. So, fund-raising and budget concerns are a big part of a presenter's job. Presenters also must consider the balance of the entire concert series they book, so that they provide a variety of offerings for the community.

Producer: A person who organizes a concert, creates the program, hires various musicians, arranges the venue, rehearsal times, sound checks, ushers, logistics.

Publicist: A person who works to get media coverage for an individual or organization. Writes and sends press releases to newspapers, radio, television, and webzines. May work for an organization, such as a label or a festival, or on a freelance contract basis for particular performers, for a performance project, or for a CD release. Challenges include gaining media attention in a highly competitive market, and finding good news angles or "hooks" that the media will find compelling.

Note: These days, the roles of managers, producers, and presenters (and sometimes artists) are becoming somewhat blurred. It's not always a straightforward buy/sell transaction. Managers, presenters, and artists, working as trusted and long-term colleagues, may explore various collaborations, festival ideas, residency projects, producing tours and shared commissioning projects.

About Booking Conferences

Booking conferences are basically trade shows for the performing arts industry. There are regional booking conferences held each fall plus the big national one held in New York City each January. The purpose is to have artist managers (the "sales" people) interact with the presenters (the "buyers"). The presenters who attend these booking conferences run the gamut. There are people in charge of small concert series at libraries and community centers, with small budgets, looking for affordable emerging artists. And there are the presenters at university performing arts centers with much larger budgets who book touring Broadway shows, contemporary dance festivals, and recitals of well-known classical and jazz artists.

At the conferences, the managers rent booth space and lay out all their artists' promotional materials. Presenters browse and visit with managers at their booths, considering artists to book for their series. These booking conferences include the full range of the performing arts: dance, theatre, and all genres of music, classical, jazz, world music, and more.

An important feature of booking conferences is showcases. These are mini performances, often twenty to thirty minutes, for performers to showcase their talents to presenters. It's great exposure for performers, as many presenters at the more prestigious series will not book a performer they have not seen perform live, either on another series, or in a showcase setting. Showcasing can be a great opportunity but also frustrating, because the showcases often happen in hotel conference rooms with poor acoustics. Furthermore, the sheer number of showcases booked simultaneously at large conferences means that many artists perform for small audiences. Still, this less than ideal exposure can result in bookings and a "buzz" about the artist.

Regional Booking Conferences are held annually in the fall across the United States. There is the Arts Midwest Conference (http://www.artsmidwest.org), Performing Arts Exchange (http://www.southarts.org/pae.htm), and the Western Arts Alliance Conference (http://www.westarts.org). In addition, some individual states hold their own smaller booking conferences, including Pennsylvania (http://www.papresenters .org), Ohio (http://www.oapn.org), and North Carolina (http://www.ncpresenters.org). And the big event each year for managers and presenters is the national conference, sponsored by the Association of Performing Arts Presenters (http://www.artspresenters .org), held in New York City each January. There are also other conferences, not primarily geared toward booking, but at which artist managers and presenters regularly meet and discuss artists, tours, and possible collaborations. These include Chamber Music America (http://www.chamber-music.org), the American Symphony Orchestra League (http://www.symphony.org), and ISPA, the International Society of the Performing Arts (http://www.ispa.org).

For performers, attending one of these conferences as a volunteer or intern is an amazing opportunity to see the business side of the music industry in action, to meet managers and presenters, to see the promotional materials of hundreds of artists, and to gain perspective on the industry. For the booking conference nearest you, contact your state arts agency (see appendix).

How Artist Management Works ■

There are many factors that go into a manager's decision of which artist to represent. Of course, a manager must believe in the musician's artistry and ability to communicate with audiences. This is somewhat subjective, a matter of taste and interest on the manager's part, but also a matter of the artist's track record of success, his or her reputation, career readiness, and personality. A manager needs to know that the artist has "booking potential"—that the manager will be able to interest presenters in booking this artist. And managers must of course consider the balance of their roster. If they already represent a solo harpist—not an easy "act" to book—it's unlikely they'd consider adding another. And if a manager is stretched thin with the number of artists she or he is already representing, it may be impossible to add more.

No matter how much artist managers love music and love working with musicians, they are business people. In order to stay in business they must make money. Managers usually take 20 percent of the gross concert fees they negotiate for their artists, plus expenses (telephone, postage, promotional materials, travel to booking conferences, etc.). The expenses are usually billed to the artist in monthly or quarterly portions. In most cases, managers have their artists sign contracts of one to three years, an agreement that details their working relationship and financial arrangement.

The three major New York management companies are CAMI (Columbia Artists Management Inc., http://www.cami.com), ICM Artists (International Creative Management, Inc., http://www.icmartists.com) and IMG Artists (http://www.imgartists.com). These firms have the largest artist rosters, and many of the most well-known artists. And these firms have the most clout in negotiating contracts with festivals, record labels, and orchestras.

There also are mid-level management firms, with somewhat smaller rosters, such as Herbert Barrett Management (http://www.herbertbarrett.com), Thea Dispeker Inc. Artists Management (http://www.dispeker.com), and Colbert Artists Management (http://www.colbertartists.com). And, finally, there are small firms, generally one- or two-person offices, far too many to list.

Musical America, the annual music industry directory, lists hundreds of artist management companies and the artists signed to their rosters. You can browse *Musical America* at your music library to get a sense of how professional management companies market their artists. It's instructive to look at which artists are on which rosters. Managers must stretch their attention and energy more or less evenly across their roster. Inevitably, not every artist's career gets the same effort.

There are also people who will work as a manager or artist representative on a retainer basis. The musician pays a monthly fee for a contracted year or more. In New York it can cost $500+ per month, plus expenses. Unfortunately, it can take quite some time to develop leads and contacts, so artists may pay for many months without getting any concerts, or may get concerts that don't end up covering all the expenses.

Like anything else, there are good managers as well as ineffective ones. Don't sign a contract or invest in management without checking references thoroughly and getting to know the manager. Ask for the names and phone numbers of past and current artists the manager has represented. A manager without the appropriate skills, contacts, and experience is worthless to your career. And, sometimes, there are just poor matches. The chemistry between artist and manager has to be right, as the working relationship is a partnership. There is usually a courting period before artists sign with a manager, when both parties are checking the other out. And after signing, it may take a whole season before the artist gets any work. Why? Because most of the midsize to larger presenting series with which a manager works book several seasons in advance, and it can take several seasons for word to get around, within the network of presenters, about this or that "hot new talent."

To find out more about how artist management works, visit the National Association of Performing Arts Managers of America website (http://www .NAPAMA.org). Read the ethical guidelines for the profession; this will give you a good idea what to expect from a manager and what questions to ask if you are considering working with a particular manager.

Are You Ready for Artist Management? The Quiz

Do you have anything to manage?

How many concerts did you play last season?

How many reviews have you received?

What was the total amount in fees you made from concerts last season?

Now, take 20 percent of that sum and ask yourself this: Would a manager be interested in signing you? In other words, have you created enough work and media attention to interest a manager? Professional managers are not in the business of growing anyone's career "from scratch" (unless you are a world-class child prodigy). Managers simply can't afford to invest time and energy in this process.

But the good news is it's absolutely possible to successfully *self*-manage your career and to book your own performances!

Competitions

Yes, there are some competitions that offer management to the winners. These include competitions sponsored by Concert Artists Guild (http://www.concertartists .org), Young Concert Artists (http://www.yca.org), The Pro Musicis International Award (promusicis@aol.com or call 212-787-0993), and Astral Artistic Services (http:// www.astralartisticservices.org). Musicians who win such competitions receive pre-professional management for a few years. Then some of these artists, if they are successful, move on to professional artist management rosters. Other competitions offer winners a certain number of concerts at prestigious halls or a professional recording opportunity. Some musicians who win major competitions are offered professional management for a year or two on a trial basis. For more information on competitions, see the appendix.

How (Not) to Get Artist Management

Musicians often prepare elaborate, expensive promotional packets and send them to all the managements listed in *Musical America*. Every week these management companies receive bushels of unsolicited promo kits with letters from artists requesting representation. By and large, these letters, packets, and demo CDs go unread, unheard. The management companies already have their hands full trying to book the artists on their rosters. So if you don't have a personal contact with an artist management, or know that a particular management is looking for exactly what you offer, don't waste your time and money sending materials that will only be discarded.

However, management companies may be interested in hearing a new or emerging artist if an esteemed performer, teacher, presenter, or coach recommends them. If you have a mentor with management contacts who feels you are ready for management, he or she can invite these people to your next concert, or write a letter of introduction for you. But without such contacts, what's an aspiring artist to do?

Self-management: Your Best Bet ■

The basic idea of self-managing your career is that *you* are in the driver's seat. Instead of hoping to win the right competition or waiting for someone else to get your career going, why not take charge of it now? Mozart did not have a manager. He composed and performed his own works, rented halls for performances, and organized his own subscription concert series. It's true, all this takes considerable work, but take heart; there's a long history of musicians as creative, successful entrepreneurs.

Booking your own concerts is not rocket science, but there are specific skills required. In coaching musicians in this process, I've found that once you break it down into manageable pieces, most anyone can do it. My best advice is to start small and local. Arrange performances in your community first. The goals are to generate an audience and media interest, add names to your mailing list, and, eventually, to get reviews. All of this can lead to further bookings at larger venues.

Many musicians build solid local or regional reputations and followings. And once they are successfully doing this, they're in a good position to either attract good professional management, or to hire and train an administrative assistant to handle specific pieces of the self-management work. Assistants might be trained and skilled in press material updates and mailings, writing contracts, managing mailing lists and websites, writing program notes and press releases, and so on. The work you have an assistant do should depend on how much you have to spend, the skills of the person you hire, your current projects and goals, and what your own strengths and management skills are. To find suitable candidates, talk to other self-managing musicians, people at small local arts organizations, and advertise at local music schools and career centers.

Alternative to Traditional Management

Nick J. is a Boston-area clarinetist who has specialized in contemporary music, premiering and commissioning many new works for solo clarinet. He had self-managed his career while in school and then pursued finding professional management to no avail. Finally, he found a friend with a background in orchestral management who agreed to work as his personal representative on a 20 percent commission basis. The first season, Nick's friend booked fifteen concerts for him! Many of these were engagements as soloist with regional orchestras in the Midwest. This made a great addition to the New England bookings that Nick had arranged on his own.

Another alternative to traditional management described in *Making Music in Looking Glass Land*, the terrific music career guide by Ellen Highstein, is artist-run group management. A group of musicians or ensembles may band together and collectively hire a personal representative to work on their behalf either on a commission or retainer basis, or the musicians themselves divide up the work, parceling out the phone work, graphic design, administrative, and bookkeeping duties according to their abilities and preferences. Ellen Highstein writes that these alternatives to traditional commercial management "can have several advantages over individual or self-management: they can enable group members to pool information and contacts, to spread the work and cost of self-management among the members or allocate it to a salaried person, allow the member musicians to control the kinds of musicians on the roster and allow the members to say, 'Call my manager,' with honesty and confidence."

The Physics of Music Career Development

Growing a performance career works in a kind of upward spiral. Inviting your network and the press to your performances is necessary to draw audiences. Sending your recording to journalists for potential reviews also helps grow your audience and create media "buzz." Having local performances may help persuade retail stores to carry your recording. All this activity will make it easier to get airplay on local radio stations, which can lead to a demand for your recordings, more audience at your performances, and more performances at more prestigious venues. It's a process, and the periodic buzz of a CD release or premiere of a new work or a special collaboration helps boost a career forward. That is how a musician's career advances from a local level, to a regional one and beyond. And, once established, an artist must make the process continue, because without new projects, new buzzes, a musician's reputation will fade.

Researching Your Opportunities ■

Ask your mentors, teachers, and colleagues for suggestions of places where you could perform. Ask the presenters where you've performed in the past, perhaps with a college or community group. There may be appropriate concert series in your area, and there may be churches, museums, or community centers with good acoustics, where people would want to sponsor a concert or start a series. The way to find out is to start asking people for suggestions.

Beyond your network, your sleuthing should include checking the websites for the past itineraries of other aspiring musicians. Where have they performed? And read the calendar and arts sections of your local newspapers. Find out who is performing where in your local area. Familiarize yourself with the various concert series and possible performance sites. If these series have websites, read them carefully. To find contacts and particulars on possible venues for performances, visit your public library and ask the reference librarian for assistance. Your local Chamber of Commerce also might be a good resource.

Where to Perform?

There are many other possible places to perform beyond standard concert series and festivals. It's a question of bringing music to an audience and connecting personally. Use your imagination in thinking which community organizations might be interested in live music or which of these host special events where your music could be a part of the program. These alternative venues may have good acoustics, interested audiences, and the possibilities of an ongoing collaboration, a series, or a residency. Check out your local:

museums	public schools	high-end condominiums
libraries	private schools	hospice centers
historical houses	boys and girls clubs	rehab centers
churches/temples	hospitals	resort hotels
community centers	shelters	civic clubs (Elks, Rotary)
colleges/universities	senior centers	adult education centers
parks and recreation	prisons	veterans' associations
chamber of commerce	alumni associations	community music schools

In addition, you should be able to get statewide lists of presenters and other music organizations from both your state and regional arts councils (see appendix). For example, musicians living in Boston have the Massachusetts Cultural Council and the New England Foundation for the Arts. These agencies support a range of initiatives, including grant programs for community projects, arts education programming in the schools, and funding for local arts agencies to run concert series, art exhibitions, and more. Check with your local, state, and regional arts agencies for information, presenter listings, and for any grant programs for which you may be eligible.

You may have more than one geographic area to research. There's where you currently live, where you went to school, or where you've lived for a reasonable length of time, as well as where you grew up. With contacts and performance opportunities in multiple locations, musicians arrange "microtours," performing the same program in several different communities to gain exposure and experience. And, often, it's the smaller cities and towns where an emerging artist can get media coverage and reviews more easily.

Think about performance spaces in your area where you have a connection, a contact, where music such as yours is presented, and places you'd like to perform. In *Making Music in Looking Glass Land,* Ellen Highstein suggests that your school alumni association might hold functions that include live music, "that the church you attended growing up, or the library in your home town, has a concert series; that your Aunt Sadie is on the board of directors of the local chamber music society. You might find a place where you performed as a kid on a special young person's concert, where they also hire professional artists. Any connection will at least get a foot in the door, and will provide something concrete with which to start your dialogue."

Beyond a Single Performance: Creating a Concert Series

To find ongoing opportunities, think non-traditional performance spaces. Researching possible community collaborations may be as simple as walking around your neighborhood and locating schools, churches, and community organizations as possible concert sites. Gather the names of these sites and then call to request their printed materials. Do your homework; it's fine to just call and ask to be put on a mailing list or to be sent a copy of their latest brochure or newsletter. Find out about the organizations: what they normally program and what their mission is.

■

Pianist Sarah Bob started a concert series at the community music school where she teaches (see http://www.SarahBob.net). New Gallery Concert Series, founded in 2000, brings together new music and contemporary visual art along with their creators. Audiences get to hear new music in a setting that showcases new visual art. Stimulating. The invitation postcards always display samples of the visual work that will be on exhibit at the concert—it makes you curious, not just to see the artwork but also to consider the relationship between seeing the art and hearing the music, how the two influence each other and you.

■

Effective Programming: Engaging Presenters and Audience ■

What are you offering? Before making actual booking calls, it's important to outline this. I've found that many emerging artists underestimate the importance of offering engaging programming ideas to presenters. In music schools, recital programming often consists of standard repertoire from four different periods, a kind of musical history tour. But what satisfies a degree recital requirement does not necessarily work well for presenters, critics, or the public.

Think about it from a presenter's point of view. A relatively unknown artist, whose name alone will not attract an audience, playing standard repertoire— does that sound like a box office draw? Who would come hear yet another Moonlight Sonata played by an unknown when the audience can stay home and listen to the work on a CD played by any five of their favorite legendary pianists? Presenters need to consider whether or not an artist will attract an audience. If name recognition won't, an innovative program might.

Developing Programs

For emerging artists, one of the best ways to interest presenters, as well as critics and audiences, is through interesting programming—unusual pieces or interesting pairings or groupings of standard and unusual works, or themed programming.

Radius ensemble director/oboist Jennifer Montbach approaches programming by first choosing a work she is in love with and wants most to perform. Then she asks herself: Does this work suggest any potential themes or ideas that could be explored in the rest of the concert program? What unusual pieces might make an interesting contrast to this work? To get ideas, you can also ask other musicians, collaborators, faculty, and music librarians.

Think about it from the presenter's point of view. You may be able to dovetail your concert with ongoing programs at the concert site, such as offering a museum a concert of music related to one of its special exhibits, say on twentieth-century American Expressionists, on African artists, or on works by women.

Explore how the repertoire you have to offer might fit with the organization's programming. If the site has any ongoing children's programs or adult education programs, you could offer to do a master class or lecture/demonstration. Do they have a special fund-raising event coming up that could use a short recital program after dinner? In preparing for your booking calls, it's important to have at least one program organized and to be able to describe it engagingly.

Programming Ideas, Consider:

- Premiering new works (especially by local composers)
- Unusual pairings of composers (i.e., Baroque and Contemporary: a program exploring the parallels between the two)
- Music from a particular country
- Music inspired by literature
- Works exploring one idea, such as war, passion, faith, love, or redemption
- Works inspired by myths and legends
- Works linked with dance or graphic arts
- A concert organized to celebrate or commemorate a local event, person, holiday, organization, or anniversary
- Collaborating with a guest artist from the local community, a musician, dancer, or video artist
- Pairing music with poetry or short fiction readings

The Boston Modern Orchestra Project (http://www.bmop.org) has consistently compelling programming that draws diverse audiences. They've done programs focused on film music, on works influenced by world music, on works using Pan-Latin rhythms, and works influenced by rock music.

Shake Up the Formal Concert

Look for ways to make your performances less formal and more audience-friendly. What about taking a few audience questions after intermission or between any stage setups? There's no such thing as a stupid question! And I've seen singer-songwriters take a photo from the stage of their audience. This can be a lot of fun! Ask your audience to say "cheese," tell them they look great, and that you want to preserve them for your tour scrapbook.

Orchestras and chamber groups looking to expand their audiences have started having special pre-concert gatherings for the twenty to thirty-five age group. There's wine, cheese, and schmoozing with some of the artists an hour before the concert. This also can be a great way to build a mailing list, and a network of future donors.

In Napa Valley, California, each August, violist Michael Adams and violinist Daria Adams run Music in the Vineyards (http://www.napavalleymusic.com). The concert programs generally have the meatier works on the first half, then intermission includes a half-hour wine tasting, followed by the concert's second half, with the more whimsical, lighter selections. The idea with all of these examples is to make the complete concert experience more inviting, more social, more personalized.

Booking Performances A – Z   ■

Once you have a list of possible venues (both traditional and non-traditional concert sites), you need to consider the presenter's point of view. Be able to explain clearly how what you have to offer compliments their needs or programs. You may be able to dovetail your concert with ongoing programs, such as offering a local museum a concert of music related to one of the its special exhibitions. If the organization has programs for children, you could offer to do a master class or lecture or demonstration.

Exploratory Calls

Once you've done your preliminary research on your list of concert series, venues and non-traditional performance sites (reading Web sites and brochures, talking to people who've performed there), you're ready for initial exploratory calls to fine-tune your information.

Some smaller series are booked by volunteers, part-time staff, or by people who have various other duties at their institutions. Presenters at large series don't answer their own phones. When you call, it's very likely you'll get a presenter's assistant or another staff person. These people can be very helpful, so be gracious. Always make a note of the name of the person you're speaking with, so that when you call back you can refer to them by name and it's no longer a "cold" call. Your call should cover the basics, as outlined here.

> "Hi! My name is _____ with the _____
> (if you're promoting an ensemble). I'm calling with just a few questions about your concert series . . .
> Can you tell me who handles the booking of artists? Can you spell that for me? And what is her/his title? Thanks! And when are good times to reach him/her? . . .
> Could I be added to your mailing list? (and/or) Could I be sent your season brochure? . . .
> Thank you! I appreciate your help!"
> *If the person is friendly and doesn't seem rushed, here are some possible follow-up questions:*
> "From looking at your recent offerings, I see your series includes classical and jazz concerts. Are they the main focus? . . .
> Do you offer family concerts or educational workshops? . . .
> What is the seating capacity of the hall? Do you use just the one venue, or others in the area? . . .
> Does your series book emerging local artists? . . .
> Thank you! I appreciate your help!"

Note: You'll need to accept the fact that this approach will not always work. Some series only book well-known artists with management. Do as much research as you can on each presenter so you've got a good sense of the professional level of the artists they book. And realize that rejection is just part of the job of booking concerts. Don't take it personally.

Through your research and exploratory calls, you should be compiling information on a number of presenters. Use a presenter information sheet like the one here to save time and energy.

With your promotional materials ready, a list of likely presenters and their info sheets, one or two interesting programs to offer, and any personal connections you've researched, you're now ready to make calls to presenters for possible bookings.

Presenter Info Sheet

Series/Hall: _____

Referred by: _____

Contact Name: (make a note of pronunciation)

_____

Title: _____

Address: _____

Phone: _____

Fax: _____

E-mail: _____

Seating Capacity: _____

# of performances/season: _____

Season includes: (genres, family or children concerts, etc.) _____

_____

Specifics on venue (piano, stage set-up, acoustics, etc.): _____

_____

Notes about presenter: (special interests? common interests?) ___

_____

People who've performed there: _____

_____

Presenter information sheet

Do's and Don'ts for Telephoning Presenters

- Do your homework first. Be informed about the presenter's series and history. Make sure you're calling a series that's appropriate for your level of experience and type of music.
- Do demonstrate that you're familiar with the series and that you can articulate how you're a good match for the series.
- Don't make booking calls on Mondays or Fridays, as those tend to be more frantic days for most people.
- Don't rate yourself or offer subjective evaluations of your performance. Don't compare yourself with other performers, or put down others to prove that you are more deserving. Instead, offer concrete information, the facts about where you've performed, who you've worked with, awards you've won, what programs you have to offer, etc.
- Review your phone skills (see chapter 2).
- Do be persistent, but don't be a pest. You may need to call two or three times to get a person live on the line. You can leave messages but most presenters get far too many cold calls and they're far too busy to return them. If after three attempts to interest them, you don't get a nibble, move on. However, you may want to keep the presenter on your mailing list, inviting her or him to your performances in the area and sending updates of your career advancements (three times a year is plenty and only if you've got real news).

Contacting Presenters

To be effective in making booking calls, you'll need a succinct, well-crafted "pitch," a twenty- to thirty-second conversation piece about you or your ensemble. The purpose of the pitch is to interest presenters in talking further with you, so you can send them a demo or promo kit they'll listen to and read. Basically, you only have the first twenty to thirty seconds in a call (or on a voice-mail message) to pique a presenter's interest. In that brief time you need to cover the five points listed here; otherwise, you'll lose the presenter's attention and she or he will end the conversation quickly.

Five Elements of a Pitch

1. Identify your name and what you do: your instrument/ensemble/genre. "Hi, my name is Jane Smith with the ABC Brass Quintet"; "Hello, my name is Jon Doe with the XYZ Jazz Trio"; or "Hi, I'm a violinist living here in Tucson; my name is Marla Thompson."
2. Establish a connection with the presenter, their series, or the commu-

nity. "Tom Smith, the baritone who performed for your series last year, suggested I call you" or "Wendy Jones, who's on your board of trustees, suggested I contact you" or "I grew up in Brookline, and have gone to many performances on your series over the years. Now, as a young professional, I've performed quite a bit in New England and I'm interested in investigating the possibility of performing on your series."

3. Give a third party endorsement: state one or two of your most recent, most impressive credentials. It's important to offer credible evidence of your abilities, your track record of success.

> "I recently won the ABC competition."
> "I recently performed on the ABC and XYZ concert series."
> "I recently received the ABC grant."
> "I graduated with honors from [well-known music school], and have performed extensively with ABC and XYZ." (ensembles or individuals)
> "My ensemble recently released a CD that got a good write-up in ABC and XYZ newspapers/magazines."
> "My ensemble has presented well-received family concerts at _____ and _____ ."
> "We performed a series of concerts in Washington, DC last year, at the XYZ library series and we've just completed a CD. We're looking to book a series of CD release concerts this fall and we'd like to include a date in your area."

4. Program idea—What specifically are you offering?
   Describe one or more of your interesting programs:

> "Our ensemble has been performing a new work written by prize-winning composer Joe Smith. We've got a program that pairs new works by this composer with well-known works from the standard repertoire. We usually discuss with the audience the similarities and differences in approach the composers use, and audiences seem fascinated, the Q and A session is great fun."

> "I noticed on your website you do family concerts and I wanted to let you know about our educational programming. We've got a concert for grades four through six and another tailored for pre-schoolers. These programs emphasize how pieces of music are built, and teach active listening skills."

> "We've got a program of works by women composers, including two local composers in residence at A and B colleges."

"We're excited about our new program that pairs one masterwork of the repertoire with early, rarely heard gems by the same composer."

5. Questions and follow-up plan
[Other useful questions for your info gathering, if you can't find these out through your pre-call research:]

"What is the hall's seating capacity?"

"Do you use more than one venue?"

"Do you collaborate with any particular schools for enrichment programs?"

"When do you usually do most of your booking for the season?"

[This is very important, because some presenters work a year or more in advance, whereas other smaller presenters may book several months in advance.]

[For follow-through:]

"May I send you some information?" "What would be helpful? Our flyer? CD?"

[Note: your full promo kit is expensive to produce. Don't send the full kit unless it's requested. Give them just what they ask for but include a note telling them what else you have if they want more information.]

"And, I'll call to follow up in two weeks." "When are the best times to reach you?"

Remember, the call should be a dialogue—back and forth, a real conversation, but these five points are the major areas you should do your best to cover.

Tip: To get comfortable with your pitch calls, you'll need to practice this with someone experienced in booking, so that they can give you constructive feedback. Ask your mentors and colleagues. This is easy to do by phone, if these people are at a distance.

The goal of these conversations is to make a connection with presenters and find out more about their series and interests. It's the start of a relationship, so your interpersonal skills are paramount. In the conversation, you'll also introduce yourself, and—we hope—spark their curiosity and interest for your promotional materials.

◼

Idea: Research your region for places within driving distance where you might be able to do a series of performances, a mini-tour of "run-out" concerts. Once you've got a great program to offer presenters, and an initial "anchor" date booked, it can be easier to interest other presenters.

An e-mail pitch with a referral might go something like:

"Dear Ms. Smith:

Ms. Jones at the ABC Concert Series in Portsmouth suggested I contact you. She's booked our string ensemble, Trio X, for her series this summer. She told us great things about your series in Portland, especially about the innovative community residency programs you do with the parks department.

We're taking a terrific program on tour in your region this spring. Here's our website, http://www.triox.com, which includes our press kit and bio. We've got some dates open for the first two weeks in July; I'd love to find out more about your program and discuss the possibility of our working together. I'll follow up in a few days. Thank you!"

◼

Follow Through

Send them what they ask for and what you promised—immediately. You can send an e-mail with a link to your website and your electronic promo kit, and then follow it up by mailing a hard copy. Send your materials with a cover letter or, if your handwriting is good, a handwritten note, with something like:

Dear So-and-so:

I enjoyed speaking with you today about your series! Here are the materials you requested—the bio, fact sheet, and CD for my jazz ensemble, Four Minus One. I was very interested in your Sunday afternoon jazz series because of the diverse audience you attract. I'll call in two weeks to follow up.

Best Wishes,

Eric Platz

If you say you'll call back, do it! To stay organized, keep a log of presenter calls so that you can track when you called, what you sent and when to make the follow-up contacts. When you call, remind the presenter who you are and that you sent her or him your materials.

Possible Outcomes to Presenter Calls

- Rejection: you'll need to develop a thick skin. A presenter may tell you straight that she or he is not interested. Be cordial and ask the presenter if she or he has any suggestions for *other* series where you might be a better fit. Thank them for their time.

    Most of the time you'll hear "no thanks." Handling rejection is part of being a professional. It's a percentage game; you have to make many calls and pitches in order to get a group of bookings. If you learn to view this as simply part of the profession, you're better off.

- Don't call us, we'll call you. A presenter may say they'll call you if they're interested, as a way to let you down gently. You should keep this presenter on your mailing list and periodically send her or him career updates and invitations to your performances.

- The presenter is interested! She or he may ask you detailed questions about your performance history, ideas for programming, number of people on your mailing list, and so on. Talk in terms of the fit your performance might make with their series. Be personable. You are building a relationship with this presenter. Sometimes a presenter is interested in a possible booking for a future season, not the immediate one. If this is the case, ask when it would be best to follow-up and then make sure you do so!

Perspective: Put Yourself in the Presenter's Shoes

A presenter, in effect, "curates" a concert series, the way a museum curator plans an art exhibition. Curators carefully choose and arrange the artwork, guided by the principle that each individual work is experienced in relation to the whole exhibition. Curators write and print descriptions of the works and they publicize the exhibition to attract, engage, and enlighten a community audience.

Likewise, a presenter books individual performances with the whole season in mind. The goal is to create a varied, interesting and balanced concert series that appeals in its entirety to potential season subscribers. So a presenter must consider carefully the variety of offerings planned, the repertoire, and the potential box office draw of each program.

So, there are many factors that go into a presenter's decisions. Being rejected may simply mean now is not the right time or that your program doesn't fit the presenter's plans for the season.

Negotiating Fees ■

If the conversation is going well, a presenter may eventually suggest a fee or ask what your fee is. Do your homework in advance. If you know people who've performed on this series, ask them what range of fees the presenter pays.

Because some presenters receive public funding, your state and local arts agencies may be able to give you a ballpark range of the fees a particular presenter pays. Many small community series have limited budgets. Libraries and community centers may pay $300–1,000 with little or no extra for transportation or lodging. Presenters of larger concert series may pay emerging solo artists $1,000–3,000 and ensembles $2,000–5,000. Keep in mind that ticket sales account for only a fraction of the costs of running a series. The fees presenters can offer are determined by their budget, factoring in the performer's experience and ability to draw an audience.

Know your bottom line. Know the total expenses you'll incur should you agree to this performance: your accompanist fees, travel, rehearsal time, and so forth. If there are any special technical requirements for your performance (drum kits, amplification, video equipment for multi-media productions, etc.), you'll need to find out what the presenter can provide and what you'll need to bring or rent. This will affect either your expenses or the presenter's. The details of technical requirements should be clarified in your negotiations and then confirmed in your written confirmation or contract. Typically, these are inserted into a contract as the "technical (or 'tech') rider."

Likewise, if the presenter can help out with travel and lodging, this can make a performance worthwhile or touring possible despite a lower fee. Presenters sometimes can offer discount recommendations for lodging, or complimentary lodging at a home of a board member or contributor. In the end, you'll need to weigh the benefits of doing the performance—the exposure and experience—against the costs to determine your acceptable fee.

Should you be asked your fee, be prepared to say something like, "My (or our) usual fee is _____," and PAUSE! Wait for the presenter to react. She or he may say, "That's fine" or "Oh, we can't pay that much" or "That's a little steep for my budget." You can then add, "I'm willing to work with you on this" or "I can be somewhat flexible."

The idea to convey is that you are reasonable, that you want to work as a team with the presenter to help her or him make a great series, and that you're easy to work with. Think long term. Remember, it's not about booking one particular gig. It's about building professional relationships with a presenter who can book you again as well as recommend you to others.

Presenters may have a board of trustees or others to satisfy. A presenter may need to get committee approval before making a firm offer for a booking. This can take several months, especially with colleges and university presenters. Musicians need to be patient through the process.

Details to Nail Down

Beyond the fee for the performance itself, these three issues will affect how reasonable the fee offered is:

1. Whether or not you can sell your CDs at the gig. It's not unusual for presenters to get a percentage of the CD sales, especially if the presenter provides equipment or staff to assist with the sales. Ask and then confirm your arrangement in writing.
2. Any use of special equipment, or lighting for the performance and who provides what (drum kit, screen and video projector, amplification, etc.). Again, this will need to be specified in the contract as your Technical Rider.
3. Transportation and lodging arrangements. For the most part, when it comes to transportation and lodging, artists are on their own. So unless the presenter has offered or agreed to provide accommodations or travel, you'll need to consider these costs as you negotiate a fee.

About Block Booking—Creating a Regional Tour

Block booking is how tours are organized. The idea is to schedule a number of performances in a specific region, in close enough proximity to reduce costs (travel, accommodation, and fees) for the performer and presenters. Organizing a tour usually starts with an initial booking, an "anchor" date. Next, the artist looks for other possible venues in the region that will make the expense of travel for this date worthwhile. Perhaps there are nearby schools that would be interested in master classes, residencies, or lecture demonstrations to "tag on" to the anchor booking. And there may be other venues in the region to build a series of performances into a week's tour. A presenter can often help the artist make contacts with the other venues in a region to build the tour.

Confirmations and Contracts ■

Once you've agreed verbally on a fee and a date for the performance, you need to get it in writing. Confirm the booking by contract or letter even if you trust or know the presenter well. Written confirmation is essential to making sure that both you and the presenter are in agreement on all the details you've worked out. Many times the presenter will send her or his contract to you. Read it carefully and if needed, add an attachment to clarify specific details. If the presenter does not send a contract, you need to. The confirmation should include:

1. Date, time, and location of the performance
2. Fee and specifically how and when it is to be paid (by check made out to the artist, received at the performance)
3. Any special equipment or arrangements agreed upon (Steinway grand piano tuned to A440, amplification, particular lighting, drum kit, page turner, etc.). These should be specified in the technical rider, an attachment to the contract.
4. Arranged times for sound check and rehearsal in hall; name and contact information for the facility's manager, the on-site person you'll be dealing with to get into the hall, deal with lights, etc.
5. Any special parking, transportation, or lodging arrangements
6. Whether or not you can sell your CDs at the performance, and, if yes, what the presenter will provide to assist with this and what (if any) percentage of CD sales is due to the presenter
7. The box office phone number
8. Cancellation policy

A sample contract follows. When using your own contract, send two unsigned copies to the presenter, who signs both and sends both back to you. Then you sign both copies, keep one and send the other to the presenter for her or his records. This method ensures that you don't first sign something that gets amended later.

Conclusion

Why wait for the prince or princess charming of artist managers to visit you? Until you find the manager of your dreams, you will most likely self-manage your career and book your own concerts. To enhance your reputation and build your track record of performances, you can start locally, finding interesting, welcoming and alternative performance spaces. Make sure you plan carefully, from creating engaging programming, to researching performance sites, preparing a script for booking calls, practicing negotiating fees, to closing the deal with a contract. The truth is, there are places in your community where you could be performing in the coming months, and YOU are the one who can to make it happen.

Music Performance Contract

From: Jane Doe
16 Chilcott Place #1
Jamaica Plain, MA 02130
617/555-1111
jdoe@aol.com

To: Ann Smith, Executive
Director
Smithtown Concert
Association
1 Main St.
Smithtown, MA 02111
978/555-2222
asmith@SCA.org

This contract is intended to confirm the following agreements:

- Soprano Jane Doe, herein after referred to as "the Artist," agrees to perform a concert for the Smithtown Concert Association, herein after referred to as "the Presenter," at the 1st Congregational Church in Smithtown on Friday, November 10, 2006, at 8 P.M. The concert will consist of the attached programmed repertoire, subject to change by the artist. The concert will last approximately 90 minutes with one 15-minute intermission included.
- The Presenter agrees to pay the Artist $500.00 for the concert, payable in U.S. dollars by Certified Check or Money Order, to be given to the Artist prior to the concert.
  If an invoice is required before payment, please state:
  ❑ Yes   ❑ No
- The Presenter agrees to furnish one Concert Grand Piano, preferably a Steinway or best Concert Grand in the area, properly tuned and in top playing condition, for use at the performance.
- Rehearsal and sound check will be 2-4 P.M. the day of the performance.

PERSON TO NOTIFY ON ARRIVAL: _____
Business Phone

_____
Address

- The Presenter agrees to provide the Artist with four comp tickets to be held at the box office.

Sample performance contract

164

- The Presenter agrees to allow the Artist to sell her CDs at intermission and immediately following the concert. The Presenter will provide a table and chair in the lobby for this purpose. The CD sales will be managed by the artist with no assistance from the Presenter.
- No recording of this engagement shall be made, reproduced or transmitted from the place of performance, in any manner or by any means whatsoever, in the absence of a specific written agreement with the Artist relating to and permitting such recording, reproduction or transmission. The Signatory Artist may enforce this prohibition in any court of competent jurisdiction.
- The Artist shall be under no liability for failure to appear or perform in the event such failure is caused by or due to the physical disability of the Artist, or acts or regulations of public authorities, labor difficulties, civil tumult, strike, epidemic, interruption or delay of transportation service, or any other cause beyond the control of the Artist.

Signed _____ Date _____
      (Presenter's signature)

Signed _____ Date _____
      (Artist's signature)

Artist's social security number or Federal ID number for payment and tax purposes: _____

Sample contract *(continued)*

■ Suggestions for Moving Ahead ■

1. List three venues in your area that might sponsor a performance for you. Think beyond the typical concert series (museum, historical home, library, etc.).
2. Describe one or two program ideas you think would interest these venues.
3. To prepare your booking calls, write your pitch statement, including the five essential elements.
4. Practice your calls with a colleague or mentor, and then go for it!

7

Building Your Reputation, Growing Your Audience: The Media, Publicity, and You

The next issue to tackle is "buzz"—how to attract media attention so that you can attract audiences. This is essentially about "telling your story," articulating and communicating what is special and interesting about you and your music. How effectively you do this will play a major factor in your future success.

Communications specialist Scott Menhinick (http://www.improvisedcommunications .com) believes that promotion can be divided into three fundamental concerns: information, communication, and dissemination. "Each carries equal weight," he says, "and each must be satisfied in order for the promotion effort to have the best chance of success. Simply put, one must have something newsworthy to say, say it clearly in an appropriate format, and say it to the right people at the right time."

Attracting an Audience ■

Once your performance is booked and confirmed, your work is not yet done. You need to help draw an audience. Once you've agreed on a date, ask the presenter what kind of publicizing she or he does for the series. Find out:

> Does the presenter have a series brochure?
> Will your performance be listed on it?
> Will there be a special mailing for your concert?

Is there an e-mail list of subscribers?

Does the presenter send press releases to local newspapers, radio stations, Internet bulletin boards, Web calendars, and magazines?

You want to find out how the presenter handles publicity so that you can help these efforts. Presenters will usually ask you to provide a bio, photo, program, program notes, and additional CDs for radio play. It is essential to have these items ready and to send them promptly when requested. There are many deadlines to meet in order for a presenter to create a season brochure, get listings in newspapers, on the radio, on Web calendars, and in order to have posters and programs printed. Have a variety of photos to offer—including a color slide. And have a variety of lengths of bios, to fit the presenter's needs. Make it easy for the presenter to publicize your concert!

Of course, you'll also want to send invitations and notices to your own network. If the presenter is doing a printed postcard mailing to subscribers, ask if you may have a stack of these to send to your own mailing list. You should personalize these by writing (in blue, purple, or green ink so that it stands out from the black print) "Hope to see you there!" And it's great to combine a printed invitation with an e-mail invite or reminder. Get the timing right. When combining a print and e-mail invitation, I'd suggest timing it so your mailing list gets the postcard about ten days before the performance and gets the e-mail reminder the day before the performance.

You and the presenter both want the performance to be a success—to draw a large and diverse audience and to attract positive media attention. But many concert series are understaffed and underfunded. Presenters may only provide minimal publicity for individual concerts. Once the performance has been booked, you need to have an open discussion with the presenter about how much work will be done by each of you to attract media attention and audiences. You need to be clear about who will do what so there are no mishaps. If the presenter can only do a portion, you may need to do the rest.

Many musicians produce their own concerts, or start their own series and festivals, handling the publicity in addition to the other duties. Typically, musicians must play the role of publicist, at some point in their careers, so it's imperative to learn the basics of publicity.

What Does a Publicist Do?
(And When Do I Need One?) ■

"A publicist is the professional you hire to be your ambassador to the media," according to Janice Papolos, author of the excellent *Performing Artist's Handbook*. Publicists can work on a per project basis, to publicize a particular concert, series, festival, or CD release, or else on retainer, on an ongoing basis, for a soloist, ensemble, or institution. A publicist's goal is to generate news stories, audiences, reviews, and a general "buzz" about the particular project. Publicists' work includes sending press releases and photos, CDs, and press kits to contacts in the media and following up with phone calls to "pitch" a story to a journalist in hopes of securing an interview and article for the artist or ensemble. When you hire a publicist, you're getting the strength of that person's contacts and reputation with the media, his or her writing ability, creativity in planning a promotional campaign, and organizational skills in disseminating information in the appropriate format at the right time. Publicist's fees for promoting a single concert or a CD release can run $500 to $1,000 and up, depending on the amount of work done and the clout of the publicist.

When should you hire a publicist? When you have a sufficient track record as a performer and have a compelling project that would warrant significant exposure in the media. Janice Papolos says, "There must be a story behind you that the publicist can work with as well as newsworthy events on the horizon such as a concert or record." So until your career is far enough along to warrant a full promotional campaign, you'll need to handle the basic work of publicity on your own. The good news is that this is very doable. And no matter where they are in their careers, performers need to be savvy about how to attract media attention and how to help build audiences.

Acquiring Media Savvy

Part of being a successful musician is being aware of current ideas and opportunities in your field. If you don't read about who's doing what and where, you are missing out on potential collaborations, bookings, program ideas, and more. Read your local newspapers, relevant music journals, Web calendars, and magazines. Get to know what the arts reporters in your area like to cover. Keep current on the arts in your community and learn what gets media coverage, what's considered *newsworthy*.

What's Newsworthy?

The media look for items of interest to readers: compelling and engaging stories. So what do arts reporters actually cover? What kinds of events attract media attention?

> *About a single performance*
> · Unusual, interesting programming
> · Premiere of a new work
> · Collaboration with a well-known artist

- Collaboration with an artist from another discipline—a dancer, graphic artist, writer
- Performance in an unusual setting (i.e., the one hundredth anniversary of the Boston Marathon)
- A local "celebrity" narrating a work on the program
- Benefit concert for a community cause
- A performance to celebrate a holiday, the opening of a new community building, or a local anniversary date
- A personal connection to work(s) on the program, for example, the performer studied with the composer, or the performer is related to the composer or is returning to this work after a hiatus of ten years

Beyond a single performance
- Winning a grant or competition
- CD release
- Starting your own concert series or festival
- Launching a tour
- Starting a competition for a new work for your ensemble
- Quirky personal stories about you or your ensemble, stories about buying instruments, being on tour, interesting "day jobs"
- Innovative approaches to teaching music

What else can you add?

Tip: Think like a publicist. Look for a news "hook" or angle that would interest the media. You may want to host a brainstorming party with colleagues and friends to help come up with ideas for attracting media attention.

Basic Types of Media Coverage

- Calendar listings—posting of arts and cultural events in a community. Calendar listings are found in newspapers, magazines, on cable television, and on websites. Also, community events are announced on radio and TV as public service announcements and community calendar listings.
- Newspaper "Pick of the Week" sections include select highlighted calendar events, recommended by the editors (e.g., the *Boston Globe*'s Thursday edition includes a special pullout calendar section, and the Calendar Choice events are listed in a centerfold spread with color photos. This is a highly desirable placement, as the Calendar Choice gets the most attention from thousands of readers.)

- Preview articles about upcoming concerts—these include bio and program details, and often a photo and quotes from artist interviews. Intended to stir interest and audience attendance, preview articles are mostly found in daily and weekly newspapers.
- Reviews of CDs
- Reviews of live performances
- Articles on broad trends and issues in the arts: funding, education, copyright, economics, and more

More Coverage

Gaining media attention helps to build your reputation in your community, to get a buzz going about you or your ensemble, and to build up your promo kit with press clippings. Beyond notices about your upcoming performances, you can and should contact the media with other newsworthy items. You can send press releases about winning a competition or grant, participating in a summer festival, going on tour, accepting a teaching position, or commissioning a new work.

The media also is interested in arts stories about broad trends and issues. You can "pitch" a journalist a story idea about a broader issue, a story that uses your ensemble or your career as an example among others. You pitch a story to a journalist by outlining the idea for an in-depth article, contacting him or her by phone, e-mail, letter, or press release.

Broader Arts Coverage: Issues in the News

What kinds of topics get coverage?

- Funding issues (private and public, at the national, state, and local levels)
- Recording industry issues (copyright, artist-run labels, internet promotion, recording technology, etc.)
- Arts education issues (including local artist/teachers, residency programs, etc.)
- Economic issues—the impact of the arts on the local economy. Interesting stories of how concerts spur other spending: dining, parking, local shopping (do your own audience poll at intermission to get statistics)
- Arts events as benefits for a cause. The cause may be the main news and the fund-raiser gala dinner may be on the society page, but the performers also can reap the benefit of the media attention.

When you start following arts coverage, you'll find it's not just relegated to the arts pages in newspapers. You'll see stories about musicians as business-people in the financial section, musicians as teachers in the education section, and interview pieces on local musicians in the city or neighborhood sections of newspapers.

■

How to Write a Press Release ■

What does the news media want? Editors and journalists want *news*: ideas and information of interest to their particular audience. You are potentially a supplier of that news. And if you want media coverage, you must learn the tricks of the trade, including how to present your information in the standard format, a press release.

A press release is an announcement issued to the media, a brief document in a specific format announcing an event, performance, or other newsworthy item. It should effectively demonstrate to newspeople why you or your ensemble merit media attention. It should outline the news story and provide pertinent background information. Arts journalists receive bushels of press releases each day and part of their job is to select from these the most relevant, compelling, and engaging news for their audience.

If you want a newspaper or website editor to consider your news item for publication, or a radio programmer to announce your listing, it's important you submit your information in the proper format. If you want your press release to stay out of an editor's wastebasket, make sure you write it correctly!

- Use double spacing and wide margins to facilitate editing.
- Put your contact information at the top.
- Put the release date immediately underneath the contact info, indicating the desired date for publication ("For Release: April 5, 2006"). If the news is ready to go, write "For Immediate Release" and the date you're sending it.
- Keep it brief: one to two pages in length. If it is more than one page, write "continued" or "more" at the bottom of page 1. Pages should be numbered at the top with five repetitions of the number, for example, "22222," or "33333"; strange, but that's the convention. To indicate the end of the release, finish it with "END" or ###.
- Include a photo only if you have a good one. Having a compelling image may help get your press release printed! $8 \times 10''$ or $5 \times 7''$ black and white is standard. If the publication uses color, include a color slide. Photos inevitably get separated from press releases. Label the back of photos and the edge of slides and don't expect to get your photos back. Do not ever write directly on the back of a photo! Use a sticky label or tape a piece of paper with your contact info onto the back.

Tip: Include a Media Kit on Your Website

Include your website address on all your press releases so that readers can easily track down more detailed information as needed. Have an online version of your promo kit—your "media kit"—on your website. Include your bio, list of press quotes, past performances, and upcoming dates—all in PDF file format—as well as a range of high-resolution photos in JPEG files, for easy downloading. Having this easy access to information online can mean the difference between getting media coverage and not. Journalists and editors unable to get the details they need may simply decide to include the next musician's news instead of yours. Make it easy on the media to get your story!

Press Release in Seven Easy Steps

1. Select a headline for your release—communicating the main focus of the news story. Make it catchy and engaging for readers. If you're from the area, it's wise to emphasize your local connections since editors are looking for news of special interest to local readers.

   Local Violinist Premieres New Work
   Award-Winning Local Brass Quintet Launches Innovative After-
      School Music Program
   Local Soprano Wins National Competition
   ABC String Trio Performs for Senior Citizens at Public Library June 15

2. Get the essential news in your lead. After the headline, the opening sentence(s) of your release should tell the essentials of the story: The who, what, where, and when (the four Ws). Your language should be succinct and direct.

   The Quintet of the Americas will present a special program of Polish music for wind quintet on Sunday, April 27, 3 P.M. at the Kosciuszko Foundation, 15 East 65th Street, between Fifth and Madison in Manhattan.

3. Consider the "Why"—the fifth "W." Ask yourself why should an average reader care? Ask yourself, What's the *story* here? Emphasize what's unusual, interesting, and newsworthy about the programming and the performers. Test your draft release with the tough questions: Who Cares? and So What? Make sure you've emphasized the most compelling and engaging aspects in your lead.

4. Stick to concrete facts. Newspaper editors are looking for news, not advertising. Don't use superlatives or "hype" to describe your own concert. Instead state your credentials, where else you've performed, awards you've won, and so on. You can include quotes from presenters or teachers, with their permission, of course. You also can quote yourself, as though you've been interviewed, as long as you have something interesting and fresh to say about the repertoire or the occasion of the performance.

> Ms. Smith is looking forward to returning to Whoville for this performance and says, "Whoville is where I got my start so I'm thrilled to be performing for the opening of the new community center."

5. Watch your language—don't use music jargon or technical terms that an average newspaper reader would not know. Find engaging ways to describe works so that non-musicians can "get" it.

> Hill's work, "Thoughtful Wanderings," features natural horn and a taped accompaniment of nature sounds and percussion instruments. The piece was inspired by the music of the Native Americans from the Plains.

6. Use short paragraphs—newspapers prefer them. Keep these to two to three sentences, in logically organized units of thought.
7. Consider structure. After the lead paragraph, the following paragraphs should flesh out the essentials with background info on the performers, details about the program, composers, and so on. Keep in mind that editors, when short on space, cut from the bottom, assuming that the essential info is in the top of the release (this journalistic writing style is called the "inverted pyramid").

   Don't forget the all-important details of ticket prices, info on the performance series, venue, directions, phone and website for further info. Leaving out a crucial detail is a common mistake and, very often, it's why releases don't make it into the paper. Have friends proofread your releases carefully.

Fine Points

- Use quotation marks to indicate titles of compositions (newspapers don't use italics)
- Months: abbreviate Aug. through Feb., and write out March through July
- Numbers: write out one through nine; use numerals for 10 and higher

Tip: Arts Consultant Jeffrey James (http://www.jamesarts.com) recommends that musicians new to media relations talk to more established colleagues. "Find out how successful groups write press releases and handle their public relations . . . find a mentor, or take a publicist or established arts professional to lunch or ask for a consultation. It's well worth it!"

Send It Out!

When do you send releases? For concert announcements, you may have several versions of releases to send: simple calendar listings, full releases, and a radio release. Pay close attention to deadlines; you may need to send releases five months in advance for monthly magazines; two weeks in advance for a weekly newspapers and radio programs; and ten days in advance for a daily paper.

More and more news outlets are accepting releases electronically but many, as of this writing, still prefer hard copies. Check before sending an e-mail release. For e-mail releases, align all the text to the left (do not use centering or tabs because your formatting most often will be lost when the text is transmitted). In the text, as you mention the performers and the presenter, include their hyperlinks, and if you're performing new music include the composers' websites.

For sending hard copies, fold your press release in thirds with the top fold facing out, so that when the envelope is opened, the reader sees text immediately; send in a standard business-size envelope. When sending a photo with a release, send both unfolded in a large envelope with a piece of cardboard inserted to keep the photo from being damaged.

How to Invite a Critic to Review Your Concert

- Have a compelling program
- Schedule your performance so it doesn't conflict with major performances in your area. Plan ahead. Get the season listings early from presenters and performing groups in your area. Mon. and Tues. nights generally are less crowded with competing performances.
- Send a release very far in advance, to give the reviewer plenty of notice
- Send a letter with the release inviting the critic. Ask the critic to call or e-mail you to have two complimentary tickets left in her or his name left at the box office.
- Have a well-regarded mentor personally invite the critic

Unfortunately, there is less coverage of the arts these days than in previous generations. There are many cities in the United States where there are no music reviewers on the major newspaper's staff. Where there are reviewers, they are invited to far more performances than they can cover. A critic's job is to cover the arts news in her or his region. A critic must sift through all the releases and invitation she or he receives and determine what's most important to cover. First, the major performing groups in the area need to be covered as well as important premieres of new works, and, when there's time, critics try to cover musicians who are doing interesting and innovative work or else the ones who have been gathering a following, who've started creating a buzz.

Note: While getting a good review can help a career, a review can't make (or break) a career. The best approach is to do what you can to get listings and preview articles for your performances. Send releases, invitations, and ideas for articles. You may need to build a track record, to be on a critic's radar screen for several seasons before getting reviewed. Be persistent, patient, and professional.

There are six good examples of various press releases and media contact letters on the following pages. The first is a press release for a single concert written by the group's publicist; the second release comes from an ensemble's director (and also the group's oboist) announcing the ensemble's season; the third announces a trumpeter's teaching appointment and a local concert, sent to his hometown newspapers; the fourth is a calendar listing; the fifth is a radio announcement; and last is a cover letter sent by a publicist requesting a review of a new CD. To read examples of a wide variety of music press releases, check out http://www.musicalamerica.com. Also, many larger performing institutions place their recent press release announcements on their own websites.

Compiling Your Media List ■

To build your reputation in your local community, you need to cultivate media attention by regularly sending the media information about upcoming performances, CDs, awards, and so on. To get started, you'll need to compile a media list. The most important media contacts to gather first are your local listings. Find out who the arts reporters are in your area. You should also add strategic regional and national publications where appropriate. Your media list should include:

- Local newspapers/journals (daily, weekly, monthly, quarterly) and their arts reporters and community calendar editors
- Appropriate radio station programmers
- Local commercial and community TV station arts reporters
- Website editors for community calendar listings

Contact: Jeffrey James Arts Consulting
(516) 797-9166 or jamesarts@worldnet.att.net
For Immediate Release
April 18, 2003

Quintet of the Americas Presents All-Polish Program in New York on April 27

The Quintet of the Americas will present a special program of Polish music for wind quintet on Sunday, April 27, 3 PM at the Kosciuszko Foundation, 15 East 65th Street, between Fifth and Madison Avenues in Manhattan.

This program will feature Grazyna Bacewicz's "Quintet for Wind Instruments," Maciej Malecki's "Suite for Wind Quintet," Alexandre Tansman's "Suite for Reed Trio" and Robert Muczynski's "Quintet for Winds" (1985).

Tickets for the April 27 concert, which include a reception with the artists following the concert, are $25 ($20 for KF members) and can be reserved by calling the Office at (212) 734-2130.

The members of the Quintet of the Americas are Sato Moughalian, flute, Matt Sullivan, oboe, Edward Gilmore, clarinet, Barbara Oldham, horn, and Laura Koepke, bassoon.

The Quintet, founded 26 years ago, has toured extensively in over 300 cities in North and South America, Eastern Europe and the British West Indies. They have twice received the ASCAP/CMA Adventuresome Programming Award, and were recipients of the Chamber Music America Residency Program Award. They are currently the Quintet in Residence at New York University. The group has released several CDs, including woodwind music from North and South America. The Quintet Of The Americas has premiered over 50 works, commissioned over 20 new pieces for the woodwind quintet repertoire, and made numerous arrangements of their own. More information about the group can be found on their website at http://www.quintet.org.

This concert is made possible with public funds from the New York State Council on the Arts, a state agency.

For more information about the Quintet of the Americas, contact Jeffrey James Arts Consulting at (516) 797-9166 or jamesarts@worldnet.att.net.

END

Example: Release announcing an individual concert

RADIUS ENSEMBLE OPENS ITS FIFTH SEASON
AT THE EDWARD M. PICKMAN CONCERT HALL,
27 GARDEN STREET IN CAMBRIDGE
ON SATURDAY, SEPTEMBER 27, 2003 AT 8 PM

September 9, 2003   Contact: Jennifer Montbach
FOR IMMEDIATE RELEASE   617.792.7234

"Radius ensemble is first rate . . . The players represent a new generation of chamber musicians, and their youth and informality
has attracted a younger, more diverse audience."

Richard Dyer, Boston Globe

Radius Ensemble, directed by Jennifer Montbach, opens its fifth
season on Saturday, September 27, 2003 at 8 pm at the Edward M.
Pickman Concert Hall, 27 Garden Street in Cambridge. The concert includes Alberto Ginastera's *Impressions de la Puna* for flute
and strings; *Amour Fou*, a piano trio by the avant-garde composer John Zorn (of *Naked City* renown), Mozart's quintet for
piano and winds; and Luciano Berio's brilliant and timely *Opus
Number Zoo* for wind quintet.

A free pre-concert talk at 7 P.M. features Mary Greitzer (Harvard University), and a free reception with complimentary good-
ies from Carberry's Bakery and Café with the artists follows the
concert. Tickets are $10 (cash or check at the door), $5 for kids
and students. Subscriptions are available. Call 617.792.7234 or
visit radiusensemble.org for more information.

Performers include director and oboist Jennifer Montbach, pianist Sarah Bob, flutist Orlando Cela, pianist Alison d'Amato, clarinetist Eran Egozy, violinist David Fulmer, horn player Anne
Howarth, cellist Mickey Katz, violinist Annegret Klaua, bassoonist
Sally Merriman, and violist Julie Thompson.

- More -

Example: Group's season series announcement

Jennifer Montbach, Director
Radius Ensemble
45 Pine St. Concord, MA 01742 P: 617.792.7234
W: radiusensemble.org E: jmontbach@radiusensemble.org
22222

Radius Ensemble has earned rave reviews and a dedicated following in just four years by reinvigorating classical music for a new
generation. A chamber music ensemble of winds, strings, and
piano, Radius Ensemble performs music from the classical period
to the modern era, from beloved masterpieces to undiscovered
gems. Its musicians are outstanding young professionals inspired
by tradition, willing to take risks, and committed to connecting
with a diverse group of listeners. Founded in 1999 by oboist Jennifer Montbach, Radius Ensemble's season includes a four-concert
subscription series at Pickman Hall in Harvard Square, a free Sat-
urday-morning family concert, and a free community ticket program offering tickets to disadvantaged children and their parents
or mentors.

Pickman Hall is wheelchair-accessible and convenient to public
transportation. We furnish large-print or Braille programs by request, and strive to provide additional accommodations as
needed. Radius Ensemble, Incorporated, is a 501(c)(3) non-profit
organization and a Massachusetts public charity.

Example *(continued)*

CONTACT: James Knabe
faculty, School of Creative Arts
(617) 641-4493
FOR IMMEDIATE RELEASE

LOCAL MUSICIAN APPOINTED TO FACULTY POSITION, ANNOUNCES BOSTON DEBUT RECITAL

BOSTON, MA—Former Iowa City resident trumpeter James Knabe, son of William and Judith Knabe of Iowa City, has been appointed to the music faculty of the School of Creative Arts in Lexington, Mass. The School is affiliated with Grace Chapel, the largest church in the New England area. This school serves numerous communities including Boston. At the school, Mr. Knabe will teach private trumpet lessons and music history courses and conduct a brass ensemble.

James Knabe will make his Boston-area solo debut at Grace Chapel in Lexington at 8:00 P.M. on Friday, May 26. The program will include familiar and unusual works by Handel, Hovhaness, Copland, Neruda, and Vaughan Williams. Artists joining Knabe for the recital are pianist Elenye German, soprano Kimberly Cone, organist Douglas Marshall and narrator Nancy Gerber.

A former student of David Greenhoe at the University of Iowa, James Knabe is now pursuing graduate studies at the New England Conservatory in Boston, where he studies with Peter Chapman and Charles Schlueter of the Boston Symphony. Knabe has performed with the Boston Civic Symphony, Boston Chamber Ensemble, and the Dubuque Symphony Orchestra. He currently plays principal trumpet with the North Shore Philharmonic Orchestra. He returns to Iowa this summer for a series of master classes and recitals. When asked about his latest success, Knabe said, "I consider myself very fortunate to have received a great musical start growing up in Iowa City and I look forward to returning home this summer to re-connect with my musical roots."

Example: Release intended for hometown newspapers in Iowa, announcing a teaching appointment and recital in Boston. It appropriately emphasizes hometown connections

collage
new music

david hoose *music director*
frank epstein *founder*

po box 230150 boston ma 02123 | www.collagenewmusic.org

FOR IMMEDIATE RELEASE

CONTACT:
Danny Lichtenfeld
Phone: (617) 325-5200
info@collagenewmusic.org

Collage New Music and Janna Baty present Exotic, Neurotic, Erotic Music of Luciano Berio, Ralph Shapey, and Fred Lerdahl

Boston, MA—Live-wire Janna Baty joins Collage New Music in her prismatic singing of Luciano Berio's vivid multi-national *Folk Songs* and Fred Lerdahl's *Eros*, an electrified and electrifying display of Ezra Pound's heated poem, "Coitus." Pianist Christopher Oldfather and percussionist Frank Epstein convene to tackle the radical-traditionalist voice of maverick Ralph Shapey in the Boston premiere of his *Gottlieb Duo*. The exotic, the neurotic, the erotic. Not to be missed.

Who	Collage New Music, with soprano Janna Baty
What	Exotic, Neurotic, Erotic: Music of Luciano Berio (*Folk Songs*), Ralph Shapey (*Gottlieb Duo*), and Fred Lerdahl (*Eros*)
When	Sunday, January 12, 2003 at 7:30 P.M.
Where	Suffolk University's C. Walsh Theatre 41 Temple Street, Boston—behind the State House on historic Beacon Hill, between Derne and Cambridge Streets. *Wheelchair Accessible*
Tickets	$20 at the door or by calling (617) 325-5200; $7 students/seniors. *Free* to students from Boston Conservatory, BU, Harvard, Longy, MIT, Milton Academy, NEC, Tufts, Suffolk, and Walnut Hill.
Info	Danny Lichtenfeld, Collage New Music (617) 325-5200, info@yellowbarn.org

Example: Calendar Listing, the most basic form of a press release; these should contain the essentials and be mailed to the appropriate calendar editors in plenty of time for their deadlines

Contact: Jeffrey James Arts Consulting
(516) 797-9166 or jamesarts@worldnet.att.net
STARTING DATE: Feb. 12
ENDING DATE: Feb. 28

PUBLIC SERVICE ANNOUNCEMENT

"NEW YORK VIRTUOSI CHAMBER SYMPHONY
PRESENTS CONCERT FEATURING
INTERNATIONALLY RENOWNED GUITARIST"

WORDS: 77
TIME: 30 seconds

THE NEW YORK VIRTUOSI CHAMBER SYMPHONY PRE-
SENTS A CONCERT ON SUNDAY, FEBRUARY 28 AT 3 PM AT
THE HILLWOOD RECITAL HALL OF CW POST UNIVERSITY
IN GREENVALE. THE VIRTUOSI WILL BE JOINED BY INTER-
NATIONALLY RENOWNED GUITARIST VIRGINIA LUQUE
(LOO-Kay) FOR A PROGRAM THAT INCLUDES A GUITAR
CONCERTO (cone-CHAIR-to) BY RODRIGO, VIVALDI'S FOUR
SEASONS AND MOZART'S EINE KLEINE NACHTMUSIK
(EYE-nuh KLINE-uh NOCKTmoozik). FOR FURTHER INFOR-
MATION, PLEASE CALL THE NEW YORK VIRTUSOSI AT
(516) 626-3378 . . . THAT'S 626-3378 FOR THE NEW YORK
VIRTUOSI.

more . . . more . . . more

Example: This is a radio release. For radio, you must include phonetic pronunciation guides for any words the average reader might be unsure how to pronounce,
especially names of performers, composers and titles of works. The word count
and accurate timing it takes to read the announcement needs to be given, and the
norm is to provide several lengths of versions. Include the starting and ending
dates for when the announcement should be aired. Radio stations are required by
law to include a certain number of public service announcements for nonprofit organizations and community announcements.

WORDS: 57
TIME: 20 seconds

THE NEW YORK VIRTUOSI CHAMBER SYMPHONY CON-
CERT ON SUNDAY, FEBRUARY 28 AT 3 PM AT THE HILL-
WOOD RECITAL HALL OF CW POST UNIVERSITY IN
GREENVALE WILL WELCOME GUITARIST VIRGINIA LUQUE
(LOO-Kay) FOR A PROGRAM THAT INCLUDES VIVALDI'S
FOUR SEASONS AND MUSIC BY RODRIGO AND MOZART.
FOR MORE INFORMATION, CALL THE NEW YORK VIRTU-
SOSI AT (516) 626-3378 . . . THAT'S 626-3378

WORDS: 45
TIME: 15 seconds

THE NEW YORK VIRTUOSI WILL PERFORM MUSIC BY RO-
DRIGO, VIVALDI AND MOZART ON SUNDAY, FEBRUARY 28
AT 3 PM AT THE HILLWOOD RECITAL HALL OF CW POST
UNIVERSITY IN GREENVALE. FOR MORE INFORMATION,
CALL THE NEW YORK VIRTUSOSI AT (516) 626-3378 . . .
THAT'S 626-3378

WORDS: 31
TIME: 10 seconds

THE NEW YORK VIRTUOSI PRESENTS MUSIC BY RODRIGO,
VIVALDI AND MOZART ON FEBRUARY 28 AT 3 PM AT
THE HILLWOOD RECITAL HALL OF CW POST UNIVER-
SITY IN GREENVALE. FOR MORE INFORMATION, CALL
(516) 626-3378.

Example *(continued)*

Beacon Communications
1753 Beacon St., Number 2   Telephone: 617.232.1212
Brookline, MA 02445   Email: KMYRON@SHORE.NET

April 27, 2002

Steve Greenlee
The Boston Globe
135 Morrissey Boulevard
Boston, MA 02107

Dear Steve,

The Shimon Ben-Shir Group will be celebrating the release of their debut CD *Shades* at Ryles Jazz Club, 212 Hampshire Street, Cambridge, on Wednesday May 29 at 8 P.M. Enclosed is a copy of the CD for your consideration for a review in the *Boston Globe*. The band is based in Boston but the members represent far ranging regions from around the world. The music reflects the individual journeys the musicians have taken to come to share a musical vision and a common language . . . jazz.

    The musicians in the Ben Shirim Group have considerable performance experience, playing in venues around the world with jazz luminaries and in two cases, playing before a king and a president. I believe your astute readers would enjoy learning about good jazz by local musicians. The CD has been getting airplay on the Jazz Gallery with Al Davis on WGBH radio and is currently available at http://www.yoursound.com, where the band is also featured, Flipside Records in Brookline and at Tower Records in Boston. Enclosed is a list of upcoming performances in the area. I hope you like the music. Thank you so much for your time and consideration. If you have any questions or would like additional material please don't hesitate to let me know.

Sincerely,

Kevin C. Myron
Beacon Communications

Example: Submission for CD review from publicist Kevin Myron to the *Boston Globe* jazz critic Steve Greenlee

- Your alumni magazine(s)
- Newspapers from your former hometown
- Appropriate national publications and media outlets (http://www.MusicalAmerica.com, www.NewMusicBox.org, and journals such as *Strings, Strad, Piano, Jazziz, the Instrumentalist*)
- Membership organizations with journals or website listings (i.e., Chamber Music America, Percussive Arts Society, American Music Center, etc.)

What's in a media list? Each contact should include:

- Name, title, organization, section of newspaper (calendar, arts pages, special column, feature writer, etc.)
- Mailing address
- Phone, e-mail, fax
- Publication schedule (daily, weekly, monthly, quarterly)
- Deadlines for receiving info

Gather your media contact information and put these in a database format so you can print labels easily. Media lists need constant updates because people change jobs, and media outlets change focus and structure. People hate to get mail addressed to their predecessor, or with their name misspelled or their title wrong. Keep your media list updated and readily accessible.

Research Your List

How do you get all this information? To research your list, visit your public library and ask the reference librarian if there's a compiled directory for local media. The librarian can help you find a range of resources including:

> Any local media directories (for smaller local media outlets)
> *Gale Directory of Publications and Broadcast Media*
> *Working Press of the Nation* (in three separate directories: newspapers/newsletters, radio/TV, and magazines)
> *Musical America* (for major newspapers and radio stations, organized by state, cities)
> *Encyclopedia of Associations* (for specialized music organizations with newsletters)

Timeline for Publicizing Your Next Concert ■

To help organize your preparations for a performance, it's a good idea to have a checklist and timeline. Check with the presenter to find out what publicity they will do and when, so that you coordinate your efforts. You need to send releases out in the right form, to the right contacts, at the right time.

Beyond your friends and the press, you should also invite other local presenters, influential musicians, conductors, artist managers, and colleagues. Even if they don't come, it's good for them to know who you are and what you're doing. Many performances pave the way for future possibilities—it's about building awareness, getting people interested in you and your music.

Six months before
❑ Research and compile your media list
❑ Update your mailing list, include influential local musicians, conductors, artist managers, presenters, and so on
❑ Send press releases to quarterly publications (check deadlines!)

Three to five months before
❑ Send releases and make phone calls to any specialized radio shows with guest interviews or live performance broadcasts. You need the lead-time because these shows are booked far in advance.
❑ Send press releases to monthly publications (check deadlines!)

Two to three months before
❑ Invite local critics

Six weeks before
❑ Send releases to radio program producers
❑ Send releases to local cable channels and Web calendars

One month before
❑ Send releases to weekly publications
❑ Send calendar listings to all

Two to three weeks before
❑ Send releases to daily publications
❑ Send Internet releases to Web calendars and magazines

Seven to ten days before
❑ Mail personalized invitations to your mailing list, perhaps a postcard with a handwritten "Hope to see you there!"
❑ Send an e-mail invitation to your mailing list

One to two days before
❑ Send e-mail reminders to your mailing list

After the Concert

Send thank you notes to everyone involved—this is one good way to help the presenter and other supporters to remember you positively and want to work with you again. Cut out all newsprint coverage you got from sending press releases and make copies, with the newspapers' masthead and date, for your promo kit.

■

Andrew Kohji Taylor, a violinist who performs frequently in the Northeast and in Japan, found that once he started sending handwritten thank you notes to presenters after his concerts in Japan, that return engagements were much more frequent. The thank you notes were a way to extend and develop relationships with these presenters. He was really getting to know these presenters as people—and they liked working with him and wanted to invite him back.

■

Conclusion

Attracting an audience to a performance takes planning, organization, and some media savvy. But with a timeline and some advance work, you can create a buzz around you and your music. By building your mailing list and sending well-composed press releases to the media, you can grow your reputation, audience, and career.

■ Suggestions for Moving Ahead ■

1. How big is your mailing list? If you haven't started one, do so. Use your address book as a start and create a database on your computer, with names, e-mail, postal address, and phone number.
2. List five local media outlets where you could send a press release about an upcoming performance.
3. Get creative; challenge yourself to create three complete performance programs. Build one concert program around an anniversary, holiday, or other celebratory date; design another program around a theme or idea; and organize the last program around a benefit cause close to your heart.
4. What's a story idea for a press release you could send this week to your hometown newspaper, in the place where you grew up?
5. Consider the last concert you played. Thinking like a publicist, write a dynamic press release for it, to attract an audience and a critic. Emphasize the most compelling features of the concert; is it performers, the occasion, the program, something else?

8

Connecting with Audiences: Residency, Educational, and Community Programming

This chapter goes beyond individual performances in formal concert settings. Here we're focusing on residencies and residency work—what is also referred to as community engagement activities, educational programming, or outreach.

What Is Residency Work? ■

The term *residency* can be confusing. Traditionally, residencies referred to artist-in-residence opportunities, long-term teaching and performance positions for ensembles (occasionally for soloists) at colleges or universities. These positions are quite difficult to attain as they are generally offered only to well-established groups. It's nice work if you can get it, but these are not the only kinds of residencies available. There are also residency positions that aim to develop emerging ensembles; some of these lead to graduate degrees or diplomas, and offer coaching with distinguished faculty members.

In recent years, the definition of "residency" has been extended to include shorter-term engagements for teaching artists, sometimes with performance and teaching activities at multiple sites. The term residency is now used to describe anything from a touring musician's weeklong stay in a community, doing several children's programs at schools, to an ensemble's concert series at a museum, or an ongoing teaching and performing partnership with a university. These are all considered residencies, no matter what the duration, and whether or not the artists actually live in the community.

Not Your Typical Residency

The jazz vibraphonist and composer Stefon Harris participated in a residency in 2003 at the University of Iowa Hancher Auditorium (http://www.uiowa.edu/hancher), one of the leading presenting series in the US. Hancher's artistic director, Judy Hurtig, invited Stefon to collaborate in a residency with poets during the International Writing Program, the university's prestigious international literary conference. Before the residency, Stefon was sent the participants' written poems and recordings of these being read by their authors, so he could get a sense of the sounds of the various languages and voices. Then over two evenings during his residency, Stefon and his band, together with the poets reading, created the music and the order for the performance. Stefon composed specific music to be performed with each poem as it was being read by its author. The works were presented in a continuous poetry cabaret-style performance at the student union. It was a big success. The poets got a chance to present their work in a dramatically new context; Stefon got an interesting creative challenge and access to a new audience. And the presenting series at Hancher got great PR and the opportunity to collaborate with one of the university's well-known programs, setting the stage for future collaborative projects. It was a win-win-win situation for all the residency partners as well as for the audience.

Defining the Term

For our purposes here, we can define residency work as any artist engagement outside of the formal mainstage concert presentation. Residency work is about *partnering* and *connecting with communities*, whether it's the community of a classroom, a hospital, a factory, or a group of museum attendees. Often, residency work is about going *to* your audience, meeting them on *their* turf, which may mean performing in nontraditional spaces, at a school gym, a shelter, or an office complex. Residency work at its best is engaging, interactive, educational *and* artistic, whether it's a single performance for a 6th grade class, a postconcert audience talk with the musicians sitting on the edge of the stage, or a monthlong residency at a community center. The common denominator in residency activities is that the purpose is to *actively engage participants with the music and with the performers.*

Alternatives to Formal Concerts

Where, how, and when performances take place all matters. For many, the formal classical concert event can be a real turn-off. The audience is asked to sit quietly in rows, at a distance from the players, without making noise or speaking until intermission, and God forbid anyone should applaud at the wrong time! All this creates a barrier between audience and artist. In recent years, presenters and musicians have been rethinking how, where, when and *why* they give performances.

The Fischoff National Chamber Music Association in South Bend, IN (http://www .fischoff.org) presents concerts by visiting ensembles in local homes and businesses, presenting chamber music the way it was intended to be heard, in intimate settings. Ann Divine, the Executive Director for Fischoff, has scheduled concerts in museums, cafés, and furniture stores, usually incorporating great food and community, to make both the music and the players approachable.

Da Camera of Houston (http//www.dacamera.org) is a producing organization that presents a mainstage series plus educational programs at schools and other community settings. Their family series includes four weekend afternoon performances at the Houston Zoo, complete with a question-and-answer session and a musical petting zoo, to give children a chance to see, touch, and play musical instruments.

And the Myrna Loy Center in Montana (http://www.myrnaloycenter.com) presents visiting musicians in turn-of-the-century landmark buildings in Helena, including performances in the cathedral, the capitol building, and the former governor's mansion. Great music heard in beautiful or unexpected settings makes for memorable experiences.

Clarifying Goals

For a presenter, the goal of the residency work may be to bring music to those who normally wouldn't go to a mainstage concert. But in many cases, goals reach beyond simple exposure to great music. For the presenter, residency programs may serve audience development, community awareness, and publicity goals. And, in many cases, residency work is focused on education, on having the audience become more familiar with the instruments, the musicians, the music, and with each other — creating a sense of community wherever the performance takes place.

Clearly, there can be more than one reason to do a residency performance. When planning any residency work, it's important to consider goals and to discuss these early on in the planning stage with the presenter and any other residency partners. Look at it from three perspectives: What would make the residency event a success for you? For the audience? For the presenter?

Why Bother? ■

Is residency work necessary? Musicians often think:

> *But if I perform really well, the audience will "get it." The music should stand on its own: After all, music is the universal language.*

Have you ever been to a museum or an art gallery and been confronted by a work you simply didn't "get"? And maybe friends and family were raving about the work but you were at a loss and felt left out? Well, many people have the same experience with art music, what composer/bassoonist John Steinmetz calls the kind of music that one has to pay attention to, be it Bach, Coltrane, Zwilich, or Shankar.

It can be difficult for trained musicians to imagine what going to a live concert is like for the general audience, for people who are inexperienced with art music, who don't read music, and have never paid close attention to it. In reality, average Americans experience music as a background effect. It's the aural wallpaper that accompanies their daily life. It's often the backdrop to their more focused activities: conversing, eating, shopping, or working.

Most people don't get *more* out of music because no one has ever helped them to engage more fully with it, to *hear* more in the music. The fundamental listening skills we may take for granted, such as hearing melody distinct from accompaniment, distinguishing instrumental timbres, changes in tone colors, tempos, and the contrasting affects of themes—these are all skills that people learn. Audiences need to practice listening in a new way in order to catch these distinctions. And it can be quite easy for people to learn how to hear more in the music—it may take only a minute—but people often need help knowing how to do it or where to direct their attention. We ask audiences to pay attention often without giving them any clue as to *how* to pay attention, or for *what* specifically. Steinmetz writes, "It's not hard to perceive musical details but often listeners need help learning how to aim their ears."

And the whole point of paying attention to art music, of perceiving details, is that it may lead to the pay-off: hearing more in the music can allow for a stronger emotional connection to it. Sometimes all a new listener needs is a chance to hear a work several times. Through repeated hearings of a work, live and recorded, a listener starts to get a sense of the shape and features of the work, starts to have the pleasure of recognizing themes, discovering new details within the familiar, and gets a chance to have the satisfaction of perceiving a work as a whole experience, with a beginning, middle, and end.

The most basic goal of residency work is to help people make a powerful emotional connection to music. It's about the relationship the listener has with the music, and how rich the listening experience can be. Let's face it: art music isn't for everyone. Exposing people to it and educating people about art music doesn't necessarily lead to converted fans. People become fans because they get an emotional charge out of something. But if people are not somehow "invited in" to this music, they may never have the opportunity to find out if they do in fact get that charge. Residency work is all about the "inviting in."

Example

The Huntington Brass Quintet (http://www.huntingtonbrass.org) first honed their residency skills through the NEA/Chamber Music America–sponsored Rural Residency program, a grant program that brought the group to Stephenville, Texas, for a yearlong residency of performing, teaching, and living in a community.

The HBQ has since held residencies in Boston at several area churches. These residencies have involved performing for special church services and holidays, and, in return, the quintet has presented their own concert series at each church. Having their own "home" series has allowed the quintet to grow their local audience base and gain visibility.

Residencies at houses of worship are not usually aimed at aesthetic education. It's not about hearing distinction and specifics in the music. When they perform as part of a religious service, artists are bringing their music to an audience that otherwise might not hear them. Whether in a church, a temple, or a mosque, artists can be heard in a context that helps listeners open their hearts to music. It's about a connection beyond words, a directly emotional connection that's about the occasion and the context.

In addition, the HBQ performs residency programs in schools, libraries, and other community settings. They've found that presenters appreciate not just their terrific playing but also their ability to talk with audiences and design interactive programs. Trumpeter Mark Emery attributes their frequent repeat bookings to their residency skills.

Primary Residency Skill: Talking to Audiences ■

For many musicians, speaking at performances is where it all begins. Being able to introduce yourself and your music from the stage is a terrific starting point for more complex residency work. Most presenters welcome an artist speaking from the stage, introducing one or more works on a program, particularly with new or unusual pieces. This applies to both mainstage performances and residency work. Don't make the mistake of leaving this area of your performance unpolished.

Tip: Recommended Attitude

What you say and how you say it can help build a rapport with your listeners, and build a sense of cooperation and community in the performance. You've been invited in to someone else's space, and others have come to meet you. Take the approach, no matter what the setting, that this is an intimate house concert, and you are the guest. Be gracious!

Context

What you say should depend on your audience, the venue, and the situation. Consider the differences between a . . .

- mid-morning concert for sixty middle school students in a school auditorium
- lunchtime performance at a hospital for staff, doctors, and ambulatory patients
- formal evening concert at a community music school; audience members include your students, their parents, your friends, and the public

Think how different both your remarks (and maybe your programming) need to be for these three audiences. It's not a matter of dumbing-down; it's a matter of adapting your comments to fit the age, interests, and curiosity of your audience.

Content: What Should You Say?

Go back to what makes the listening experience enjoyable. One of our most basic musical pleasures is recognizing familiar tunes—think how you feel when you hear a favorite song on the radio. In introducing new work to the audience it can be very helpful to play "previews" of some of the themes during your remarks so that when the piece is performed, the audience will be able to recognize these themes as they would an old friend.

Rattling off various dates and biographical tidbits about the composer won't necessarily help the listener to connect with you or with the music. Your remarks need to be more than just sporadic, disconnected "points of interest" about a work. Gear your remarks toward the experience of the performance—the more personal the better. You may do well to keep your remarks relatively brief and stick to matter that falls under the broad heading of "why you find this work fascinating." Get specific, demonstrating what you mean by "the first time I heard this movement, I was amazed at the effect the composer got in the opening; it sounded like a hallucination, with a kind of out-of-focus underpinning underneath a reeling melody. Here, let's play a bit of this . . ." Take the listener into the music and into your experience of it. The more you can invite the audience into the work, using active listening skills, the deeper their experience may be.

Ideas: What to Talk About

Remember that the purpose of your remarks is to help the audience make a personal and emotional connection with the music. Your remarks should help make a bridge between the listener and the music. Think about what in the work you find intriguing, and what drew you to it initially. Consider what specifically you love about the piece and consider what your audience might find interesting. Think of what features may stand out for the audience and what might help them hear more in the music.

- Stick to experiential issues, how the music can be perceived and experienced by listeners.
- Highlight personal reactions, histories, and stories around a work, both your own and the composer's.
- Remember this is not a music theory or history class. Your remarks should not be about teaching facts or delivering information; they should be tools to aid in the listening experience.
- Strike a balance: don't use jargon or technical terms, and don't be too simplistic. Assume there will be a range of expertise in the audience, from people new to the music to the musically sophisticated. It's easy to alienate novices simply by using technical terms like contrapuntal, cadenza, sonata form, dominant seventh chord, and so on.

Designing Residency Programming: Basic Ingredients ■

Beyond speaking from the stage, the next step is designing actual residency work. People who book artists for this work are looking for programs that are interactive. This does not simply mean that the musicians ask a few questions of the audience. For educational events, the baseline goals of residency work are to:

- Engage the participants
- Cultivate active listening skills
- Let the participants in on the "secrets" of what makes this music great

"What makes it great?" is in fact the title of a series of innovative and acclaimed programs the pianist/composer/educator Rob Kapilow has presented across the United States. Here's Rob's description (from the website for his ongoing residency work in Kansas City, http://www.chambermusic.org/ whatsgreat.html): "During each What Makes it Great? Program we will take a piece of great music, tear it apart and put it back together again. We will rewrite it, sing it together, tap it, clap it, in short do everything in our power to get inside of it to see what makes it tick and what makes it great. Then on the 2nd half of the program we will hear the piece performed in its entirety— hopefully with a new pair of ears." For listeners, getting a handle on what's actually going on in the music can allow for making a deeper emotional connection to the music.

Questions for Planning Residency Work

Is the goal for the audience to learn something, to experience something, or both?

What specific repertoire would you like to use? *Why?*

Who is the audience? A local high school, a retirement home, the local Rotary club?

What specific ideas or concepts do you want to address with each work or movement? *Why?*

What kinds of participatory activities do you plan to incorporate and why?

What will the audience get from this? What specific skills do you want the audience to develop?

What is the learning you would like to have take place?

How can you help your audiences to actively connect with the music?

Residency Work with Adults ■

Residency work with adults happens on college campuses, at libraries, museums, historical societies, community and civic clubs, bar associations, businesses, and many other places. And whether your audience is college students or factory workers, if you're doing residency work for general adult audiences— people without musical training—it's wise to find links between what they are familiar with and the points in the music you'd like to discuss. In doing so, you may be providing a way of linking seemingly disparate disciplines. Provide a point of reference and a connection between one kind of thinking they are familiar with and successful in, and the new area, the music you're presenting. What's great about this approach is it helps make meaning. We live in a culture in which we're constantly bombarded with facts and information. So any chance we have to make connections among disciplines and find meaning in our work, in our lives—well, that just about beats everything.

For example, when you're looking for ways to link specific repertoire to the audience's experience, you might want to brainstorm, do a free association exercise. You can do this on your own or with friends, including non-musicians. Listen to a recording or play through a movement of the work and then talk. What associations come to mind from the music? Chaos theory? The composer's spiritual or religious background? The political realities in the world at the time? The fragility of life? The nuances of dialogue, of musical "conversation"? Whatever the music brings to mind may be a great launching pad for a fascinating discussion with your audience. Part of what you can do in residency work is to name these associations, to reveal parts of your own associative process to your audience. In a sense, by your example, you can encourage the audience to explore their own associations—that's a big part of how and why people love music. This process can make both you and the music more approachable.

Adult Residency Programming

The String Trio of New York (a violin, guitar, and bass jazz ensemble; see http://www.s3ny.com) offers a series of college-level educational programs called "The Human Residency." These programs were developed to highlight the natural links between music and a variety of subjects including mathematics, philosophy, art, psychology, sociology, business, and more. For example, the trio's program "The Mathematics of Jazz" includes a discussion of the use of numbers in music, from the overtone series, rhythmic subdivisions, intervals, and figured bass. Their program "The Business of Collective Initiative," designed for economics and business classes, involves the discussion of how the ensemble is organized, and managed as a collective group. The trio has presented these innovative sessions on many campuses, including Dartmouth, Penn State, and Stanford University.

With adult audiences, it's especially important to make sure your approach is not condescending. Adults can be very self-conscious about their familiarity with music. They can be reluctant to ask any question that might reveal their ignorance about a subject. It's up to the artist to create an atmosphere of fun, open inquisitiveness, and exploration in any residency activity. The artist should be on a learning journey along with the audience, curious about their reactions and insights.

Residency Work with Seniors ■

Residency work with seniors can be especially gratifying. Seniors often make the most appreciative audiences. Performing for seniors can be an excellent way to gain experience with residency work. If you're just getting started with talking to audiences and designing interactive programs, you might want to start by offering a program to a local senior center, and work with their activities director or music therapist if they have one, to plan a satisfying experience. Keep in mind that not all facilities have excellent pianos or acoustics, so you'll need to check on these. Visit the site to meet with the activities director, meet the seniors, and maybe sit in on an activity so you can get a real sense of your audience.

In doing your residency work for seniors, make sure you project your voice or use a microphone—you need to be heard. And be prepared for interruptions and distractions. There may be individuals who speak out during a performance or come and go from the room and you'll need to be able to continue and not be thrown by these disruptions. Residency work requires flexibility, humanity, and resilience.

Your local senior centers, assisted living facilities, nursing homes, and Alzheimer's units are all possible sites for residency work. These facilities offer a range of care and programs to elders with varying health needs. All of these have activity directors who work at organizing and providing interesting social and cultural programs for their residents.

Some retirement homes want formal concerts of strictly classical music and have very well-informed audiences. More often, homes look for a mix of classical or jazz and familiar standard repertoire from musical theatre and the Great American Song Book. If you have, at least for encores, arrangements of standards by Gershwin, Cole Porter, Jerome Kern, and others, and can get your audience to sing along, that's great. Think of programming at least some familiar music that your audience knew when they were growing up.

Residency Work with Children ■

When it comes to the goals for residency work in K–12 schools, a sponsor may look to residency programming to provide a context for:

practicing self-expression
developing self-esteem
building teamwork skills
learning specific curriculum through the arts
gaining different perspectives on oneself, others, and one's own life situation

To work successfully with K–12 schools, it's important to be aware of school culture. Teachers and school administrators are very busy with many competing demands. Schools are under tremendous pressure these days for accountability, and standardized testing often drives curricular decisions. Funding is tight and time is short, and this means that artists wanting to do residency work should design programs that enhance, reinforce, or extend the school's curriculum. Note that every state's mandate and required curriculum is different: see the Arts Education Partnership website (http://www.AEP-arts .org/policysearch/searchengine) for each state's arts requirements, assessment policies, teacher certification information, and more.

So, whether it's for a forty-five-minute assembly program or a month-long residency, you need to design programs that link to the curriculum and to the goals of the teachers and school districts. Effective residency work helps make links between the arts and other areas of learning. Examples include programs that connect math curriculum with music, such as exploring fractions in the context of musical notation, demonstrating how music is organized in time, and how the overtone series is based on mathematical properties. Other programs connect science with music, exploring sound properties, sound waves, and how musical sounds are produced and perceived.

Musical Super Heroes

The Music Center of Los Angeles County (http://www.musiccenter.org) offers a wide variety of residency programs to schools in the area. Here's a brief description of one of these programs.

> *"Musica Angelica's* program entitled *"Musical Super Heroes"* introduces grades K–6 to the world of ancient Greek and Roman mythology. The ensemble—a soprano, tenor, and lutenist, all highly accomplished professionals based in the Los Angeles area—play intriguing instruments, perform opera scenes, dances, and instrumental music of the Baroque period. Colorfully costumed and highly interactive, the program invites audiences to participate as it shows how these marvelous myths are relevant to the family of man."

To get acclimated and to understand the culture, ask to spend a day visiting a school. Spend part of the day with a teacher of music, math, history, English, or science. Spend some time with the administrators, in the gym, and on the playground to see how a school really functions, and to think through how your program might fit in.

Beyond Schools

There are other great venues for children's educational programming, some with fewer bureaucratic and scheduling difficulties. There are summer camps, after-school programs, community music schools, and preschool programs. For the pre-K crowd, check out the Fischoff Association's (http://www.fischoff.org) program, which introduces great books to preschoolers through musical reenactments by chamber ensembles. The performers use their instrumental "voices" to represent the story's characters, emotions, and ideas. Musicians narrate the story and often use props for additional drama. These interactive programs incorporate music, reading, art, storytelling, drama, and imagination.

Effective K–12 Residency Materials: Study Guides for Teacher Preparation ■

One way to ensure that your residency program has some real impact is to create supporting materials for teachers to use before and after your visit. The best materials are those that teachers and students can immediately put to use.

From a presentation at a Chamber Music America Education and Residency Institute in Chicago, 2003, below are suggestions from Brooke Thompson, musician and teacher in the Chicago Public Schools, and Catherine Larson, faculty in the music and music education departments at DePaul University.

- Keep materials and instructions brief, because teachers have so little time.
- Keep these user-friendly for non-musician teachers (who may be intimidated if they have little familiarity with music)
- Offer relevant activities that teachers can do with their students before and after your program visit
- Include brief but clear instructions on how to do these.

Consider including:
- ❑ Biographical information on the performers, with photos
- ❑ Labeled drawings of the instruments for easy photocopying
- ❑ Brief explanations of how the sounds are produced
- ❑ Vocabulary lists (names and parts of instruments)
- ❑ Selected bibliography (include a list of resources and websites)
- ❑ Syllabus (for extended residencies)
- ❑ Evaluation form for teachers
- ❑ Evaluation form for students

Possible pre- or postevent classroom activities include:
- Vocabulary fill in the blank questions
- True/false questions
- Crossword puzzles
- Expository essay question
- Discussion topic suggestions for after the performance

To read others' teacher study guides, see http://www.quadcityarts.com/study-guides.html and on http://www.ums.org/index.htm (click on education and check online educational resources).

Getting Residency Work ■

Where can you find local opportunities to present a residency program? In looking for venues, think about your own community connections. Do you have colleagues, friends, or family who are connected to a college, school, or civic organization? Start with your network as you explore leads. Ongoing residencies are built on partnerships, on relationships between the musicians and a partnering organization.

Once you have some leads, work through your personal contacts. Just as you would if booking a concert, it's about preparing your "sales pitch," calling, sending materials, and making return calls. Especially if you're looking for an extended or ongoing relationship with an institution, making an in-person visit is a good idea, once your contact has expressed some interest. You want to be familiar with the institution, the site, and your potential audience.

Possible Community Partners for Residency Work

libraries	hospitals
festivals	correctional facilities
churches	retirement homes
after school programs	hospice
museums	day care, Head Start program
Boys and Girls Clubs	parks and recreation departments
public schools	rehabilitation centers
private schools	shelters
historical societies	colleges/universities
community clubs: Kiwanis, Lions, Rotary	

It's quite possible to create your own ongoing residency. A residency partnership might involve starting a concert series, a community music lesson program, or a summer festival. Partnerships with schools, museums, libraries, community clubs, social-service agencies, and more are possible.

Beatrice H.—a mezzo-soprano with a regular church choir section leader gig—needed a place with a piano to teach. She couldn't afford to rent a studio. She was friends with the church choir director and asked if it might be possible to use the church basement rehearsal room two afternoons a week to teach voice. It worked out well. Beatrice ended up bartering for the use of the space. Because of the good relationship she built, Beatrice is now co-presenting a recital series at the church and starting a children's choir; these are the seeds of a residency.

Beyond looking for residency work on a case-by-case basis, through developing relationships, there are also a number of organizations that can help you find work. These agencies hire or facilitate the hiring of musicians to perform in schools and alternative performance sites.

Getting Residency Bookings

Your state arts agency most likely has an arts-in-education program that funds performances and short-term residencies in schools; check the appendix.

County and city arts agencies are funded in part by State arts agencies. These smaller local agencies often fund a variety of community arts projects.

Young Audiences (http://www.youngaudiences.org) is a national nonprofit organization that arranges performances and residency programs in schools. There are thirty-two chapters and affiliate organizations nationwide.

Local organizations devoted to music performances in schools. Check what's available in your community: ask any K–12 music teachers, check with the local parent-teacher organizations, or inquire directly at schools.

VSA Arts is a national organization that works to make the arts accessible to people with disabilities. The organization has network affiliates in forty-nine states; see http://www.vsarts.org.

Funding Sources for Residency Work

Chamber Music America (http://www.chamber-music.org)
Association of Performing Arts Presenters (http://www.artspresenters.org)
Meet the Composer (http://www.meetthecomposer.org)

American Composers Forum Continental Harmony project (http://www.
   continentalharmony.org)

■

Planting Seeds to Establish a Long-term Partnership

Start with a single event: a concert, a fund-raiser, a master class, or lecture/
demonstration. If the event works well, you can explore a residency, an ongoing relationship with the organization.

   If you organize a residency directly with an institution, you should use a
contract that stipulates what each party agrees to do for the other. An institution may offer rehearsal or teaching space and concert promotion in exchange
for a certain number of formal concerts, residency events, or amount of teaching per year.

Marketing Yourself for Residency Work   ■

Concert presenters are becoming more sophisticated and demanding in terms
of their expectations for residency activities. Because residency work can be
fairly well paid and competitive, musicians need to market their educational
programs effectively. Typically, experienced teaching artists have a specific
flier or brochure for their residency work that can be included in their promotional kit or sent separately.

■

Residency Fliers or Brochures Should Include:

Contact information for the artists and how to get more information
Brief bio info and where you've presented your residency work
Testimonials, quotes from presenters who've booked you
Concise and compelling description of the programs you offer:

   For each, describe the benefits, what will the audience get from this?
   Appropriate age group for which each program is tailored
   Recommended audience size

For in-school performances: describe how the program is tied to the curriculum.
   This is essential for principals and teachers who must justify the class time
   given to these activities. In schools, in order to get the funding for an arts residency event, there needs to be a clear and specific educational value.

   Note: Some school administrators say they only look at brochures that include
   the price range.

■

Quality Control: Evaluating Your Residency Work ■

Getting objective feedback and constructive evaluation is the only way to know whether your residency work is meeting your own or your partner's standards. Building evaluation into your residency work will help make for continued development.

If you're working on a new program, do several trial runs with friends, family, mentors, a church group, or a local day care facility. Ask for specific, concrete feedback, such as, "I didn't quite follow the explanation of . . ." or "I'm not sure your audience will all understand the terms you used: . . ." or "The balance of talking to playing was generally good but I thought you went on a bit too long before the third movement" or "I'm not sure why you demonstrated . . . or what it had to do with . . ."

Ask to have a member of the host institution's staff observing every (or at least most) of your residency visits. Informal feedback can sometimes give you the best help in improving your programs. When people know you are open to hearing critical feedback and you really want their input, they are more likely to give it.

You may need to ask for this feedback after the fact, by e-mail or phone if you are rushed after the event. Good questions to ask include:

When did the participants seem most engaged?
When were they least engaged?
Was there anything you noticed that would help me improve the session?

The school or institution that hires you for this work will need concrete evidence of the effectiveness of the program. This is used in reporting to funders who support residencies. Of course, evaluating yourself also allows you to improve and develop better programs. The evidence of your effectiveness is also important for marketing purposes for future bookings and media attention, essential for your continued career growth. You'll want to gather comments, letters of recommendation, and testimonials, along with the constructive feedback for improvement.

For K–12 Work

You can use portfolio assessments for participants. Have children keep a journal for extended residencies, in which they write about what they experienced in each session. Depending on the age range, the journal can include drawings of what they did with the visiting musician that day, or for older participants, they can write about what they did with the visiting musician; what they liked most and least and why; and what they'd like to do next with music activities, either on their own or with the musician.

You can and should collect evaluation evidence in a number of ways, some more formal than others. You can videotape your program (ask a friend to not just film you but to try to catch audience reactions and response as well). Get written thank you's from participants, teachers, staff and use copies or excerpts of these with evaluation materials (and for marketing purposes). You can record (write or use audio or visual recorders) any informal verbal feedback you get from participants, staff, parents, or teachers. Take photos (good for documenting the work, audience reactions, and good for publicity). Note: To take photos, you'll need to get permission from the partnering institutions in advance. And of course, you can design a brief evaluation form for participants and guest observers, administrators, and teachers. Tailor the form to fit your program.

Tips for Residency Work

from Nancy Christensen, former education director for Chamber Music America and now managing director for MCM Artists.

1. "Talk to other musicians who are experienced and successful with this kind of work." (Need referrals and contact info? Check with your state arts agency, Young Audiences, or with Chamber Music America; see the appendix).
2. "Observe successful musicians doing their residency programs." (Most people are flattered to have a fellow musician ask to observe their work and most would be happy to spend time with you afterwards discussing residency work opportunities.)
3. "Before doing any residency work do your homework. Before the gig, call and talk to your contact at the residency site—the presenter, the classroom teacher, or activities director. Find out about your audience, the community, and about the performance space. If it's a school performance, make sure you know what the students are studying now. Find out if the school has a music teacher, any other local arts organizations working with the school, or no music or art instruction at all."
4. "Use humor, be genuine. Your audience wants to respond to you personally."

Biggest challenges musicians face in doing residency work? Nancy says:

1. "Spontaneity, being flexible, able to adjust a program and a plan on the fly as needed. You need to meet the audience *where they are* (emotionally, intellectually, and developmentally). Musicians may come prepared with a par-

ticular program, and invariably there are surprises." (An audience that doesn't respond as expected; a last-minute change of venue; an audience double the size expected; a performance in an auditorium when the group had expected a group of thirty in a classroom. This is the real test of this kind of work—you need to be able to handle curve balls.)

2. "Musicians need to keep their residency programs interesting, evolving, and fresh. Audiences—especially kids—sense immediately when you're not giving 100%." (Musicians need to challenge themselves and experiment with their programming in order to keep their standards high and their enthusiasm up.)

Summary

Audiences want to be actively engaged and musicians can help through the way they speak from the stage and through the educational programs and residency activities they create. Developing residency skills and opportunities takes time and effort but the rewards can be more performances, more engaged audiences, and the possibilities for ongoing institutional support. The good news is that there are resources, models, grants, and programs to help along the way. Musicians may sometimes feel that their residency work pulls them too much *away* from formal concertizing, away from the music. But in the end, it's this very work that often brings musicians closest to the reason why music matters, and reminds them of the power of the art.

Resources for Residency Work

Make Money Performing in Schools by David Heflick published by Silcox Publications, Orient, WA: A terrific, detailed, and practical book

Kennedy Center ArtsEdge, http://www.artsedge.kennedy-center.org: ArtsEdge is the Alliance for Arts Education at the Kennedy Center for the Performing Arts, a resource center for arts in education programs. Resources include standards, model programs, and assessment guidelines for designing curriculum, materials, and programs. Check the national and state curriculum education standards on this site so you can appropriately gear your program to your audience.

Lincoln Center Institute, http://www.lcinstitute.org: LCI is an arts and education organization whose approach is based on aesthetic education and the writings of such innovators as John Dewey and Maxine Greene. LCI works in partnership with pre-K through grade 12 educators and degree-granting teacher education programs, and provides numerous professional development opportunities.

Young Audiences, http://www.youngaudiences.org: See the national site, and my favorite, the Massachusetts chapter: http://www.yamass.org. Read descriptions for arts education programming in music, theatre, and dance.

Carnegie Hall's education program: http://www.carnegiehall.org, click on Explore and Learn.

The Metropolitan Opera Guild's Creating Original Opera program, in which students take on the entire production, from the libretto, to the music, costumes, set, casting, organizing rehearsals and publicizing the performance, http://www.metguild.org/education/educators/creating_original.aspx.

Arts Education Partnership, www.AEP-arts.org/policysearch/searchengine: lists each state's arts requirements, curriculum frameworks, teacher certification information, etc.

The New England Conservatory Journal for Learning Through Music, second edition, download off the Web: Contains articles and roundtable discussions http://www.nec-musicined.org/journal-two.html

State Arts Agencies' website for descriptions of arts education programs in your state (contact info on each state arts agency is listed in the appendix).

The Teaching Artist Journal, Eric Booth, editor (available at http://www.erlbaum.com)

■ Suggestions for Moving Ahead ■

Brainstorming for residency programming

1. Imagine you are going to perform for a group of business people at an awards luncheon honoring the retiring president of the company. You've been hired to perform this person's favorite piece. Because most people in the audience are unfamiliar with this work, you've decided to say a few words. What could you say in a two- to three-sentence introduction to help the audience connect to this work? [You choose the piece]

2. Same piece, new audience. Now you're performing this work for a retirement home's concert series. How would you introduce it?

3. Same piece, new audience. How would you introduce the work to a class of twenty-five sixth graders?

For finding residency work partners

4. List three organizations in your community that you're curious about, to explore partnership possibilities. Forget about traditional concert series and halls, and instead think about places where there are groupings of people, possible new audiences for you. Perhaps they have an un-

usual performance space, or a membership base that might also be interested in your music. For ideas, read your local newspapers, talk to neighbors, search on the Web. Think broadly and creatively (science museums, historical societies, civic organizations, etc.).

5. Research the three community organizations you listed above. Find out about their resources, programming, and any current partnerships. Visit the organizations, read their printed brochures and websites. Look at staff listings to see if you have any contacts working at the organizations. Check with your alumni office. To make an initial contact, it's especially helpful to start with a personal connection.

6. Take a work in your current repertoire and design an initial offering for an organization. Find the appropriate person at the organization and make an appointment, hopefully with the help of an introduction from someone you both know. The idea of the appointment is to explore the idea of an initial performance presentation (with or without pay), as a trial balloon for exploring an ongoing residency.

9

Performing At Your Best

The topic areas of this chapter revolve around how musicians achieve and convey peak performances. How musicians use their bodies and their minds to perform at their best. The specific topics for this chapter are stage presence, performance anxiety, and performance health—issues often avoided in music schools and among professionals. Typically, vocalists in music schools are coached on their stage presence, but not instrumentalists. Most often, musicians think of stage presence as something you either have or you don't. As for how to deal with performance anxiety and performance injuries, these topics are often taboo. It may be fine to discuss these issues quietly with a trusted friend but not in public. It's unfortunate, because virtually all musicians deal with both performance anxiety and performance injuries at some point in their careers. It's high time to openly discuss these subjects, because so much can be done to help, with access to good information and resources.

Stage Presence ■

How you present yourself is a big part of the audience's experience. It's part of why they're there—to *see* as well as hear you perform. In *Stage Presence from Head to Toe* author Karen Hagberg defines stage presence quite broadly, as the total " . . . visual aspect of a live performance: everything from a performer's walk, bow, facial expression, and dress, to an ensemble's portrayal of a single, unified entity; from the condition of the chair, music stands, and piano, to the mechanics of smooth stage management."

In a way, we're all naked when we walk out on stage. How we feel about ourselves, the audience, and about performing is part of what we communicate in a performance. The audience picks this up loud and clear. We wear our emotions in the way we carry our bodies, in our walk, the direction of our gaze, and in our facial expression. Some people have a natural charisma and a charm that is communicated immediately in their everyday self, in their curtain walk, and in their performance itself. That's fine, but for the rest of us, the majority of musicians, there are specific ways to help "unlock" our best stage presence, to retool our presentations and become more at ease in any performance situation.

Hagberg describes good stage presence as a clear expression of a musician's "respect for the music, for the audience, for other musicians and for himself." Working at whatever is getting in the way of a musician's ability to convey this, that's what improving stage presence is about.

Think about an artist whose live performances you've seen a number of times and whose stage presentation you admire. How would you describe the impression this artist makes when she or he walks on stage and bows? Professional? Confident? Assured? Welcoming? Happy to be here? Aristocratic? Humble? Preoccupied? Unprepossessing?

Now, how do *you* want to come across to your audience?

True Story

Hands down, the worst stage presence I've witnessed was a concerto soloist who exhibited an extreme case of stage arrogance. When he strode on stage he barely acknowledged the audience's applause, giving just a perfunctory nod in the manner of a high school jock about to compete in a sports competition. During the orchestral introduction, his body language screamed studied boredom mixed with impatience. He actually nodded to himself after several of his own solo passages—either nodding yes, as if he approved, and in a few cases nodding from side to side and looking disappointed in his output. His body language and facial muggings were a kind of blow-by-blow commentary on his performance. And how was the playing? To be blunt, he sounded arrogant, even when I closed my eyes to blot out the visuals. His antics were so exaggerated this would have been comical but for the fact that this musician was not a child but an adult professional. I realized either no one had taught him this was unacceptable behavior or else if someone had tried, he didn't realize or care about the impression he was actually making.

Coming across as arrogant on stage is not the only way you can go wrong. Some performers convey their nervousness and unease, forecasting an unsure performance to the audience before they've heard a note. Others have unconscious physical habits or facial tics that the audience may interpret as anger or discomfort. Most musicians are not such extreme cases, but then, most of us don't actually know how we come across in performance. Which brings me to the first recommendation.

Have someone videotape your next performance, including the walking on and off stage and the bows. It can be very hard to be objective when you watch yourself, so view the video with a trusted mentor and discuss it together. You may need to turn the sound down in order to really focus on the stage presence and not the musical performance or the quality of the sound recording. As you watch, ask yourself, are you conveying the image of a professional who welcomes the opportunity to share music with the audience? Many performers have facial mannerisms and physical habits that are unbecoming, but these can be overcome. It's worth working on because it's a big part of the audience's experience. Stage presence is an important piece of what you communicate in a performance.

NOTE: Many of the specific pointers below come from the noted stage director and coach Janet Bookspan, from the workshops and seminars for musicians she's given at numerous conferences and schools of music. It can be especially helpful for musicians to work with an experienced coach to improve their presentations because we often need an objective third party to help us sort out our own issues.

Take a Bow

The purpose of an entrance bow is to greet your audience and to acknowledge their applause. It's the equivalent of a handshake and a greeting when you meet someone new. When you walk out from back stage, walk straight to your performance position, with your head and chin up. Turn to the audience and make eye contact, not fixing on one person, but catching eyes as you let your eyes sweep over the crowd, and smile. The eye contact conveys your sincerity. Have in mind something like "I'm so happy to see you here!" because that's the message you should convey. This may help put you more at ease if you have the attitude of welcoming the audience to your music-making. Then bow from the waist to about 45 degrees, keeping your hands relaxed at your side. Look down as you bow; it's a sign of humility. When you come up, again make eye contact with the audience. Hagberg writes that when you don't complete all these components of the bow, it's "equivalent to meeting someone and shaking hands without making eye contact, or turning to walk away before the handshake is finished—either of which would be dismissive and rude."

More Bowing Tips

- After performing, bow and acknowledge the audience. Convey that you appreciate their thanks, and smile, *no matter how you feel the performance went.* When returning for curtain calls, return to stage center.
- If you are given flowers, accept them graciously and bring them backstage. If there is another curtain call, leave the flowers backstage—don't bring them back on stage with you.
- For soloists with orchestras: enter before the conductor, go to your spot and wait for the conductor to get on podium before acknowledging applause (this shows respect to the conductor, who is considered the bigger "star"). Make sure you appear interested and involved, even when you are not playing (in the orchestral tutti sections). When the performance is done, first shake hands with the conductor, then the concertmaster; say thank you to the orchestra, take conductor's hand and bow together. Curtain calls: the second time out, simply shake hands with the concertmaster. Third time out, with conductor, let her/him signal for the orchestra to rise (it's not your job). If you've ever seen Yo-Yo Ma in a concerto performance, you'll have an image of how to be a gracious soloist. Audiences, orchestras, and conductors appreciate good manners.
- Gender issues on stage: for stage exits, it looks better if the males let the females go first. For entrances, however, if it's an ensemble group, enter in the order you will seat yourselves or stand while performing. If you are a male singer doing a recital and your pianist is a woman, you should enter first (it's your recital, you're the "star") and exit second (demonstrating that though you're a star, you're still a gentleman). Chivalry looks good on stage.

Stage Presence Do's and Don'ts

- Smile! Check your posture.
- About page-turners: they should enter unobtrusively after the performers and should bring music to the stage. If entering the stage on the usual side, stage left, they should walk behind the piano.
- If the audience applauds between movements, don't frown, glare, or roll your eyes. Instead, if you simply lower your head a bit, you can wait until the audience quiets, then proceed with the performance.
- About encores: should you announce or not? This should depend on the size of the hall and the quality of your announcing voice—have a colleague at the back of the hall at your run-through listen to you announce and tell you frankly what's best.

Tips For Ensembles

- Everyone should move at the same speed during exits and entrances. Pick a leader to cue the beginning and end of bows and choose leaders for stage entrances and exits. Clarify this before each performance. This can mean the difference between looking like a cohesive professional group and looking like a bunch of freelancers who have just met to sight-read a gig. When returning to the stage for curtain calls, return to stage center, in front of stands and chairs (as long as there's enough room to do this comfortably).
- Figure out a tuning order and do it quietly, quickly and accurately. If possible, take care of your tuning offstage.
- Be careful of the way you sit: Make sure that all ensemble members' faces can be seen—the audience wants to see your expressions and your eye contact with each other (audiences are often very aware of the nonverbal communications among ensemble members).
- Look at your partners during their solos—show your involvement in the music. Don't count rests—audiences can always tell if you're not involved in the music.
- You need to consider how your ensemble looks together. You don't necessarily need to wear the same suits or colors, but you need to create—with the help of your clothing—an impression of a cohesive unit.

Concert Attire

What you wear needs to be appropriate for the performance site and occasion. For a morning residency performance at a middle school you'd wear something different than at the formal evening concert on a presenter's series. It's important to get objective opinions on your concert attire from people who go to and who give lots of concerts. We all think we have great taste and that we know what is most flattering on ourselves, but the proliferation of television makeover shows is evidence to the contrary. We've all been to concerts where the performer's choice of attire was less than optimal and made a less than optimal first impression. Get objective, expert advice.

A Few General Tips

- Make sure your concert clothes allow you to move and breathe freely and look good when you are moving in performance (musicians often wear concert clothes that are too tight or constricting).
- Pay attention to the quality and line of clothing; you want to convey your professionalism in every detail of your performance.
- Even wearing all black, it's possible to look chic, elegant, distinctive, and

attractive—but your clothes should not stand out so much that they distract the audience from your music-making.

- Shine your shoes! And because onstage your socks or hosiery are usually partially visible, make sure you're not flashing bare shins, runs, odd-colored socks or stockings. Coordinate your colors and make sure your hosiery doesn't scream discount store.
- For men: your jacket should be buttoned when you enter and exit the stage. Unbutton the jacket just before you begin playing, as you take your seat.
- Watch out for hairstyles that hide your features—the audience wants to see your expressions because it's an important part of their experience of you as a performer.

Just for Women

Remember: your performance is not a fashion show. Whatever the fashion this season, your attire should help the audience focus on you and your music, not your dress. Your dress needs to flatter your body type and allow you to perform and move comfortably. The line and drape of a gown can help accentuate the positive and minimize the negative of any figure. Shop for your potential concert gowns with a colleague you trust, someone who'll be brutally honest *before* you buy anything.

It's usually best to stick to one solid color because it's less distracting and will help elongate your line. The color, of course, should be flattering to you but should also help make an impact (for instance, dark reds and greens can look wonderfully rich on stage). The quality of the fabric matters; it's very apparent under stage lights. Keep the distracting accessories to a minimum: no belts, watches, or dangling earrings. Other distractions include jiggly upper arms. Many women of all ages have them. If you do, avoid sleeveless gowns and wear loose fitting sleeves that cover the upper arm. Be careful about lengths of dresses for daytime concerts: mid-calf may be the safest. If you sit to perform, stick with fuller skirts. Cellists and harpists need full skirts, full length, or pants with a flattering drape. Make sure your audience can concentrate on your music-making and not on the knees, legs, or thighs you may be flashing or the bodice out of which you may be falling!

Preparation: Checklist for Before the Performance
- Check the stage lighting carefully so that any spotlights don't blind you, or create too much heat on stage. Check that the lighting is flattering to performers.

- In your dress rehearsal, carefully arrange the chairs and stands the way you want in the performance. Make sure your set up allows the audience to see all ensemble members. Make sure that all performers can see each other and have enough space to perform. If the stage crew needs to move any of your set-up before the concert, have the floor marked or "spiked" with tape so the set up can be recreated easily. Do whatever you can to help make smooth stage transitions and to minimize the time between your stage entrance and the first note.
- Make sure all page turns are workable and planned out (photocopy and/or cut and tape pages as necessary).
- Pianists—if at all possible arrange the chair or bench height *before* you walk onstage. (Your audience does not want to see you adjust the bench on stage.)
- For ensembles: use folding metal stands—they don't block the sound and they don't obstruct the audience's view of you and your instrument.

Remember that the audience experiences the performance as a totality, including your bows, your facial expressions, your speaking, your clothing, your attitude at the reception, and your general demeanor. Also, the printed program, the hall, the ventilation, and the parking situation may all contribute to either a pleasurable or less than pleasurable experience. From the audience's point of view, the "concert" is much more than just how the music sounds, so make sure that their total experience is a good one.

"You can not give an audience or anyone something you don't own. It is your own vision of the music that makes it your truth."

—Janet Bookspan, stage director and performance coach

Performance Anxiety ■

Stage presence is actually directly linked to performance anxiety issues. Your level of anxiety often determines your stage presence. This section deals with performance anxiety and practical techniques for overcoming it. Whether it's a big issue for you or a just an occasional discomfort, there is practical information you can apply to help move you toward more peak performance experiences.

What Is Peak Performance?

When performing artists speak about their best performances, their most creative moments, they often describe these as peak performances. Athletes call this state of optimum performance being in the "zone" or being in "flow," like being in a meditative state. There's a loss of self-consciousness and musicians sometimes say it's as though the performance were going on without any interference from them, without effort, as though they were almost channeling the performance, not having to make it happen. While in the "zone," time can seem suspended, you can feel a freedom in your music-making, and feel your body working easily and your mind remaining in a calm receptive state. This is the peak performance experience musicians seek. It doesn't happen regularly, it's not something you can chase. Instead, the best most musicians can do is help themselves clear the clutter of thoughts and negative self-talk to allow for these peak performance experiences to occur, whether they happen in a phrase, a movement, or an entire concert. Working on reducing performance anxiety is all about reducing the clutter of thoughts, feelings, and physical symptoms that get in the way of peak performances.

If you have ever experienced any performance anxiety, rest assured, you are not alone. Every performing musician experiences performance anxiety to some degree. The *way* each person experiences it, though, is unique. The extent to which anxiety affects one's playing is individual, as are the combinations of symptoms. Musicians also report that their performance anxiety changes over the course of their career; it can have peaks and valleys.

This section on performance anxiety is divided into three parts: the first deals with the causes and symptoms of performance anxiety; the second, with self-assessment; and the third, with interventions and practical treatment methods.

What Is Stress?

Let's start with a basic: stress, it's our mental, physical, and emotional reaction to events and situations in our lives. Losing a job or a loved one can cause stress, just as winning a competition or an audition can. Stress is a basic part of life; without it our lives would be routine, predictable, boring. Stressors (the events and situations we react to) make life challenging, exciting, and memorable. It's the *way* we react to these stressors that can be problematic.

Experiencing stress before a performance can be positive: it means you care about the performance and are excited to be performing. It can give your performance an "edge." Musicians look for a balance between having no excitement in their performance and having too much.

You probably know people who lead very busy, pressured lives and yet their general demeanor is relaxed and happy. Other people "make mountains out of mole hills," blowing small issues out of all proportion. These extremes can be attributed to personality traits, genetics, or temperament, but no matter what your natural disposition may be, you have a *choice* in the way you react to stressors. You can change your attitude toward any difficulty or predicament in which you find yourself. Changing your attitude, your perception of a situation, is a powerful tool—*change your perception and you change your reality.*

What Is Performance Anxiety?

Performance anxiety can be broken down into four areas, or types of symptoms. Performance anxiety manifests itself with any one or any combination of these.

1. *Physical symptoms* such as shortness of breath, dry mouth, sweating, increased muscle tension, rapid heart rate, trembling, nausea, or dizziness.
2. *Cognitive indicators*: thoughts, worries, dwelling on negative assessment of the situation, negative thoughts about the performance and oneself.
3. *Emotional indicators*: feelings of inadequacy, fear of disapproval, fear of the fear itself, or an irrational exaggeration of the performance situation (it becomes a test of one's worth as a person, or a life-or-death situation).
4. *Behavioral changes* in response to the symptoms above, such as avoidance (deciding not to do the audition, postponing a recital, etc.), or denial (procrastinating in planning for, practicing, or rehearsing for a performance).

People who experience high levels of performance anxiety tend to concentrate on their symptoms, which in turn causes more worry, more negative thought patterns, more feelings of inadequacy, and an increase in the severity of these symptoms. Musicians can get stuck in a performance anxiety loop, or a downward spiral.

The paradoxical nature of performance anxiety is that it has nothing to do with the performer's actual ability. World-class performers as well as rank amateurs can experience debilitating performance anxiety. The sense of vulnerability comes from within; it has little to do with how an audience might assess the performer's abilities.

Fight or Flight

Our body's extreme reaction to stress is called the fight or flight response, an instinctive physical response that includes an increase in heart rate and blood pressure, and a rush of adrenaline. Biologically, humans are programmed for the fight or flight response for self-preservation purposes in life-threatening situations. But unless you're playing in a war zone, a performance is not a life-threatening situation. If we react in a performance situation with the fight or flight response, it's a clear indication we need to examine our thoughts and feelings and make some adjustments in order to alter our perception and our response.

Competition and Career Stress

Career stress adds to the stress of any one performance. Competition is an inherent element in the lives of musicians. We compete and are judged throughout our careers—to win scholarships, to go to festivals and schools, and beyond graduation, we compete for grants, awards, and jobs. Musicians want to perform at their best, to realize their potential, and to become the best they can be. Musicians learn early on that their career depends almost entirely on their success in performance situations. This reality magnifies the pressure we feel over any individual performance. There can be an exaggerated perception that if the next performance goes poorly, it may mean the end of one's career. So the inherent competition in the profession can produce a general job stress that is cumulative and contributes to performance anxiety.

Most musicians realize that stress and performance anxiety to some degree come with the profession. But most people don't realize they have the ability to change their reactions to stress. The first step on the road to change is self-assessment.

Case Study: Part 1

Steve O., a talented flutist, found that his performance anxiety had increased over the past four years and it was becoming disabling. Before a performance he would typically find his hands trembling and his mouth so dry it became nearly impossible to start the performance. The weird thing was, once he got started, the symptoms usually subsided and he was able to perform adequately—not as well as he could in a practice room, but better than he feared he would before the performance. Read on for more of Steve later in this chapter.

Self-Assessment: Check Out Your Attitudes ■

Overcoming performance anxiety is a process that begins with self-assessment. It's necessary find out what kinds of conscious and unconscious thoughts and feelings are contributing to the anxiety. Seeing a professional counselor can be tremendously helpful in this process and you may want to find a therapist who specializes in treating anxiety.

Your attitudes toward yourself (your confidence and self-esteem); toward your instrument (is it a love/hate relationship?); toward performing in general; and toward your audience, are important factors and may be contributing to how you experience performance anxiety. You need to find out what's really going on in order to do something about it. There are specific thoughts, associations, experiences, feelings and concerns that cause the range of symptoms any musician develops.

Attitude toward Self

Performers tend to view themselves as musicians first and as people second. In his article "Resuscitating Art Music" (read at http://www.mumb.com/artx2 .html), John Steinmetz writes, "Many of us musicians . . . have made the terrible mistake of letting our sense of personal worth and our self-esteem get wrapped up with the quality of our performances. Somewhere along the line we decided that we have no value as people unless our performances are really good. If not, we are worthless scum." If all of your confidence and feelings of self-esteem are tied up in the last performance you gave, you are setting yourself up for trouble.

Perfectionism Is a Trap

We all aim for ideal performances, and we are all critical of ourselves. Musicians are often perfectionists. At the extreme, they may engage in all-or-nothing thinking—that a performance must be 100 percent "perfect" to be acceptable. But mistakes are inevitable, as humans are not machines. A performance should be about artistry, about taking chances, about making music, not about executing a technically perfect account of a work. If you realize that perfection is not for humans, and that mistakes are inevitable, you may give yourself the leeway to take risks in your performances. Give yourself permission to fail and you may surprise yourself and feel a new freedom in your performances.

Artists are often between a rock and hard place: we necessarily set our sights on unattainable goals for our artistry and so we may be constantly disappointed in our "failure" to reach these goals. Instead of striving for perfection in a performance, we can more realistically strive for excellence. Pablo Casals said, "We must be grateful for even one beautiful phrase." Be careful what you are actually expecting from yourself and of how you evaluate your performances. It's easy to get so wrapped up in our profession, our idealism, and our ambition, that we lose track of our basic stance toward life and toward ourselves. It's a good idea to check in periodically, to examine your thoughts and feelings on these issues.

What Does Performing Mean to You?

Is it about sharing? About telling a story through the music? Is it about trying to achieve perfection? About self-esteem or self-worth? About proving something to yourself or to others? About being better than someone else? Most musicians would not have just one answer here. Unfortunately, if there are some negative issues for you around the motivation for performance, and you don't deal with these issues, this can cause more performance anxiety.

How do you react to the compliments people give you after a performance? Do you shrug them off? Do you immediately say or think, "Yes, BUT . . ."? What you may perceive as glaring mistakes or faults may mean very little to your audience. It's important to be gracious to others' compliments but it's also important to be able to recognize what is good, what is valuable in your performances, and what your strengths as a performer are. We are far too good at analyzing our deficiencies and are often unable to articulate or appreciate our positive qualities.

Attitude toward Audience

How do you picture your audience, as friend or foe? When you are performing, what do you imagine your audience to be experiencing? Do you imagine them at all or is the performance all about you and your own standards of excellence? Can you imagine your audience as a supportive group of friends and family? Can you feel their support, their interest, and their gratitude? Are you able to acknowledge their applause instead of slinking off stage because of a few missed notes?

The foundation of performance anxiety is the fear of public humiliation. Unfortunately, in a competitive environment the festive aspect of performances can seem to disappear and we get caught up in judging ourselves and in worrying over how we may be judged. It's easy to forget why someone comes to hear you perform in the first place. Audiences are not there to judge you; they want to hear your interpretation of some great music. Your audience wants to be moved by your performance. Don't project your fears and negative thoughts onto your audience—they are on your side.

Examine Your "Self Talk"

What goes on in your head during a performance? Negative self-talk often comes in predictable flavors:

"I can't believe I just f–d up that easy passage . . ." or
"Well, that was a disaster, and there's no excuse, it went great in the last rehearsal. What is my problem?"
(Obsessing over a mistake instead of letting go and staying in the present)

"Who do I think I'm fooling; I can't play this piece!" or
"This is going really bad; this whole performance is going to suck."
(Overgeneralizing, "catastrophizing")

"Oh my God, here comes that passage I always screw up . . ."
"Yikes, here's where I had that memory slip last week."
(Anticipating disaster: often making it a self-fulfilling prophecy)

These thoughts, our self-talk messages, are often lurking just below our consciousness and may be habitual or automatic. We may be unaware of these messages, yet they exert a powerful effect. These thoughts produce negative feelings: worry, fear, feelings of inadequacy, and these feelings in turn incite the physical symptoms of performance anxiety. In other words, we react to our perceptions of reality rather than to reality itself.

Case Study: Continued

When Steve started to self-assess, he started by noticing his thoughts in the practice room, what he was thinking while preparing for the next concert with his quintet. He started to keep a practice room journal and, as part of his practice, imagine that he was warming up backstage for the next concert. He noticed his thoughts tended to center around worry over particular passages. He also noticed his self-talk before actual performances. Steve noticed his thoughts raced with frantic thoughts like, "The third movement is not good, that fast passage is a mess!" or "What if I screw up that cue like I did yesterday?" or "I have to concentrate harder on intonation!" As for his thinking about himself and his audience, Steve reported that, right before walking on stage, he'd have a fleeting sense of panic, like he wasn't qualified for the performance, like he was a fraud and had no business doing the performance and that the audience was going to "see through him" and judge him as incompetent. Steve wrote all this up in his journal. He was surprised at how negative the thoughts were and how extreme. He was discouraged because his negative self-talk seemed so ingrained that he doubted he could change. Read on, Steve makes a breakthrough.

Take Your Performance History

What were your first performance experiences like? As a youngster, did you like performing? Many of us began studying and performing as children in very supportive atmospheres. Recitals may have been held at a teacher's home, a church, or at a local school. These performances may have had a festive party atmosphere, with a family celebration afterward. Or, in a more competitive environment, you may have felt pressure at performances from your earliest concerts. Chances are you would not be a musician today if performing has always been a struggle.

If your early performance experiences were positive, you can reclaim that experience. And if your early performance experiences were less than positive, you can learn new responses. Remember, you are in the driver's seat in terms of how you react to stress.

Interventions and Treatment Methods ■

There is, unfortunately, no magic bullet cure for performance anxiety. There are some medications that alleviate some of the symptoms of performance anxiety, but to treat the cause of the anxiety, there's no quick fix. The good news is that there are a range of methods and coping techniques that can be extremely effective. But changing our ingrained habits, the way we react to stress, takes time. Finding what works takes patience and experimentation. It also takes a willingness to look frankly at your underlying feelings, thoughts, and emotional baggage. And, because each musician is unique, what may work well for your colleague may do nothing for you.

A range of coping techniques and methods follow. Keep an open mind and experiment with these suggestions to find a combination or adaptation that works well for you. Consider your practice room your laboratory. This is the place you can experiment with new kinds of "self-talk," with visualization techniques. You can simulate performance situations in your imagination so that "the real thing" goes the way you'd like. The information below includes ideas and coping strategies you can incorporate into daily practice to build new habits in the months before your next major performance.

> *Check your community resources:* Reach out to others. Don't isolate. In talking to others, both musicians and non-musicians, you may pick up many good ideas as well as the comfort of knowing you're not alone. Talk to people and ask about resources in your community. Find out if there are stress management courses available near you. Many community centers, clinics, and hospitals offer these.
>
> *Preparation:* Excellent preparation for your next performance will do a lot to increase your confidence. Create a plan for the months and weeks preceding the performance. Include a schedule of practice time and deadlines for completing work on each piece. You may want to schedule lessons with mentors to make sure that you're fully prepared and do not have undue concerns over your abilities to perform the program.

Desensitization is the process of gradually building up resistance, and increasing tolerance to stress. This is the same technique doctors use to treat allergies, and therapists use in treating social anxiety and panic attacks. The idea is you start with lower stress performance situations, playing a mini-concert in less-pressured atmospheres and gradually build up to the "real" performance. Start with just playing a small part of your program for one or two friends. You can "up the ante" regularly, systematically increasing the number of people and the level of stress in each performance situation. Arrange to perform at a local church, community center, or nursing home. The object is in part, to learn more about what is going on in your thinking as you perform and, most important, to become more accustomed to handling your symptoms as you experiment with various coping strategies.

Visualization: this is the technique of creating a positive mental picture that will influence your thoughts, feelings, and actions. Visualization is a powerful tool to aid in concentration, but like anything else, it takes practice and experimentation. Here are three different visualization exercises:

1. *Recreating a performance:* Think back to a performance you had that you felt satisfied with. The idea is to recreate your performance experience in every detail in your mind. Remember what you saw, smelled, heard and felt. How did your arms and legs feel as you were performing? What was your breathing like? What thoughts were passing through your mind? What feelings were you aware of? You can practice recreating this state of mind in your practice room, gradually increasing the amount of time you can stay in the remembered state, in the recreated sense of calm, focused concentration. With practice, musicians learn to bring back this desired state of mind and body at will, so they can use this technique in performance.

2. *Direct your own movie*: In your mind, you can create a movie of the ideal way you want to perform a particular passage, a movement, or a piece. Again, use your imagination to detail all your sensory experience. Imagine how your arms, fingers, neck, shoulders, spine, legs, and feet feel. In your ideal performance of a particular passage, what would you see? The conductor, a colleague, the music? What would you hear? What would the sound be like in the hall? What exactly do you notice about how the passage sounds to you? You may want to close your eyes as you do this.

Start first with just a phrase then build up your movie-making ability to a complete piece. Make sure that you are not just replaying a favorite CD or DVD in your head—this visualized performance has to be yours, with all the nuances, inflections, and physical movements involved in your optimum performance. When you create such a movie in your head you are teaching your mind and body how to recreate this performance in reality.

3. *Circle of Excellence:* Composer Michael Colgrass writes about this exercise in his article "Performing at Your Best" (http://www. michaelcolgrass.com/71.html). Simply draw or mark a circle on the floor, using chalk or tape, or in a carpeted room, you may be able to "draw" your circle in the carpet's pile with your finger. Now step into your circle of excellence. Michael Colgrass writes, "Inside the circle is your own personal excellence, what makes you unique. If even for a split second you feel less than your best, you step out of the Circle, quickly do what's necessary to regain your optimum state, and step back in again. The Circle is like a force field made of your own energy, and it's impenetrable. You can visualize the Circle anywhere you need it—on stage, in the practice room, at auditions—and it's always with you because you carry it in your head. Performers claim they feel an almost electrical power in their Circle of Excellence, a feeling very like their peak performance state." You need to practice this for it to work. You need successful "circle" experience in the practice room so that your imagination can use it effectively in front of your audience.

Keep a performance journal: keep track of your preparation and performances by keeping a journal. Like our case study, Steve, you can record in your journal your self-talk and emotions in practice sessions and rehearsal. Record whatever visualization techniques you used and how they worked. This way you can track your progress and your use of various techniques. For performances, record how you felt after the performance and specifically what other people said to you about the performance. It's important to know one's strengths as well as one's weaknesses. It's important to be able to appreciate what's good and what's working well. Writing down these positive comments should help you let them "sink in."

Thought stopping: This is the technique of consciously stopping negative self-talk and replacing it with positive phrases. For this to be effective you have to be vigilant since most of us are unaware of our self-talk; it's a backdrop to our daily activities. Cognitive therapy is based on the theory that your thoughts determine your feelings and therefore your behavior. Negative thoughts kick off the cycle of performance anxiety symptoms. So when you stop these thoughts and replace them with new positive thoughts, you trigger positive feelings of confidence and reduce the physical reactions to the stress. The main point is that you can control the self-talk and choose which "voices" to follow, the negative or the positive.

For instance, if you find yourself thinking things like, "I can't do this" or "There's no way this is going to be good" or "Oh my God, my hands are starting to sweat again," you need to squash these thoughts. You may need to shout in your head, "Stop!" and then replace the negative with positive talk such as, "I have prepared well," or "I have a good performance waiting to unfold," or "I have a story to tell through my performance and I want to share it with this audience." Self-talk is powerful; it determines our emotional states. If you want to change your emotional state, you need to change your self-talk.

Learn to let go. During your performances, are you able to stay in the present? If you make a mistake can you let it go, and not dwell on it, and stay focused on the present? Do you notice what goes well or only what does not?

I've often noticed a difference in the general attitudes that jazz and classical musicians have toward performing. Improvising is all about being in the present moment and there's not a sense of chasing a fixed sense of perfection. If you don't improvise, consider taking a class or some lessons with an improvising musician. Or take a theater class in improv—it can be a great way to start feeling more comfortable in your body and with the experience of being in the present.

Take a deep breath: Better than any pill is using the technique of deep abdominal breathing. It's the best antidote for the fight or flight response. Slow diaphragmatic breathing will slow your racing heart, help regulate the surge of adrenaline, and help to calm and focus your thoughts. Make it a habit to practice this breathing twice a day. Start by practicing for two minutes at a time, and gradually increase your capacity. The practice will pay off: your body will adopt the *relaxation response* as a habit, a part of your routine that you can "turn on" as part of your performances.

The Relaxation Response is a simple practice that once learned takes ten to twenty minutes a day and can relieve stress and tension and help you towards a healthier, more satisfying life. The technique was developed by Herbert Benson, M.D. at Harvard Medical School, tested extensively and written up in his highly recommended book *The Relaxation Response,* published by HarperTorch in a reissued edition, 2000. Here is the description, reprinted with permission.

1. Sit quietly in a comfortable position.
2. Close your eyes.
3. Deeply relax all your muscles, beginning at your feet and progressing up to your face. Keep them relaxed.
4. Breathe through your nose using diaphragmatic breathing. Become aware of your breathing. As you breathe out, say the word, "ONE" silently to yourself. For example, breathe IN . . . OUT, "ONE," – IN . . . OUT, "ONE." etc. Breathe easily and naturally.
5. Continue for ten to twenty minutes. You may open your eyes to check the time, but do not use an alarm. When you finish, sit quietly for several minutes, at first with your eyes closed and later with your eyes opened. Do not stand up for a few minutes.
6. Do not worry about whether you are successful in achieving a deep level of relaxation. Maintain a passive attitude and permit relaxation to occur at its own pace. When distracting thoughts occur, try to ignore them by not dwelling upon them and return to repeating "ONE." With practice, the response should come with little effort. Practice the technique once or twice daily, but not within two hours after any meal, since the digestive processes seem to interfere with the elicitation of the relaxation response."

Meditation usually begins with the practice of slow breathing. The basic idea is to consciously empty the mind of thoughts. People practice meditation by focusing on their breath or on just one thing, such as a single syllable mantra or visual image, in order to aid in relaxation or concentration. The relaxation response above is a form of meditation and can be learned and practiced either alone or with a group. Yoga and Tai Chi are disciplines that are based on meditation and both can be tremendously helpful for musicians. When you regularly practice meditation, you train your mind and body. Performance itself can be a kind of meditation, being in the zone or being in flow are kinds of meditative states. So, by practicing meditation, musicians can exercise the same state of mind they need for peak performances.

Memorization: to prepare a piece you plan to perform by memory, it's important to recognize there are four ways we memorize. Build all four methods into your practice sessions, as they will help build your confidence and resilience to anxiety.

Intellectual: you know the piece's structure: you know where you
are in the piece, at the recap, in the development, etc.
Auditory: you can hear the music, hear what's coming next
Visual: you can visualize the printed music, seeing it in your
mind's eye
Kinesthetic: your body memorizes the motions, the fingerings, the
position, etc.

You can work on these multiple memorization strategies by practicing without making a sound, by visualizing the score and hearing
the work in your inner ear, or by imagining all the physical motions
involved and playing through the work again, away from the instrument.
The most secure memorization relies on more than one method, so that
if, for instance, you momentarily can't hear what's coming next, or can't
see the page in your imagination, and your body knows the motions.

Medication: Beta-blockers are drugs that stop the body's response to
adrenaline. Inderal is commonly prescribed to musicians for performance anxiety; it's also used to treat high blood pressure, angina,
certain heart conditions, and migraines. Beta-blockers treat physical
symptoms only (they can reduce the sweating and slow down the
racing heart). Beta-blockers do not address the causes or the thinking
that may be preventing you from enjoying the experience of performing. Beta-blockers may be psychologically addicting, have varying side effects, and possible drug interactions with anything else you
may be taking. Because of this, don't ever use someone else's pre-
scription! Some musicians only rely on beta-blockers for special occasions, for important auditions or particularly stressful performances. The problem is you need to know how your body will react
beforehand. Don't risk the outcome of a performance on an unknown result. If your performance anxiety is such that you feel the
need to try medication, have a thorough medical exam first and then
try taking the medication with a lower stress performance situation
so that you can gage your response.

Case Study: Final Installment

At first, Steve read several books about performance anxiety. While he found these
to be interesting and informative, and he tried the recommended exercises, he felt
he needed some outside assistance, tailored to his specific difficulties. He worked
with a therapist and a performance coach to get at the bottom of his performance
anxiety. With these professionals, Steve was able to analyze what was going on in

his head around the start of performances. He worked on thought stopping and meditation, on visualization techniques, and he developed a specific routine for pre-performance preparation. In order to work on this program, Steve created new performance opportunities for himself in low stress situations, volunteering to play for the local elementary school music classes and at a nearby nursing home. Steve reports that his performance anxiety is now manageable, that he feels much more in control, and often finds himself enjoying his performances and taking pleasure in a way that's new for him.

Stress-Busting Tips

To manage your overall "general life" stress:

- Exercise every day (and practicing doesn't count!)
- Get enough sleep
- Eat healthy, take real breaks for meals
- Notice the beauty and nature around you
- Exercise your sense of humor
- Use a daily planner and keep your to-do lists short and reasonable
- Know yourself, pay attention to the signals you give yourself when you're overloaded
- Be aware of daily stressors
- Learn to say "No." Don't overcommit; delegate when you can
- Know your own core values and make sure you're living in "sync" with these
- Don't isolate—get feedback, suggestions, encouragement from your family and friends
- Don't be a slave to your phone or e-mail—block out your "down time" to return messages
- Identify pleasurable activities that don't take a lot of time and *do* them regularly
- Own your successes, give yourself credit and celebrate
- In a stressful or emotionally charged situation, shift to being "curious" about the situation, instead of letting your own emotions take over
- Meditate or use progressive relaxation exercises
- Remind yourself why you like your work, why you love music
- Remember: You deserve to be treated well so take good care of yourself!

The Bigger Picture

It's important to celebrate your daily successes and the small joys: a productive rehearsal, a useful contact made, a good afternoon of teaching, along with a beautiful sunrise, a friend's smile. You should feel good about how you choose to spend your time; if not, that's an indication you need to make some changes. Benchmark your progress toward your goals by acknowledging the daily progress you make.

On your way home each day, pick a spot on your route where you can, in your imagination, dump each day's stresses. You want to make sure that when you leave work, it doesn't come home with you in the form of worry and anxiety.

To summarize, you will need to experiment with a range of techniques to find the answers to your own situation. This self-assessment and experimenting can lead to more satisfying performances and to a deeper understanding of how music fits into your life.

Performance Health ■

Performance anxiety is only one piece of a larger subject: performance health. Taking good care of your body and your mind is essential for your career and your life.

Preventive care for musicians is very important. Musicians spend countless hours and years training their bodies in very intricate, precise muscular/ skeletal movements and positions, much the way athletes do. Unfortunately, musicians do not usually give their bodies the same consideration that professional athletes do. To achieve peak performances, your body and mind need to be in excellent working condition.

■

Performance Health Quiz

Do you warm-up carefully each time you practice?	Yes ❏	No ❏
Do you take frequent breaks in rehearsals/practice sessions?	Yes ❏	No ❏
Do you evaluate your technique regularly?	Yes ❏	No ❏
[Check if your posture is tension-free and if you're using unnecessary tension or force. Are you straining in any way while you practice?]		
Have you videorecorded your practice sessions?	Yes ❏	No ❏
[Practicing in front of a mirror is not the same; you need to see your playing objectively, in action. Watching yourself on video can make it easier to spot areas of tension.]		
Do you have good nutritional habits	Yes ❏	No ❏
[You need to fuel your body with a balanced diet.]		
Do you smoke?	Yes ❏	No ❏
[If yes, have you started a smoking cessation plan?]		

Do you manage your performance anxiety and other stresses
   well?   Yes ❑   No ❑
      [Take special care during high-risk times for developing
      injuries: when preparing for an important audition, or when
      adjusting to a new instrument, repertoire, or technique.]
Are you getting plenty of sleep?   Yes ❑   No ❑
Do you exercise regularly?   Yes ❑   No ❑
      [Practicing doesn't count as exercise. Take a walk every day!
      Include stretching and strengthening as well as cardiovas-
      cular exercise in your routine.]
Is your attitude toward your playing and toward music positive?   Yes ❑   No ❑
      [Perfectionism and ambition can cause too much stress and
      tension.]

Musicians are a special risk group for repetitive motion injuries. And beyond their music-making, musicians should periodically evaluate their other activities. Problems may be caused or aggravated by computer use, sports, carrying children, hobbies, and excess effort or tension in other daily activities. Pay attention to what your body is telling you all of the time, not just when playing. And depending on your other activities and interests (as in the case of instrumentalists also using computers), risks may be compounded and complicated. Instrumentalists' injuries are often the same as computer overuse injuries: Carpal tunnel syndrome, tendonitis, and trigger finger or thumb are particularly common among keyboardists, fretboardists, flutists, and string players. Incorrect posture, nonergonomic technique, excessive force, overuse, stress, and insufficient rest contribute to chronic injuries, pain, and disability. Singers may be at risk for vocal nodes and other difficulties of their vocal chords.

Performance injuries are fairly common. I've seen estimates that as many as 82 percent of orchestral musicians experience performance injuries at some point in their careers. Many musicians go through performance related difficulties—once you start asking around you'll find many people who have been injured go on to make full recoveries. So, if you are experiencing discomfort or pain, you are not alone. Again, the good news is there are preventive measures as well as effective treatment methods.

Warning Signals

Any kind of discomfort, muscle, or joint pain may signal overuse or a need to re-examine your playing posture or your technique. The first symptoms may be a slight twinge, a dull ache, a sharp pain, a weakening or slowing of dexterity, numbness, or a "pins and needles" sensation. Vocalists may notice a limit to their range or an inconsistency in tone color. If you experience any of these while performing, or as a result of performing, it's wise to take a breather, temporarily suspend your work and call your doctor.

The pain is your body sending you a message. The pain is a signal that you are not treating your body well, that you need to make a change in the way you're treating it. Sometimes this is just a simple matter of overuse: you need to rest your muscles, tendons, and joints. Sometimes it's a matter of the basic way you are using your body when you play—you may need to change your playing posture to allow you to play with more freedom of movement, more balance of weight and muscle tension. Sometimes the pain is a signal of something more serious. You won't know unless you get it thoroughly checked out and you're best laying off performing until you can get the difficulty sorted out.

Unfortunately, many musicians who develop injuries wait before seeing a doctor. Injuries often develop at the least convenient times (while preparing for important auditions or concerts) and musicians typically try to "tough it out." While a musician delays seeking help his or her injury tends to get worse. Some musicians just want to deny there's a problem, or assume they're simply fatigued, and they may practice even more to compensate and then exacerbate the problem. Don't wait and worry, see a doctor. *Early intervention is the best route to a quick recovery.*

Your general physician is fine for starters. She or he can either determine what the difficulty is or at least rule out some possible causes (simple overuse, as opposed to carpal tunnel syndrome, bursitis, arthritis, etc.). Your doctor may refer you to a specialist and you may want to get more than one opinion. When being referred, it is often helpful to consult with people who treat musicians, who will understand your particular concerns and difficulties. There are medical clinics for musicians' injuries in many cities, see Performing Arts Medicine Clinics in the United States at http://www.yourtype.com/survive/clinics_for_performers.htm.

Tip: a terrific resource is the Musicians and Injuries site: http://www.eeshop.unl.edu/music.html

---

A good doctor, in addition to a thorough exam, will take a detailed history of your practice and performance habits, and ask about which specific movements cause you difficulty. And it's important that your health care professional see you play. Your doctor also should ask about your nutritional and exercise habits, your emotional state of mind, your sleep pattern, and any other physical exertions beyond playing that may affect or contribute to your injury. It's typical for doctors to prescribe anti-inflammatory medicine to reduce swelling and pain. Typically, doctors also prescribe a period of rest in order to allow your body to heal and to gage the severity of the difficulty. Then, depending on the nature of the injury, your doctor may recommend a range of treatment methods.

Suggestions for Preventing Injury in Musicians

From Dr. Michael Charness, Director of the Performing Arts Clinic at Brigham and Women's Hospital, Boston, and Associate Professor of Neurology at Harvard Medical School. Dr. Charness (who is also a pianist) recommends for all musicians:

1. Avoid playing more than twenty-five minutes without a five-minute break. Try recording the last five minutes of a session and use the five-minute break to listen critically.
2. Stretch, warm up, and work gradually into practice sessions.
3. Compensate for increased playing intensity (recording sessions, preparation for an audition or recital, difficult program, stress, new instrument, altered technique) by reducing total playing time.
4. Intersperse repetitive rehearsal of individual passages throughout a practice session to avoid overworking one set of muscles. Learning and safety may be enhanced by playing a passage five times every ten minutes, rather than . thirty times in a row.
5. Begin to increase practice time weeks to months in advance of recitals or auditions.
6. Return to work gradually after a layoff.
7. Begin slowly and increase gradually any unaccustomed use of the hands (e.g., gardening, typing, sports).
8. Avoid unnecessary muscle tightness when you play. Excessive shoulder elevation or neck twisting may lead to muscle spasm and reduce the fluidity of movement in adjacent muscles. The burden of supporting the weight of instruments can be reduced by straps, posts, pegs, shoulder pads, and chin rests. Violinists and violists should adjust their supports so that the instrument can be held without *any* elevation of the left shoulder.
9. Be attentive to posture. Slouching in a chair for hours daily will eventually take its toll in back and neck problems. Good posture will reduce the work of small forearm and hand muscles by enabling larger shoulder and back muscles to support the combined weight of the arms and/or instrument.
10. Don't neglect your general physical and mental health.

What about Alternative Medicine or Treatments?

Below is a range of treatment methods and practices that musicians have found helpful. Remember, what works well for one person may not work well for the next. Also, any alternative treatments you consider should be checked with your doctor so that you do not aggravate your condition. In general, most musicians in recovery from a performance injury use a combination of western and alternative treatments. Treat your body well.

· Alexander Technique	· Massage therapy	· Acupuncture
· Chiropractic	· Acupressure	· Swimming
· Feldenkrais	· Nutrition	· Yoga
· Rolfing	· Exercise	· Physical Therapy
· Reflexology	· Tai Chi	· Occupational/Hand Therapy

Note from Judith Ciampa Wright, an occupational therapist and certified hand therapist at Nashoba Valley Medical Center in Ayer, Mass.:

"Musicians tend to jump from a path of treatment before giving it time to work." *Your recovery demands your patience!* "Too frequently, musicians seek treatments that involve their passive participation (like massages) without addressing posture, strength, flexibility, and activity modification—all of which are necessary for effective long-term injury management. A multifaceted treatment approach is often the most effective. For example, one might combine a 'bodywork' technique (such as massage therapy) with a direct treatment technique (such as Physical Therapy or Occupational Therapy) and also a great whole body exercise program (such as yoga or swimming)." *But keep your doctor informed and thoroughly discuss ALL the treatment methods and kinds of activities you engage in that might affect your injury. If you jump from one treatment plan to another, experimenting with all kinds of traditional and nontraditional treatments, you may never know what is actually helping or what is adding to the problem.*

Depending on what your doctor(s) advise, you may need to take a break from playing for a period of months and then resume practicing only at very short intervals, say five to ten minutes at a time, paying close attention to what specific movements cause the pain to reoccur. You need to be a detective, finding clues to what isn't working right and searching for alternative ways to work without causing strain.

Reworking Your Technique

Be aware that most musicians, in order to recover from a performance injury, must rework parts of their technique and change their practice habits or the way they hold their instrument. This is the part of your healing where you are most in charge. Your doctor and a teacher may be able to assist, but ultimately, it's up to you to find out what works best for your body, because you have direct body feedback. Think of the practice room as your own mini-biofeedback lab. You will need to develop real awareness as you experiment with ways to reduce tension in your playing. You are the one that will find your solutions, with the help of qualified professionals, through experimenting in the practice room, your "laboratory." You need to be patient and inquisitive as you work toward your solutions.

About Recuperation

Very often performance injuries are compounded by the accompanying worry and stress. People may feel like they'll never play again, that their career is over. Sometimes musicians feel ashamed, as if they've done something "wrong." In other words, we can be our own worst enemy by becoming depressed and more stressed out, making the pain actually worse.

Talking to others about your situation is important—getting advice, counseling, and support. The relationship of the mental to the physical is crucial. It's very important to talk to others and to have a support system during this time.

Use your imagination. You can actually use dreams and visualization to help your healing. Before falling asleep, when your body and mind are very relaxed, your mind is in a suggestible state; you can say to yourself, to your subconscious, "I'd like to know how it feels to play with ease; without stress or tension or pain." Imagining the new improved playing and "memorizing" the sensations away from the instrument can help you reach your goals by creating the sensory image you are working toward.

Take care of yourself in this difficult time by getting enough sleep, eating well, getting exercise, and taking care that you keep a positive attitude about your recovery. As you can't practice as much, you should be getting inspired by going to lots of performances and listening to music outside your repertoire. Improve your mental and imaginative skills, analyze your music and fine-tune your interpretation away from the instrument—this can be a great way to spend practice time. Also, take time to get inspired beyond music—visit museums, explore the other arts as a way to enrich your music-making.

Summary

In all three areas, stage presence, performance anxiety, and performance health, the common denominator is the body/mind connection. Being a musician is about far more than the ability to produce pleasing sounds. The performance skills and abilities that go into building and maintaining a career are complex. Taking care of your body and mind is essential in order to have a lifetime of satisfying performance experience. Musicians do well to cultivate their own awareness and curiosity about these issues, to get reliable feedback and accurate assessments, and to be open-minded and resourceful in looking for solutions to challenges.

■ Suggestions for Moving Ahead ■

1. Describe how you want to feel as you take the stage to perform:
   How do you want to feel physically?
   What kinds of thoughts do you want to be having?
   What emotions do you want to be having?
2. How would you like to come across to your audience? What image do you want to convey through your stage entrances, exits, and bows?
3. Have you recently videotaped a performance and then watched it with a mentor to discuss your stage presence? If not, when might you be able to do so?
4. How does performance anxiety manifest itself in you? What specific symptoms do you experience?
   a) physical:
   b) thoughts:
   c) emotions:
5. Which techniques for handling anxiety described in this chapter do you plan to try?
6. What are your physical "trouble spots," the places where you've experienced physical discomfort during or after practice? What have you done as a result of feeling this discomfort?
7. How often do you take breaks during practice sessions? How long are these breaks? What do you do during these breaks?
8. To help ensure a lifetime of healthy music-making, what else (beyond taking breaks during practice sessions) can you do to help safeguard your performance health?

10

The Freelance Lifestyle—Managing Your Gigs, Time, and Money

Most musicians spend at least a portion of their careers as self-employed professionals. Freelancers perform as substitute players or guest artists with various ensembles; they also may perform at weddings, corporate parties, restaurants, and hotels, or for more extended commitments, such as recording projects, musicals, and festivals.

Freelancing can make for an interesting and varied work life. But the freelance lifestyle also means not having a steady paycheck, or an employer to provide benefits, paid vacation time, or a regular schedule. So for freelancers to be successful, they need to manage their gigs, finances, and time effectively. Most musicians learn the ins and outs of freelancing the hard way, by making mistakes. But many mishaps can be avoided. The freelance lifestyle can be made easier with the right information, planning, and networking.

The Tale of Joan, Bootstrapping in the Freelance World (Part 1)

Joan B., a bassoonist, started freelancing while a graduate student. It started with her teacher and friends recommending her for a few orchestral gigs. Joan also played woodwind quintets with friends. They did several gigs together—four weddings and a funeral, in fact—plus a party for a local political bigwig. But, after graduating, Joan found this sporadic work was not enough to pay the bills. So she auditioned for the sub lists with several regional orchestras. She also asked her former teachers for the names of local contractors—the people who contract freelance musicians to play pick-up orchestra gigs. Joan called these contractors, sent them her résumé, and two of them asked her to audition. All good.

Meanwhile, Joan was struggling to pay the bills, including her student loans. Some weeks and months there'd be plenty of work and money coming in, and she could afford to go out with friends. But at other times, she was doing the starving musician, ramen noodle thing. To compound matters, her aging car had twice stalled on the way to gigs and Joan couldn't afford a new one. Not so good.

Joan realized that though she was building her reputation and getting established as a professional, it would still be a while before she could manage solely on the freelancing. So she looked into getting private students, coaching woodwind sectionals for local youth orchestras, and teaching in the community music schools. A friend referred several students to Joan and told her about a part-time opening at a music instrument and repair shop. She got the job, and found the job had an added perk. On the job she met more freelancers and teachers who could refer yet more students to her. With some regular salary from the day job and teaching, Joan got her car overhauled and started saving for a new one. Things were looking up. Read on for more on Joan, later in this chapter.

━━━ ■

The Basics: Freelancing and Gigs 101 ■

Freelancing can be extremely varied, from orchestral and choral concert work, to background music for social functions. The more you can offer, the more work you may be able to get. Do you only perform classical, or other genres as well? Can you do arrangements of "light" classics and pop tunes? For vocalists, can you sing Gospel, Broadway, perform early and twenty-first-century music? Do you have enough repertoire to play a four-hour corporate party gig? Flexibility and versatility are good things for a freelancer. But don't overstate or promise what you can actually deliver—offer the repertoire you are skilled in and comfortable performing.

Another approach is to specialize in a particular niche area, a specific musical period or repertoire. If you offer something distinctive and marketable, it differentiates you from the competition, and can help establish your reputation. The catch is your specialty area needs a niche market, an audience. For instance, for a group that plays early American music, it makes sense to seek bookings at historical societies and house museums. And a group specializing in swing music may do well going after gigs for corporate holiday parties, hotels, and wedding receptions. For classical pianists looking for accompanying work, having specialized skills and repertoire in coaching singers is a niche. Networking with voice teachers and choral conductors can help with getting referrals and work. The kind of work you seek should determine your marketing strategies, with whom you network, how you describe your skills and experience, both in person and in your marketing materials.

The Nitty Gritty: How to Get the Work

For freelance work with orchestras, choruses, and opera companies, you need to audition for contractors or conductors. If there are no current openings, you may be considered for the sub list, to be hired as a substitute player. Most metropolitan areas, especially those with top music schools and an active music scene, are glutted with experienced players. Contractors understandably like to rehire the tried and true each year. The trick is to be recommended as a sub, and when you get called for a gig, do a great job. Networking (see chapter 2) can lead to getting recommended as a sub. Talk to your colleagues and teachers, find out who is playing where, and get to know the players who may be in a position to refer you.

The Tale of Joan (Part 2)

In her first years freelancing, Joan noticed several things. She saw who got the calls and the gigs, and who didn't. At first she was surprised that it wasn't always the best players getting the work. But the more she freelanced, the more it made sense. Some of the people not getting calls for more work were friends from school. Although these friends were top-notch players, Joan realized that some non-musical issues outweighed how well they played. Some of these friends had shown up late for a rehearsal or two. One was a bit of a slob; even in concert attire, he looked disheveled. And another one could be a difficult personality, came across as a bit of a prima donna, arrogant and argumentative. Joan saw that this behavior was hurting her friends' ability to get work. For Joan this was a wake-up call to keep her own act cleaned up.

She also paid attention to the folks who *did* get the work. Some of these "A" list freelancers also were contractors for gigs. They all seemed to know each other and were generally pleasant, no matter what happened in rehearsals or performances. No big egos or temper tantrums, even though a conductor might be having both. These pros got to gigs early, always prepared, and somehow handled their busy schedules well. Joan took note.

Besides relying on referrals, you can call the larger performing organizations in your area and ask when they hold auditions. This is usually at the beginning or end of their seasons (September and May). Check on the audition repertoire and prepare carefully.

Musician Unions ◼

There is a set of performers' unions which were formed to protect the rights and interests of musicians. In general, the work of these unions is to negotiate and enforce collective bargaining agreements that establish equitable levels of compensation, benefits, and working conditions for performers. They establish pay scales and offer various benefits such as pension plans, and health and instrument insurance. Union membership is most often a contract requirement for the better paying steady performance gigs, from opera and chorus work, to orchestras, touring musicals, radio, TV, and studio recording work. There is usually an initiation fee and annual dues for members.

The type of union you may join is determined by the kind of music you perform and where you perform it. Most musicians join the appropriate union once they've won an audition for a "union" job. The primary union for instrumentalists and the largest musicians' union is the American Federation of Musicians (AFM). But for vocalists doing opera or musicals, and for all musicians working in recordings, television, film, radio, or nightclubs, there are other unions, described below. Note: unions are not employment agencies; they do not provide work to members. Rather, unions exist to protect the rights of member musicians once they are working.

Alphabet Soup: The Unions

Musicians generally note their union membership on their résumés, signaling to contractors and conductors in the audition process a certain level of experience.

AGMA, the American Guild of Musical Artists, primarily represents singers and singing actors in opera, ballet, oratorio, concert, and recital work. Musicians join AGMA when they've been offered a contract with a production requiring AGMA membership. See http://www.musicalartists.org.

AFTRA, the American Federation of Television and Radio Artists, covers live and taped TV programs, taped commercials, radio shows, and recordings. AFTRA is for all performers in these areas except instrumentalists. See http://www.aftra.org.

SAG, the Screen Actors Guild, is for feature film work, filmed TV shows, filmed commercials, or industrial films. See http://www.newsag.org.

AEA, the Actors' Equity Association (AKA: Equity), is for performers in legitimate theatre productions, either musicals or dramas. A singer seeking work in musical theatre must first win an audition for an equity show, apply to be an equity candidate, perform for the length of their contract and earn credit toward an equity card and full membership. See: http://www.actorsequity.org.

The AFM, the American Federation of Musicians, is an international organization with more than one hundred thousand members and five hundred local affiliates in the United States and Canada. The AFM publishes *International Musician*, a monthly publication listing auditions worldwide for orchestral and other work. This is the union for most instrumentalists' work. The AFM offers a number of benefits and services with membership, including instrument and health insurance, plus legal, travel, and mortgage services. Your local chapter of AFM may be a good networking resource. See: http://www.afm.org.

Timetable for Building a Freelance Lifestyle

The rule of thumb is to be patient. It takes time to build your reputation. For classical musicians doing orchestral and small ensemble work, below is a rough timetable for "getting connected" in a large culturally active city. This time frame assumes of course that your playing and networking skills are excellent.

   1 year to get your "sea legs," to get a sense of what's out there

   3 years to get hooked up in the new environment (paying your dues)

   5 years to get enough work to be in control of your life

   10 years to be subcontracting other musicians for gigs and to have stability

---

Concerts versus Gigs ■

Gigs are different from concerts. Gig clients typically are looking to "purchase" your music as background atmosphere for an event or occasion, such as a wedding, an anniversary, a corporate holiday party or a memorial service. Most often, your music is just a part of the evening's entertainment. Clients are viewing your music as a service, a product to be purchased at an hourly rate or a flat fee. And just like other service jobs, the customer is always right. Or, at least, they are if you want a good referral for future gigs.

Managing gigs is similar to self-managing your concerts, in that you need to be organized about your contacts and arrangements, marketing, negotiating fees, and your use of contracts. But the actual marketing for gigs is different from concerts. For instance, musicians looking to play wedding gigs often advertise in regional wedding directories or in the annual newspaper inserts devoted to wedding services. Wedding musicians also market themselves using the Web, business cards, brochures, word of mouth, as well as booking agencies, and postcard mailings to wedding planners, hotel function room managers, caterers, florists, and to church music directors.

Getting the Gigs

· Think about the people you know and where they work; think what institutions in your area sponsor events that need music.
· Develop a targeted list of local prospects, a list of organizations that you think might be interested in hiring you or your ensemble.
· Send an introductory e-mail, or use the postal service to mail a card, flyer, or brochure to people on your list.
· Follow up with a phone call and a face-to-face meeting during which you can offer your demo and other marketing pieces. People like to hire by word of mouth and like to know the people they hire, so it's good to get out and meet them.

Listed below are general occasions, types of gigs, and types of organizations that hire musicians for their events. Use the list to brainstorm for specific prospects in your area.

Occasions	Organizations	Institutions
Anniversaries	Chambers of	Convention centers
Association meetings	Commerce	Churches/
Bat/Bar Mitzvahs	Civic clubs (Elks,	synagogues
Expositions	Lions)	Coffee houses
Fairs	College student	Cruise lines
Fund-raisers	groups	Military bases
Mall promotions	Community Cable TV	Museums
Memorial services	Country clubs	Newspaper
Political conventions	Government	Companies
Trade shows	agencies	Private schools
Weddings	Hotels/motels	Public schools
	Local corporations	Radio stations
	Summer camp	Resorts
	programs	Restaurants
	Teen clubs	
	Private clubs	
	Women's clubs	

Tips for Gig Success

Expect the unexpected: be flexible and able to deal with unforeseen changes; be able to "cover" if and when things go awry.

Know and review the order of the music you intend to play before the gig.

Have more than enough music: You may be asked to, and want to, play overtime.

Look and sound like you enjoy what you're doing!

Marketing Materials ■

Do you have the appropriate marketing materials for your freelancing? The rule of thumb is to tailor your materials to the reader's interests and to the situation. For auditions for conductors and contractors, have a performance résumé that emphasizes your freelance work, not your solo concertizing (samples later in the chapter). Singers need a résumé and a photo (see chapter 3). For day-to-day networking and gigging, all musicians need business cards.

Marketing materials for gigs should be different from your press kit for your concert work. From what to put on your demo, to what to emphasize in a rep list and bio, you'll need to think about it from the reader's point of view. Someone looking to hire a string quartet for their wedding is not interested in the same things as a presenter considering your program for a formal concert series. You may find that putting together an inexpensive flyer for your solo or ensemble gig work is useful, a kind of quick all-in-one piece. A flyer can include a photo, brief bio, a list of sample gig repertoire, an "Engagement list" of where your group or individual members have performed, and a few quotes from satisfied customers. Some ensembles make trifold brochures specifically for wedding gigs, with a menu of repertoire choices, and details on how the group can provide a demo and contract, making the wedding planning easier, and enhancing the couple's special day with music tailored to their requests. Know what you have to offer. You will need to evaluate what you plan to sell and whether or not there is a demand for your product.

Résumés for Freelancers

You'll need a résumé to audition for conductors and contractors, as well as to apply for festivals, competitions, and grants. An effective résumé highlights the details of your background and experience that are most relevant to the particular situation and reader. Do not use the "one size fits all" approach! It's typical for musicians to have several versions of their résumé. The one résumé you send to a conductor or contractor should be different from the ones you use for a teaching position, for a grant application, or for a day job in arts administration. If you're sending a résumé to request an orchestral audition, then your orchestral experience should be listed first and most likely, they won't be interested in your teaching or arts administration experience, so you'd leave that off. But because many orchestras these days are including community engagement activities as part of the contract, it's smart to put your chamber music and residency work experience on the résumé. For singers looking for musical theatre roles, their résumé should reflect their stage experience first, before their choral or solo recital information.

Résumé Strategies

- Keep it to one page; it's not your life history, it's the highlights of your background most relevant to the specific situation for which you're applying. The exception to the one page rule is if applying for university teaching positions, where a "C.V." or curriculum vitae is expected—an expanded résumé of two to five pages.
- Make it easy on the eyes, since studies show that employers spend less than ten seconds scanning résumés. Make it easy to take in the essentials. Use an eye-catching, professional-looking letterhead. Present your credentials in titled sections. For the body of the text, use an easy to read, standard seraph font such as Palatino or Times. Keep the eye distractions to a minimum; use these sparingly: underline, parentheses, bullets, bold, all caps.
- Use titled sections to present your experience in logically organized categories, such as:

Orchestral Experience	Choral Experience
Chamber Music Performances	Honors/awards
Solo recitals	Education
Premieres	Principal teachers
Accompanying	Conductors
Recordings	Coaches
Opera Experience	Master Classes

Think over your background and look through your past concert programs. Make sure you include your most interesting, impressive, and relevant experience. The categories you choose to use should reflect your experience and your preferred emphases. For instance, if you've performed a lot of early or contemporary music, these may be categories to use. Place the sections in the order that reflect the *reader's* priorities.

- To date or not to date? Dates are important to include when listing your degrees and the honors and awards you've received. When using dates in a category, list items in reverse chronological order, the most recent to the least recent. When it comes to solo and chamber recitals, dates are not as important, so you can leave them off and instead list these performances in order of most impressive to less.

• What details do you include? For recital work and chamber music performances, list *where* you performed: the venue and the concert series, city, and state or country if outside the United States. If you've performed with impressive individuals, in chamber music performances or in a jazz ensemble, you may want to list these names in a category titled, "Has performed with" or "ensemble collaborations."

• If applying for orchestral auditions, list orchestral experience first, and then list the remaining relevant categories in an order that presents you best, including your education, principal teachers, conductors, and so on. Keep in mind that for orchestral auditions, the reader wants to see orchestral experience, not extensive lists of chamber and solo performances. Tim Tsukamoto, Boston Symphony Orchestra Personnel Coordinator, recommends clearly indicating whether you were a section player, titled player, or substitute/extra player, and also including dates of employment for your orchestral experience.

• Especially for singers: if you're seeking auditions for opera or musical theatre roles, you need to include crucial casting information at the top of your résumé with your letterhead (height, weight, plus hair and eye colors). The first category on your résumé should be a listing of stage experience. Clearly note the full roles and the partial roles or scenes performed. Roles are usually presented in columns, first with the role you performed, then the title of work (and composer, if not well known), the company or school where you performed the work, and the date. Some singers leave off dates so that they can present the most substantial and impressive roles first. Others recommend listing the places where you performed only if these are impressive. You will need to decide for yourself. My sense is, if you're being considered for a role, the music director will want to know about your experience, not just what you've sung, but with whom and when. You also can have a category for "Roles Prepared" or "Current Repertoire" to highlight works you have ready but have not yet performed. If you're auditioning for choral or recital work, you can organize another version of your résumé, with the initial category being either solo performances, concert work, or choral experience.

• Spell-check is not enough! Always have several people proofread your résumé before you send it. Double-check the spelling of the names of teachers, conductors, and awards. It's easy to miss the most obvious or embarrassing mistakes.

Samples: on the following pages are examples of performance résumés geared for freelance work, both instrumental and vocal. These examples, composites of various musicians' résumés, are designed to illustrate a variety of formats and styles. Notice on each example what is emphasized, how many details are provided, and the order of the categories and listings in each. Instead of following these as templates, and trying to make your résumé look like someone else's, use these as suggestions for rethinking your own. Because musicians' résumé differ from those used in other professions, get feedback from qualified professionals, people who hire musicians regularly. Once you have a draft for a newly improved résumé, show it to several experienced musician mentors and get feedback, and if your alma mater has a career center with professional advisors skilled at counseling musicians, use it.

Take the Big Gig Quiz

Are you freelance-ready? Do your actions say, "I'm a Pro"? Test your gig savvy below. The quiz covers the range of freelance work, from orchestra and large ensemble jobs, to weddings, corporate parties, and other background music gigs.

- ❑ Is your playing up to the standards for the kind of work you seek as a freelancer? One way to check is to take a lesson or two with the top freelancers in your area and get feedback. This may also be a way to get work. If they like how you play, they'll refer work to you.
- ❑ Are you on time for rehearsals and performances? Do you arrive thirty minutes in advance of the start in order to warm up properly? Contractors won't rehire anyone who shows up late.
- ❑ Do you come to rehearsals prepared? Do you know your part cold at each first rehearsal?
- ❑ Are your sight-reading skills competitive? Is sight-reading part of your daily practice routine? Professionals, particularly for playing shows and doing recording or jingle work, are expected to sight-read parts perfectly the first time, with all the nuances and in the appropriate style.
- ❑ Are you prepared to audition at any time for contractors and conductors? Do you keep your skills in top form? Do you have the appropriate audition repertoire ready?
- ❑ How are your people skills? How's your networking? If you socialize with your freelance colleagues, and go to their concerts, they'll be that much more likely to refer work to you. Are you easy to get along with? Are you tolerant and respectful of other people, their musical (or political) opinions, and varying levels of playing abilities? As a freelancer, you'll encounter a wide range of people; not everyone will be your preferred collaborator, but you need to

Ippei Takahashi, Violinist
100 Canadian Terrace Ste. 3 • Toronto, Ontario A1A 2B2 • (647) 590-1234 • ippeitaka@earthlink.net

Orchestral Experience

Tanglewood Music Center Fellowship Orchestra, 2004
Schleswig-Holstein Symphony Orchestra, Concertmaster, 2003
Isabella Stewart Gardner Museum Chamber Orchestra, Boston, 2003
Boston Modern Orchestra Project, substitute, 2003
Boston Philharmonic Orchestra, 2002-03
Hartford Symphony Orchestra, substitute, 2002
Columbus Philharmonic, IN, 2000, 01
Evansville Philharmonic, IN, 1999-00

Solo / Chamber Recitals

Merkin Concert Hall, NYC
King's Chapel Concert Series, Boston
Pickman Hall, Longy School of Music, Cambridge, MA
Ichigaya Lutheran Center, Tokyo, Japan

Education

New England Conservatory of Music, Boston, MA
Graduate Diploma in violin performance, 2003

Indiana University School of Music, Bloomington
Bachelor of Music in violin performance, 2001

Principal Teachers	Coaches	Masterclasses
Malcolm Lowe	Eugene Lehner	Miriam Fried
Stanley Ritchie	Louis Krasner	Michèle Auclair

Honors

Prizewinner, Japanese American Association Music Award, 2002
Fellowship, Asian Cultural Council Award, 2000

References Available Upon Request

Sample orchestral résumé

244

James Fortunato, Guitarist – Flamenco, Jazz, Classical
6435 21ˢᵗ Ave. NW, Seattle, WA 98195
cell: (206) 784-1234 jfortunato@hotmail.com

Solo Performances
Zeitgeist Gallery, Cambridge, MA
Peabody-Essex Museum, Salem, MA
Museum of Fine Arts, Boston
New England Conservatory, Boston
First Church Congregational, Wellesley, MA

Ensembles
Amaya, Flamenca Sin Limites, flamenco dance troupe
Hankus Netsky Klezmer Ensemble
Carlos Campos Afro-Cuban Ensemble

Flamenco Performance Venues
Boston College, MA
Palace Theater, Manchester, NH
University of Massachusetts, Amherst
Boston Ballet
Boston Center for the Arts
Westbrook College, Portland, ME

Jazz Performances
Middle East, Cambridge, MA
Ritz Carlton, Boston
Copley Plaza, Boston

Dance Class Accompanist
Boston Conservatory, MA
Dance Complex, Cambridge
Walnut Hill School for the Arts, Natick, MA

Education
New England Conservatory of Music, Boston, MA
Bachelor of Music in Contemporary Improvisation, 1999

Principal Teachers   **Master Classes**
Robert Paul Sullivan   Eliot Fisk
Hankus Netsky   Sharon Isbin

References Available Upon Request

Sample résumé, guitarist

14 Pinckney St. ◆ Boston, MA 02108 ◆ (617) 534-1112 ◆ jpark@hotmail.com

Solo Recitals	Gardner Museum, Boston
	Kings Chapel Concert Series, Boston
	All Saints Episcopal Church, Salt Lake City, UT
	Harvard Music Association Concert Series
Concerti	New Bedford Symphony Orchestra, MA
	University of Utah Symphony Orchestra
Chamber Music	Brookline Public Library Concert Series, MA
	First Presbyterian Church, Salt Lake City, UT
	All Newton Music School Young Artists Series, MA
Accompanying	Studio pianist for Eric Rosenblith, violin faculty,
	New England Conservatory, 2003-04
	Studio pianist for Russell McKinney, trombone faculty,
	University of Utah, Salt Lake City, 1998-00
Recording	*Music of the Baroque*, Educational DVD, for Oxbridge Records, 1997
Awards/Honors	Scholarship, New England Conservatory, Boston, MA, 2003-04
	Prizewinner, Harvard Musical Association Scholarship Award, 2002
Education	New England Conservatory, Boston, MA
	Graduate Diploma in Piano Performance, 2004
	University of Utah, Salt Lake City
	Bachelor of Music in Piano Performance, 2000
Principal Teacher	Patricia Zander
Master Classes	Stephen Drury, Wha Kyung Byun
Coaches	Irma Vallecillo, Kayo Iwama

Sample résumé, pianist

Michelle Santiago
Soprano

4444 W Walton St. #2
Chicago, IL 60622
(773) 773-7349
msantiago@aol.com

Ht: 5'5"
Wt: 130
Hair: Brunette
Eyes: Blue

Performance Experience

Roles performed

Pamina	The Magic Flute	Utah Opera, 2004
Adele	Die Fledermaus	New England Conservatory, 2003
Jenny	Down In the Valley	Boston Lyric Opera, 2003
Laeticia	The Old Maid and the Thief	New England Conservatory, 2002
Witch	Hansel and Gretel	Milwaukee Opera Theater, 2001
Celie	Signor Deluso	Lawrence University, 2000

Scenes performed

Polly	The Threepenny Opera	New England Conservatory, 2002
Donna Elvira	Don Giovanni	New England Conservatory, 2002
Belinda	Dido and Aeneas	Lawrence University, 2000

Musical Theatre Roles

Maria	West Side Story	Papermill Theatre, Lincoln, NH, 2000
Meg	Little Women	
Anne	Anne of Green Gables	

Concert Performances, Boston area

Handel *Messiah*, Trinity Church
Mozart *Requiem*, St. Paul's Episcopal Church
Solo Recital, Federal Reserve Bank Concert Series

Education

New England Conservatory, Boston, MA
Master of Music in Vocal Performance, 2003

Lawrence University, Appleton, WI
Bachelor of Music in Vocal Performance, *cum laude*, 2000

Principal Teachers	Coaches	Masterclass
Patricia Misslin	John Moriarty	Martin Isepp
Susan Clickner	Dale Morehouse	

Awards/Honors

Prizewinner, Rose Palmai-Tenser Scholarship Awards Competition, 2000
Second Prize, NATS Southern Regional Competition, Graduate Division, 2000
First Prize, NATS Southern Regional Competition, 1999
  Governor's Award for Most Promising Talent for a Professional Career

Sample résumé, vocalist seeking stage work

get along with everyone. Keep all criticism to yourself. If you need to talk about people, make it positive.

❏ How are you on the phone? Do you sound professional? Are you articulate, do you sound confident? Does your phone message sound professional? If you are in charge of bookings for your group, is the name of the group included in your phone message?

❏ How's your follow-through? Are you taking care of business? Do you return phone messages promptly? Do you send your demo out promptly after offering to? Do you have an organized way to keep track of your schedule, and the details on each gig? Do you deliver the performance you promise to your clients? Are you using contracts to ensure you'll be paid for the work you do?

❏ Do you look the part? Dress appropriately for both rehearsals and concerts; convey an attitude of success—that you care about yourself and your work. Do you or your ensemble look professional? Shoes polished, tuxes pressed, everyone clean, combed and upscale? Remember, audiences and clients see you before they hear you.

❏ For small ensemble and solo work: Is your sheet music organized and presentable? Members of your ensemble can use black folders or binders with everything in the order you plan to play to avoid false starts and shuffling for lost music on separate sheets. Make sure page turns work well.

Negotiating Fees

You should have an hourly rate per musician that you quote to clients. Make sure your hourly rate is appropriate and competitive with what similar groups are charging in your area. Call your local chapter of the AFM, ask other musicians what they charge, or call a competitor ensemble and pretend you're a prospective client. As of 2004, the New England Conservatory's Music Referral Service (the school's gig office) quoted clients the rate of $100–125 per musician per hour. The rates in various regions differ, so ask around. You can be flexible with your fee but you should know what your absolute minimum is and stick to it. Don't sell yourself short. If you're traveling a distance for a gig, you should charge extra to compensate for the travel. Have a policy to quote to clients for travel beyond a certain number of miles.

Freelance Savvy

Robert Paul Sullivan, a classical guitarist, plays as a freelancer with the Boston Symphony Orchestra, as well as with most of the New England regional orchestras and the contemporary music groups in the area. A veteran freelancer, he's played acoustic and electric guitar, banjo, mandolin, mandola, and lute in clubs and hotels, for opera productions, weddings, and wine tasting events—you name it, he's done it.

Bob's tips on freelancing? He makes it a point to not quote a fee to a client until he's heard *all* the particulars on the gig. He asks lots of questions about the travel, any special repertoire requests, the performance site itself, and so on, because these details help determine his fee. And Bob doesn't haggle with clients. If a client doesn't like his price, he cordially says, "Let me give you the names and numbers of some other excellent guitarists and maybe you'll find what you're looking for with someone else." He gladly refers work to others and they reciprocate.

Weddings are always high maintenance gigs. So Bob makes it a point to arrive extra early, and checks in with his contact to go over where they want the musicians set up and the timings and cues for playing.

In demand as a freelancer, Bob has had gig date conflicts occur a number of times. For example, he gets called to do a performance of a new work with a contemporary music group; he's free, the money's ok, and he says yes. A few days later he's offered a much better gig for that same date—in one case, the second gig was with the Boston Symphony at Tanglewood. What does Bob do? He makes it a point to honor his first commitment. He turns down the second gig because he'd already given his word to the first client, and because his word is a big part of his reputation as a professional. What does he say to the second client, the contractor? Bob explains that he's already committed for that date and refers them to someone every bit as good *if not better than* he is. The contractor is the pipeline for future gigs. Bob wants to be remembered as reliable and professional, so that the next time around, the contractor will again call Bob.

It's All in the Details

A big part of being a pro is handling details. Once you've got a client who wants to hire you for a gig, you need to clarify many details. Both you and your client want *no* surprises. Professionals use checklists to make sure they stay organized. This can be a list you develop to fit the kinds of gigs you play. You can keep your copies of your list in your date book and fill in the particulars each time you're booking or confirming a gig by phone and then as you create the written contract to confirm your agreement.

Don't assume anything: clarify all the details with your client first by phone or email, then by written contract. The use of a contract is a sign of professionalism. It solidifies the details you've negotiated and it assures both parties that the gig will go as planned. *You and your client need to clarify:*

❑ Date and time of the gig plus the starting and stopping times for the performance.

❏ Repertoire: make sure you are clear on the type and genre of music the client is expecting and any specific requests. If you agree to play repertoire that demands that you produce your own arrangements, you should charge extra for the gig.

❏ Dress: make sure you know what the client specifically means by "formal" or "casual."

❏ Breaks: it is typical for performers on a gig to need and take a ten-minute break for every hour played; make sure your client understands this and agrees.

❏ Lighting: make sure it is adequate.

❏ Seating: is there adequate space for your ensemble, and the appropriate type of chairs (armless)?

❏ Piano? Is it a grand, upright, electric; will it be tuned?

❏ Acoustics: Will you need to be amplified? If yes, what equipment will you need to bring?

❏ Extras: Do you need electrical outlets, extension cords, adapters? Are these available at the venue?

❏ For outdoor performances, you may want to specify that the musicians will perform under a canopy or roofed deck to be in the shade or that you will not perform outside if the temperature is outside certain parameters. Here is contract language you may want to add:
   "the client shall provide adequate shelter to protect the artist and the artist's equipment in the event of inclement weather." Or "The temperature in the performance area should not exceed 85 degrees F or drop below 65 degrees F, for the protection of the artist(s) and their equipment."

❏ Contact info: the client and performers need to know how to reach each other, exchange phone numbers, e-mail addresses, correct spelling and pronunciation of names, plus addresses for sending contracts. If you are your group's leader then you should be doing all the dealings with the client to cut down on any communication glitches.

❏ Directions and any special parking: Get explicit directions to the gig and always leave plenty of extra time for traffic. Double-check the directions using the Web and keep a detailed atlas with street index in your gig bag.

❏ Payment: agree on who will pay you, when, how, and how much: per hour and the total; if there's an additional charge for travel, add this to your fee. Most giggers prefer to get paid at the gig, directly before or after performing. Specify in your contract if payment will be by check, cash, or money order. Most often, the client will pay the group leader who must then divide up the fee for each member.

If requesting a nonrefundable deposit, state how much and when is it due, or state that the "Payment will be made in full on day of performance by check or money order" (For government or other agency clients that must requisition funds, payment can be delayed. Make sure you discuss this explicitly in advance.)

❑ Deposit: it's smart to get a nonrefundable deposit from the client to secure the date (typically 50 percent of the gig fee). Have the client send the check along with the signed contract. Then, should the gig be canceled, at least you've got half the fee.

Remember, the key is to be explicit and precise about all your expectations. Do not assume that the client will know to provide anything, from electrical outlets to advance deposits, unless you ask for it and they agree to it when you negotiate and then put it in writing.

The Tale of Joan (Part 3)

Another big lesson Joan had in her first years freelancing was about using contracts. Joan found out the hard way just how important these are. She'd been called for a pick-up orchestra gig, two rehearsals and a concert at a church in a nearby suburb. Mozart and Brahms, no problem. But two weeks after the concert, Joan still hadn't been paid. She called the contractor several times over the next month and the check was always "in the mail." Joan never got paid and because there was no contract and this was not a union gig, there was nothing she could do about it. After this experience she joined the union and from that point on, whenever Joan booked her own gigs, whether for a wedding, a school residency, or a memorial service, she always used a contract and got a deposit in advance. The adventures of Joan continue.

Gig Contracts ■

As covered in chapter 6, the particular details you've verbally agreed upon for a performance should be confirmed in a written contract. Gig contracts differ from those used for concerts in terms of the types of details you may need to cover. Using contracts for gigs is probably even more important than for concerts because gig clients (especially for weddings and corporate events) are typically people unaccustomed to hiring musicians, so clarifying details is all the more important.

It's easy to make your own contract template that you can quickly modify for each gig. Your professional letterhead goes at the top with all your contact info. The details added in for each particular gig are the client's name, the date of the gig, time, location, fee, special requests, performance area set up, and so on.

A contract is also a freelancer's security for being properly paid. With a properly executed contract, if a client refuses to pay, you can take her or him to small claims court and sue for the money you're owed. But without a contract, you have no proof of the agreement and no recourse. While it's convenient to communicate by e-mail and phone, to make a legally binding agreement, a signature must be put on paper and the two parties need hardcopies. Once you've booked a gig with a verbal agreement, simply write the details in your contract, and send the client two unsigned copies. The client signs both copies and sends both back to you. Then you sign both and return one to the client. If you're producing the contract, make sure you sign both copies last, *after* your client does. This is to ensure the client does not amend or modify the document after you've signed it. This business of who signs when is important since the contract only become legally binding once you've both signed.

The general simple performance contract on the next page is a template. Create your own contract template with your letterhead or logo at the top. Adapt this to fit your needs and particular situations, adding additional clauses for the specifics from your checklist.

Make It Easy on Your Client

To insure that your client sends back the contract with the deposit promptly, you can send a note that subtly applies polite pressure. Maurice Johnson, the author of the excellent *Build and Manage Your Music Career,* recommends sending your client two copies of the contract with a self-addressed, stamped envelope and including a brief cover letter with something like this:

Dear Ms. Smith:

Thank you for selecting the Mirabeau Quartet for your upcoming event. We look forward to performing for your guests. When you have a moment, please fill out the enclosed contract and return one copy along with your deposit check. I am anxious to confirm your event in our calendar as soon as possible. If you have questions, please contact me at (617) 534-9999.

Sincerely,
Jessica Smith
The Mirabeau Quartet

With your contract signed, you're ready to play the gig. Before leaving home, what should you make sure you have with you? Instead of frantically

Contract for Performance

_____ , herein referred to as "the artist," agrees to perform

musician or ensemble name

for _____ , herein referred to as "the client," on _____

        client's name   *date*

from _____ to _____ at _____ .

       time   *time*   *location*

The artist will arrive no later than _____ .

                                     time

The client agrees to pay the artist $ _____ per hour for playing time/time on site, and the total fee will be $ _____ . A deposit of _____ %, or $ _____ , is required _____ days in advance, and the balance is due on the day of performance, payable by money order, cash, or check.

Signatures:

_____

                    Client

_____

                    Musician

The agreement of the musician(s) to perform is subject to proven detention by sickness, accidents, riots, strikes, epidemics, acts of God or other legitimate conditions beyond their control. On behalf of the client, the artist will distribute the amount received to other member(s) of the artist's group as necessary.

    By executing this contract as client or artist, the person executing said contract, either individually or as an agent or representative, has the authority to enter into this agreement, and should she or he not have such authority, she or he fully and personally accepts and assumes full responsibility and liability under the terms of this contract.

Sample gig contract

grabbing things last minute for each gig, how about having a gig bag ready in advance? Keeping a checklist, buying a bag just for gigs, and packing in advance the morning of every gig may help you stay organized.

■

Pack Your Gig Bag Right! What to Bring—the Checklist

❏ Appropriate performance attire
❏ Folding music stand(s)
❏ Any other equipment: keyboard, amps, adapters, extension cords, etc.
❏ Sheet music for all players, plus extra emergency copies
❏ Music stand clips or clothespins for windy outdoor performances
❏ Clip-on stand lights (for poor lighting situations and emergency black outs)
❏ Extra strings, valve oil, reeds, rosin, etc.: instrument emergency items
❏ Tuning device
❏ Map and directions
❏ Copy of the contract
❏ Cell phone
❏ Client's contact phone number(s)
❏ Phone number of the place you're playing in case you get lost

---
■

Time Management ■

As a freelance musician, having good time management skills is important. But how are you supposed to fit everything you need to do into the day and the week? How can you find enough time to practice, freelance, teach, work a day job, and take care of the business side of your career? Admit it, to do it all you'd need to live without sleep. Not possible!

How do people manage time? Some folks are compulsive list makers and daily schedulers. Others take a more flexible, open-ended approach, fitting things in over the course of the week. You need to find an approach that fits your lifestyle and temperament. And if you're not staying on top of things now, it's time to experiment.

There are many time management tools—fancy day planners, scheduling systems, palm pilots, etc. But none of these will give you more time in the day. You still only have twenty-four hours. All the time management books and tools get at one essential point: time management comes down to making decisions about what you will do and won't do. You manage your time well when your daily time management decisions reflect your priorities.

The Time Management Quiz

Could you be managing your time better? Are you (circle one):

having a lot of interruptions? distractions?	Yes	No
constantly feeling tired?	Yes	No
frequently late for appointments or rehearsals?	Yes	No
making time for your real priorities, your most important projects?	Yes	No
getting enough practice time in?	Yes	No
having enough "down" time, to retool, recharge, and refresh?	Yes	No
making time each day for exercise or other activities important to you?	Yes	No

Be honest, did you answer "yes" to any of the first three questions or "no" to any of the last four? If so, you may want to take a closer look at the way you use your time.

Good time management is about planning, but this does not mean all work and no play. It's not about policing your time. It is about being more effective as a human being. Who is the person you want to become? What's it going to take to get there? The idea of managing your time is to make sure that you tend to the stuff that matters most to you. In planning the present, you determine the future: How you spend your time this week has everything to do with what you may be able to accomplish next month and next year.

The Tale of Joan (Part 4)

As she got busier, Joan found that managing her time was one of her biggest challenges. She found it increasingly difficult to make time for her own practicing and recital projects on top of the freelance work, teaching, and part-time job. She asked some veteran freelancers how they fit everything in, how they organized their schedules. An oboist practiced yoga regularly to stay sane; a percussionist reserved two hours every morning for practice, no matter what; and a soprano swore by a time management system programmed into her Palm Pilot. They'd all struggled with managing time and balancing their work lives and each had found different methods and strategies. Stay tuned for more on Joan.

Reality Scheduling

If you struggle with recurring scheduling decisions—around practice, net-working calls, or working out—that's a signal that your scheduling is not working. The idea of scheduling is to make a plan for taking care of the basics, when to take care of what, so that each day you don't have to worry and waste time on choosing what to do and when. This is not about scheduling in everything down to the minute, but about plotting out the basics, being realistic about what you can fit in.

Dana Young, a time management consultant and organization specialist, presented a workshop at New England Conservatory years ago and presented a version of the exercise given here, which is excellent for rethinking how to manage your time. On the chart, add in your regular activities for next week. The grid divides up your activities into four quadrants, including the scheduled, fixed activities (nondiscretionary) and the as-yet unscheduled (discretionary) ones you plan to do. Be realistic!

Time in Four Quadrants

Fill in the chart with your fixed schedule activities and your as yet unscheduled activities for the coming week. It's helpful to see your regular commitments and activities laid out, to see clearly what you can control in scheduling and what you need to schedule around.

Nondiscretionary: Career/professional *(i.e., time determined activities: teaching, day job, fixed rehearsal times)*	Discretionary: Career/professional *(i.e., practicing, career projects, networking)*
Nondiscretionary: personal *(i.e., scheduled healthcare appointments, childcare, etc.)*	Discretionary: personal *(i.e., socializing, groceries, laundry, etc.)*

Now, with your activities down on paper, the next thing is to organize a schedule that accommodates these. Planning saves you time, energy and worry. Instead of each morning thinking, "What do I have to do, and when will I fit it all in?" you can have already planned a realistic schedule. You can devote your thoughts and energy to living instead of constantly making lists in your head or rearranging your daily schedule.

On the weekly schedule, first write in your fixed commitments, your nondiscretionary activities, both professional and personal. Dana Young suggested you write these in ink. Next add in the discretionary activities using pencil so that you can rearrange as you think it through.

In fitting in your discretionary activities, think about your daily highs and lows of energy. When is your concentration best? What time of day is best for practicing? You may not be able to get in a solid three-hour block for practicing each day, but you can do an enormous amount of good work with a regularly scheduled hour of peak concentration. And to fit in the less challenging activities, like laundry and groceries, schedule these to fit your periods of lower energy and concentration.

Sun.	*Mon.*	*Tues.*	*Wed.*	*Thurs.*	*Fri.*	*Sat.*

Good time management is like juggling, keeping all these balls in the air, all the different areas of your life that require regular attention. If you've "dropped the ball" in one area, you feel out of balance. The trick, like in juggling, is adjusting your attention so you can see the bigger picture, and track all the balls. If you're practicing six hours a day, and consequently find that you're neglecting exercise, friends, and your nutrition, then things aren't in balance. Likewise, if you're taking care of all the basics but never seem to find the time to work on managing your career, you'll have very few concerts to play, and your longer-term goal of career advancement will suffer.

Urgent versus Important

Separating urgent from important tasks is essential to good time management. An urgent task is one that requires immediate attention, such as paying the electric bill because the company has threatened to shut off the juice unless they get the check tomorrow. Or, my favorite, you need to do laundry because you have no more clean underwear.

Important tasks, by contrast, are those nonscheduled activities that need to happen to fulfill your larger career or personal goals, such as grant research, booking calls for concerts for next season, updating your promo kit, contacting potential collaborators, and networking. These tasks are easy to push aside unless you make time for them, unless you make them a priority. It's easy to have your schedule be out of control because you're constantly taking care of the urgent, never getting to what's important. Take a look at your schedule, and make sure you've accounted for both the urgent and the important tasks.

With a reasonable weekly schedule, the remaining unscheduled things are most likely the daily "extras," the nagging chores, errands, or phone calls you may be putting off. These are the stuff of to-do lists. The problem with these lists is they can quickly get out of hand. The rule of thumb is, keep to-do lists short, specific, and do-able for the day.

Project Management

Beyond planning a weekly schedule with your regularly recurring activities planned out, the other important element to time management is working on long-term projects. Whether the project is recording a CD, planning a recital tour, or applying for a grant, the trick is to break it down into small, doable daily or weekly tasks. To stay on track, you need to see yourself making regular progress. Dana Young suggests thinking of a project as a big Tootsie Roll— you can break it up into bite-size pieces and deal with these one at a time. Completing the task and crossing it off your list by the end of the week will feel great and you'll be charged up to take on the next one. You'll build confidence and motivation as you finish each step of the project. Setting mini-deadlines, getting feedback and support along the way, and rewarding yourself regularly are ways to help stay on track.

In beginning any large project, the first hurdle is to get started, and then there's the sticking to it. Ask yourself, what's a reasonable starting point, a to-do step to get accomplished this week? Schedule some time for this task and write it down. Not sure where to start? Ask people who've done similar projects or simply start with your best guess—because the action itself will lead to more steps, and other people, information, and resources.

True Confession

Writing this book has been by far my largest project to date. It's required more time and effort than planning, producing, and playing concerts, writing grants, or organizing conferences. The writing (and rewriting) has taken several years and has taught me more than I ever wanted to know about managing projects.

Writing this book had been a long-term goal of mine, but having the goal as an idea was a lot easier than actually getting it done. My "day job," running the Career Services Center at New England Conservatory, is busy and full time. So to get the writing done I had to *make* the time for it outside of my job.

At first I tried writing in the evenings and on weekends. But after work I was often too frazzled to write, my mind cluttered with other concerns, or else my competing social plans would win out over the writing. The work was not getting done. I knew I needed to write every day in small installments, just like practicing. Eventually, I realized the only way this would happen was if I wrote first thing each morning. So I get up (still) at 5 A.M. (ouch!) Mon.-Fri., and write for about 1.5 hours. I'm no morning person; I'm not good for conversation at 5 A.M. But my mind is clear and my energy at that hour is better than it is after a long day at work. If I write at 5 it means I can still fit in my morning walk before going off to my job. Surprisingly, I've found that on the mornings when I miss doing either the writing or the walking, I simply don't feel as good during the day. The regular pattern of writing *and* walking helps me start the rest of my day with less stress.

What else did I do to manage the book project and keep focused? The deadline from my editor helped motivate (and scare) me into working. I also went to several writers' conferences—the equivalent of summer music festivals—for perspective and inspiration. Like practicing, writing is solitary and isolating work. Without regular feedback and support from others, it's easy to lose all perspective on a project, to become discouraged and filled with self-doubts. So one of the best things I did was to join a local writers group. We meet twice each month to critique each other's work, and cheer each other on. To cope with the "overwhelm" factor of the project I concentrated on just one chapter at a time (my bite-size piece of the Tootsie Roll) and set myself deadlines for completing each. I had the added incentive of submitting each chapter to my writers group and I also sent chapters to my colleagues for more feedback. My "reward" for meeting these deadlines was the comments, advice, and support I got from others.

How might this apply to you? Perhaps early morning practice sessions would provide you the consistent concentrated work time you need. Perhaps finding colleagues or a mentor to play for regularly will provide needed feedback and support. And with long-term fund-raising or recording projects, you too may need to focus on short-term goals and give yourself deadlines in order to stay focused and motivated.

Effective Practice ■

Perhaps the toughest time management question any musician has to face is "Am I using my practice time effectively?" Time in the practice room is especially precious. We never have enough of it and we're never sure we're using it wisely. Most of us are not taught how to practice and so we spend a lifetime trying to figure out how best to work at our playing.

Much of practicing is a kind of conversation with ourselves, analyzing what we hear, imagining what we're going after in a given phrase or section, thinking through what's not meeting our goals and how to improve it, and refining our "output." When we practice, we are enforcing habits—physical habits, as well as habits of hearing and thinking. The habits we reinforce may be good or not so good. The more unconscious we are during practice, the more our mind wanders or we are on "auto pilot," the less we are in control of the results. And so, the more fully conscious we are in the practice room, the better we're able to achieve our desired results.

Musicians spend a significant portion of their lives in practice rooms; we imagine we should be experts at practicing. And yet most musicians are not completely satisfied with the way they practice. Examining how you are actually spending your practice time can help you improve the results. Consider the following questions.

Practice Room Questions: You're the Expert

Take a specific passage you're working through and ask:

1. How do you want this passage to sound? Can you hear it clearly in your imagination exactly the way you want it?
2. How does the passage feel when you perform it? Is there tension in your body? Are you forcing? Are you producing the sound with ease or do you strain?
3. How accurately do you hear yourself? Do you record your practice ses-

sions regularly? Do you play back what you've recorded and listen objectively? This is one of the best ways to ensure focused and objective listening and thus, steady improvements.

4. Once you've isolated a particular difficulty in a piece, what do you do to analyze and then solve the problem? If a passage isn't working as desired, do you have the patience and creativity to take it apart, find the specific stumbling block(s) and build it back up again?

5. In playing through this passage, what are you focusing on? Can you turn your focus to one area at a time (i.e., to intonation, articulation, tone quality, etc.)?

6. What's going on in your head? Is your attention wandering? Are your thoughts racing? Are you fully conscious of what you're doing? What parts of your practice are being done on "auto-pilot"?

7. Do you really know and hear when the passage you've worked on has improved? Do you leave a practice session with a clear sense of what you've accomplished?

Going beyond how you practice a particular passage, here are four bonus questions for considering your practice time in general.

Practice Time Analysis

1. When and why do you use repetition as a practice strategy? How conscious are you when you're repeating a passage?

2. How do you approach a new work?

3. What are your practice routines? How much of this is *conscious* work?

4. How are you managing your practice time? How much time do you spend on warm-up, sight-reading, études, technical work, problem solving, and expanding your repertoire?

Financial Management ■

This next section explores the final issue in this chapter: how to manage money, an important concern for most musicians. On top of paying their living expenses, many young musicians are juggling student loans and credit card debt. Managing money is not easily done on freelance income, since work from month to month is unpredictable, and there's no steady paycheck. So it's important for musicians to have a good system of managing their finances.

What financial strategies work? First, it's essential to come up with a budget, which means knowing what your expenses are week-by-week and month-by-month. Most people don't know where their money goes; it just seems to disappear. And people are shocked at how much they spend on daily "nothings," on lattés, snacks, and eating out. The only way to really get a fix on your finances is by tracking them.

Track Your Spending

The easiest way to track your finances is to get and keep receipts for all your daily purchases and expenses. Each evening when you return home, empty your pocket of receipts and tally them in a notebook. It takes thirty seconds each evening. If you do this for a month and add in your fixed expenses (from checks or automatic bank transfers), you'll know exactly where your money is going. You can do this with paper and pen or with the highly recommended computer program Quicken (http://www.quicken.com), which is widely used by musicians for organizing and tracking finances.

Monthly spending (Your budget should account for all these areas):

Rent/mortgage: _____
Utilities (heat, electricity): _____
Internet connection: _____
Phone: _____
Cable TV: _____
Groceries: _____
Dining out: _____
Other entertainment: _____
Movies: _____
Clothing: _____
Laundry/Dry cleaning: _____
Home insurance: _____
Car insurance: _____
Car maintenance: _____
Other transportation: _____
Health insurance premiums: _____
Health care appointments: _____
Prescriptions: _____
Health club membership: _____
Loan repayments: _____
Credit card debt payment: _____
* Music/scores: _____
* Instrument maintenance: _____

* Lessons/Coachings: _____

* Instrument insurance: _____

* Concert tickets: _____

* Professional Membership dues: _____

Other: _____

Total = _____

*Examples of music career-related tax deductible expenses

Once you've tracked your expenses for three or four months, you should have a reliable monthly spending average. Beyond having an accurate tally of your spending, this tracking makes you more aware of each purchase, and that's good. When you're more conscious about everyday choices, you have the freedom to change your spending habits.

Savings

With limited income, the idea of *saving* money—whether it's for a music project, a vacation, or for your retirement—may seem impossible. But most people say they could manage to save $20 a week (it's $3 dollars a day, the cost of an indulgent coffee concoction). Saving $20 per week amounts to $1,000 a year. If you were to continue to save at that modest rate each year and invest the money for the long-term, in a fund or account that provided a rate of return of 7 percent, compounded monthly and taxed at 28 percent, your savings would grow in ten years to $14,360; in fifteen years to $24,055; and in twenty years to $36,550. Check it out, see the savings calculator on the MSM money website: http://www.moneycentral.msn.com/investor/calcs/n_savapp/main.asp

One way to make sure you start saving is to set up an automatic deduction plan attached to your checking account. This way you don't need to remember to save, it's done automatically for you. Ask at your bank; your money can be diverted to a savings, money market, or mutual fund account. You'll need to be clear on which kinds of accounts give you immediate access for withdrawals (these accrue less interest) and which accounts are for long-term savings (these accrue more interest).

Suze Orman, the financial guru and author who has done several televised PBS programs, recommends that people keep an account with seven to eight months' worth of living expenses as liquid savings, with ready access. This is for emergencies and unemployment. For many, the thought of saving this much while struggling to pay off debt can seem impossible. But this can be done incrementally. Paying off high interest loans, such as credit card debt, is for many people the first priority. For debt-reduction advice on consolidating loan payments and negotiating reduced payment plans with lenders, contact the National Foundation for Credit Counseling (aka: the Consumer Credit Counseling Service) at (800) 388-2227 or visit http://www.nfcc.org. And Ms. Orman's site (http://www.suzeorman.com) has an extensive resource listing with information and links for a wide range of financial questions.

To understand your options and to create a plan for your long-term financial health, it can be very useful to meet with a financial planner. This can be a one-time appointment, a financial "check-up." At the meeting, the planner can review your financial situation and map out a plan for budgeting expenses, reducing debt, and handling savings or investments. If you meet with a *fee-based* financial planner you'll be charged an hourly rate for the appointment, for a professional assessment and unbiased recommendations for how to handle your finances. There are also financial planners who work on *commission* and who recommend only the stocks or mutual funds for which they receive a commission. Ask everyone in your network for recommendations for financial planners in your area. You want to find an experienced professional through reliable referrals.

Record Keeping

Beyond tracking expenses to get a handle on your budget, freelance musicians need to keep ongoing income and expense records for tax purposes. Why keep these records? There's both a carrot and a stick. For musicians who keep good records and are tax savvy, there are substantial tax benefits. And for those who do *not* keep ongoing, accurate records, there's the threat of being audited. The IRS can and does ask citizens to produce their records and receipts as proof of their finances, and will also, if necessary, examine bank accounts as part of the investigation. If found in the wrong, you have to pay not only a fine and the back taxes owed but the interest on these as well!

Taxes 101   ■

Americans pay a lot in taxes. For most, their total federal and state taxes amount to roughly a third of their income. To keep this in perspective though, tax dollars pay for roads, schools, national parks, social service programs, welfare, Medicare and Medicaid, social security, national and state defense, federal and state arts programs, and more. A third of your income is plenty to pay, but most musicians—because they don't understand the tax laws and the deductions they're entitled to—significantly *overpay* their taxes. Don't let this happen to you!

Tale of Joan (Final Installment)

When Joan did her taxes that first year as a freelancer, she got clobbered, and owed the IRS $1,000. So she asked friends about handling finances. That's how she first learned about making a budget, keeping receipts for business deductions, and visiting an accountant for help with her taxes. That same year, her boss at her day job, the music instrument shop, added bookkeeping duties to Joan's workload. Consequently, she became more skilled with her own finances and started saving. The payoff came years later, when Joan was able to afford a new instrument, buy a new car, and put a down payment on a condo. Joan's first years were tough, but she was a quick study. The school of hard knocks teaches some unforgettable lessons.

How does this tax stuff work? Each April 15 we pay taxes on our income made the previous calendar year. If you have a day job, or a full-time orchestra gig, most likely you receive paychecks with some taxes already taken out. When you started the job you filled out a W4 form asking for your social security number and how much in taxes you wanted withheld from each paycheck. Then, after January 1 each year, your employer mails you a *W2* form stating the total amount you were paid in the previous calendar year and how much was withheld in state and federal taxes. You use the W2 in filling out your tax forms. If you only receive W2 income and have no other gig income (and don't own rental property or have complex investments) then your taxes should be relatively simple and you can most likely use the 1040EZ (short) form.

But for musicians with multiple income streams, doing taxes is more complex. The IRS considers freelance performance and teaching work to be self-employment, that you as a self-employed musician are equivalent to a small-business owner. Because you are paid directly in cash and personal checks, without taxes being removed, the IRS may scrutinize your income to make sure you pay the proper amount. Many musicians have combination careers. They are *both* employed by an established business (receive W2s with taxes already withheld) *and* self-employed workers (who receive payment without the taxes taken out).

For reporting freelance income, instead of getting the W2 form after January 1, musicians are sent the 1099. This is the reporting form used by clients, contractors, or other organizations that hire you for gigs or part-time work totaling $600 or more. The 1099 form states, for the previous calendar year, the amount a person or organization paid to you and that no taxes were withheld. So every year, after January 1, organizations file with the IRS the appropriate W2 or 1099 for each worker paid the previous year and they send a copy to the worker for tax filing purposes. What you are taxed on is your combined total income, from 1099s, W2s, and amounts received in cash and personal checks.

The Musician's Tax Quiz

Did you know:

- You are obligated to file a tax return if either:
  you made a minimum of $6,300 last year as a salaried employee, or you
      made $400 after expenses as a self-employed individual.
- You need to declare the income from a paid gig or professional service; the
  client or employer may have notified the IRS at the end of that year, even if
  you did not receive the 1099 form in the mail.
- If you make a mistake in filing your tax return, the IRS may notify you up to
  three years after the fact—and charge you three years' interest and a
  penalty in addition to the tax owed!

Tax Deductible Receipts = Substantial Savings!

The issue of how much you can save in paying taxes on your musician income has everything to do with the records you keep. Tracking business expenses means keeping receipts and records of all music career-related expenditures such as music equipment, scores, CDs, the cost of traveling to gigs and auditions, and more. Why do this? These expenses are *tax deductible*. This means you can *deduct* music career-related expenses from your income, and significantly reduce the amount of taxes you pay. If you keep records and receipts for these expenses, you can save many thousands of dollars over the course of your career. The IRS recognizes that small business owners must invest in their businesses, that self-employed workers must spend money in the course of doing business. And so the IRS gives people a break on their taxes for their business expenses. However, these expenses must be documented.

You can deduct these self-employed business expenses from your taxes only if you use the correct forms: the 1040 (long form) with schedule C for self-employed income and expenses showing a profit or loss. Many musicians mistakenly use the 1040EZ form, which allows for only a standard deduction, and they miss out on the many deductions to which they are entitled.

Help from an Expert

Because these forms are complicated and the rules about what you can and can't deduct can be confusing, my best advice is to have your taxes done by a professional who specializes in working with musicians. The folks at the large chain tax preparation firms may not be aware of all the varied deductions available to musicians. And note: Your tax preparation fees are deductible, too!

To Declare or Not?

Many musicians mistakenly think they'll get ahead by simply not declaring all the income they earn. But, in talking to the musician tax specialists at Donahue and Associates in Boston, I'm told that musicians who fail to declare parts of their income are typically the same musicians who fail to declare many legitimate expenses, out of laziness or ignorance. In order to take these deductions, you need self-employed income to declare against it, so you're better off avoiding tax audits by keeping accurate records and reporting all the income so you can declare all your deductions. Your tax return should reflect that you are a professional musician, should show your full income and full deductions, whether or not you also do any other non-music work.

Musicians' Business Expenses

Tax Deductible Items include:
Membership fees: professional organizations, union dues, etc.
Instruments, repairs and supplies
Music, scores, parts
Books on music: history, biographies, theory, career (this book, for example!)
Music-related journals and magazines
Publicity: photos, brochures, promo kit materials, flyers, posters
Concert attire and cleaning, along with stage cosmetics
CDs
Recording equipment and studio stereo equipment
Agent/management fees
Accompanist fees, substitute fees
Tickets to concerts (for professional development)
Costs of making recording
In-home studio expenses (percentage of rent, utilities, repairs, insurance, etc.)
Meals where professional music career issues are discussed, in your hometown as well as while away overnight on business
Travel (air, bus, taxi, etc.) to your gigs, auditions, concerts, festivals
Self-produced concert expenses (hall rental, equipment rental, promotion, reception costs, flowers, etc.)
Telephone (music business-related long distance calls)
Postage, mailings (of promo kits, press releases, demos, grant applications, etc.)
Business gifts (thank you gifts to accompanists and colleagues)
Lessons, coaching, workshops, classes, seminars

(Note: these are considered professional development for established professionals; undergraduate tuition is not deductible, nor is graduate tuition unless you established a professional career after a bachelor's degree and then returned to school.)

_____ ∎

It's in the Bag

For tracking expenses, Ed Donahue, of Donahue and Associates, a Boston-based tax firm with years of experience working with musicians, recommends the beautifully simple "shopping bag in closet" technique. This involves saving receipts for all business-related expenditures each day. At home at the end of the day, empty your pockets of receipts, write an explanatory note on any receipt that doesn't note the specific purchase, and put the business-related receipts in an open shopping bag you can keep on the floor in your bedroom closet. Easy!

Why document all this? Because if you're audited by the IRS, you'll be asked to produce proof to substantiate your declared income and deductions. Beyond the daily purchases, you'll also need to save credit card and check receipts, plus phone bills for business calls as well. When it's tax time, you'll have the necessary receipts ready and you simply organize these into categories.

Checks

Canceled checks can be used to document your professional expenditures. Keep your monthly bank statements, so that if requested, you have a record of the expense in question. And some musicians open a separate bank account strictly to track their business purchases. This is certainly the route to go if you are handling the finances for your ensemble.

Datebook

For expenses where you do not receive a receipt, such as tolls, gas, parking, mileage, or business meals under $75, your calendar datebook may suffice for keeping records. Simply enter the amount you spent, or number of miles driven on the appropriate day, with an explanatory note. If you keep accurate records of these "small" expenses in your datebook, you'll be surprised at how fast this adds up!

Ledgers

A ledger is a simple way to track business expenses and income. The purpose of keeping records is so you can know where you stand financially; what you have earned to date, what you have spent to date, and whether you are spending more than you earn. Computer programs such as Quicken (http://www.quicken.com) can be used for this purpose, or you can use the old pen and paper technique.

For tracking expenses, the next step beyond the simple paper bag in closet technique is to make an expense ledger. This can be a simple expense sheet, a chart with columns to record the date, an explanatory note about the purchase or expense, and the amount. This way, you'll see how much you're spending on business-related items and be able to track this by the week, month, and year.

Income Records

For tax purposes and sound financial decisions, you'll also need to track your music income. You may be getting paid in cash, personal checks, by organizations, or individuals. No matter how you're paid, you need to track your income in order to make sound financial decisions. You need to know what projects you can afford to take on, and what savings or investment plan will work for you. You can use a computer program or create your own ledger for tracking your music income. For the do-it-yourselfers, make up a sheet with columns that reflect the types of income you have coming in (lessons, gigs, recordings, royalties, commissions, etc.). Simply record the date received, from whom, the type of income, any special notes, and the amount, as shown in the example.

Date	Received from	Lessons	Gigs	Other	Explanation	Amount

A good reason to keep records of your income is so that you can track any seasonal patterns in the peaks and valleys of your income. For many freelancers, there are certain predictable months with little work. Being able to forecast this in advance can help you manage your finances and time to best advantage.

Conclusion

This chapter examined the freelance lifestyle in terms of three major areas: managing gigs, time, and money. In all three areas, you need to pay attention to both the small details and the big picture view of your career. In the end, it's all about the direction you want to take in life and the everyday actions you make toward that direction. Whether you're managing a project, organizing your schedule, or tending to your finances, in order to be most effective, your plans and actions should directly reflect your goals.

■ Suggestions for Moving Ahead ■

1. List three people you could contact to network with about freelance opportunities. These may be colleagues, teachers, conductors, or contractors.
2. List five organizations in your area that are likely sponsors or clients for future gigs.
3. If you do not have a performance résumé, write one. If you have one, ask yourself, how might you improve the layout or the format to better highlight your experience and accomplishments?
4. If you haven't been using a contract for gigs, create a contract template for future gigs, with your letterhead and any specifics needed for you or your ensemble.
5. For managing your time, ask yourself, on what are you spending too much time? On what are you spending too little time?
6. Design a schedule for next week's activities. Put the fixed scheduled items (nondiscretionary) in ink, and use pencil to organize the discretionary activities. Make sure you've reserved time for your top priorities.
7. In what ways would you like to improve your practice time use?
8. For handling your finances, it's never too late or too early to start tracking your expenses and income. Start saving your receipts for daily expenses and tallying these at home. Save the business-related receipts in a file or paper bag. Set up a ledger to record your freelance performance and teaching income. And, last, get expert help with doing your taxes!

11

Raising Money
for Music Projects

Rachel needs to buy a new instrument.

Charlotte's been accepted to a prestigious overseas festival and needs funds to cover travel and living expenses.

Matt is making a CD and needs money to cover the graphic design and recording studio time.

Casey and her ensemble want to start a new music concert series.

These are typical dilemmas musicians face. Rachel, Charlotte, Matt, and Casey are each in a bind. They have great ideas and plans, but lack the money to make things happen. When I meet with musicians in these kinds of situations, they often want or expect a quick fix, either a list of sponsors with deep pockets, or a sure-bet grant program that will provide immediate funds. And it's my job to deliver both the good and the bad news.

The good news is there are ways to raise money for projects and many musicians are successful doing this. The bad news is raising money usually takes more time and effort than people anticipate. Getting informed and savvy about the process will save time and effort in the long run. And if done right, raising money for a project can lead to larger and longer-term career benefits, beyond the scope of the original project.

There are generally two routes to pursue when seeking money for projects: by researching and applying for grants, or by developing a fund-raising campaign, that is, raising money from individual donors. For a particular project, one route may clearly be more appropriate. But, often, musicians will raise money using a combination of both grants and fund-raising methods.

Mapping Your Project ■

No matter how you pursue funding, the first step is to map out the specifics. Delineate all the resources needed to complete your project. Write everything down. The more concrete you are, the easier it will be to get and stay organized, to make good decisions, to find people to help, and to successfully complete your project. You can map your project by answering the eight questions below. Your answers form the foundation for both grant proposals and for fund-raising project statements.

1. *What is the goal of your project?*
   What *specifically* do you want to accomplish?
2. *Why are you doing this project?*
   How will it benefit you and others? How will it impact your community? How does this project fit in with your long-term career plans or your ensemble's mission?
3. *What specific activities will take place as part of this project?*
4. *What is your "track record" of success so far?*
   What awards, honors, performances, and so on have you done that demonstrate your ability to succeed with this project?
5. *Who will be involved (other performers, composers, etc.)?*
   What are their backgrounds and credentials? What is the nature and level of their participation?
6. *How long do you anticipate this will take?*
   Over what time period do you plan to execute this project?
7. *What will be the achieved results?*
   How will you measure your success? How will you know you've succeeded?
8. *How much money is needed?*
   Write out a detailed budget. You may need to "guesstimate" but do some research (i.e., get quotes on recording studio costs) to be is as accurate as possible. You can't go after funding if you don't know how much to ask for. Your budget should include nonfinancial needs as well, such as performance and rehearsal space and services, from printing to catering. Some of these you may be able to get as donations but they should be included in your budget just the same.

What's Next?

Once you have your project mapped, the next thing is deciding how to proceed, by seeking grants or with a fund-raising campaign aimed at individual donors. Most people would rather lose a limb than ask others for money. And people often assume that applying and winning grants is the easier method. Not necessarily true.

Keep in mind that most grant programs have specific requirements, guidelines, application deadlines, and time frames for making awards. Sometimes grant programs just don't fit the needs of a project. Charlotte, who wanted to go to a summer festival in Italy, found that most study abroad grant programs are designed for the entire academic year abroad, and the deadlines for applying are one year in advance of these yearlong programs. Charlotte found no grants to fit her project but she did raise the money, as detailed later in this chapter. It's a reasonable approach to first do some grant research for your project. If your project fits with a grant program, that's great. If not, you can then proceed, like Charlotte, with a fund-raising plan.

■
_____

Clarify Your Terms

Development: the cultivation of relationships; the process of building involvement and commitment to your endeavor.

Fund-raising: the organized activity of soliciting and collecting funds for a project, organization, or cause.

Grant: an award of money or other resources, given for a specific purpose. Grants are awarded by foundations, government agencies, companies, church and community organizations to fund education, research, or other particular projects. Grants are usually awarded through a competitive process, involving an application, proposal, and supporting materials.

Nonprofit organization: Nonprofit or not-for-profit status is a specific legal and tax designation: 501 (c)(3). Nonprofit does not mean the organization doesn't make money! Rather, the money that is made by the nonprofit is used to pay its expenses, fees, salaries, and administrative costs. A corporation, by contrast, pays its shareholders a percentage of its profits instead of reverting those funds to the organization. Nonprofits are organized with a board of trustees and a director who together work at the mission, goals, and long-range planning for the organization. Nonprofits have missions to improve communities.

The primary reason an ensemble might incorporate as a nonprofit is financial. Nonprofits can receive individuals' tax-deductible donations and nonprofits are exempt from paying federal and some state and local taxes. And many grant programs *only* fund nonprofit organizations.

Ensembles often struggle with whether or not to incorporate as nonprofits in order to be eligible for grant funding. Becoming a nonprofit takes time, effort, paperwork, and a lawyer. If your ensemble is just starting out, and unless you have a lot of time to devote to the project, it's probably best to develop a track record first, self-managing for a few seasons, before incorporating. In the meantime, you can seek grants restricted to nonprofits if you partner with an "umbrella" nonprofit and apply for the funding through this part-ner organization. To investigate these options further, check out Volunteer Lawyers for the Arts, a national organization that offers helpful publications and workshops on the issue of nonprofit status; see http://www.vla.org.

What Kinds of Projects Are Funded by Grants?

- Study in the United States and abroad (degree programs or private study)
- Research projects: i.e., studying manuscripts, traditional musics, instrumental techniques, ancient and folk instruments, and more
- Commissioning new works
- Copying scores, parts of new works
- Going on tour
- Making CDs
- Technical support and consulting on issues such as promotional materials, long-range career planning, fund-raising
- Starting, expanding, or maintaining a concert series, festival, or after-school lesson program

Researching Grant Opportunities ■

Go to your local public or university library and ask to see the grant directo-ries. Grant directories list descriptions of grant programs: what kinds of proj-ects are funded, how much money is awarded, deadlines for applications, contact information, and more. Use each directory's index to find programs appropriate for your project. You can look up grant programs by area of in-terest, such as music, education, the arts, or, more specifically, recordings, ethnomusicology, composition, and so on. Beyond the area of interest, each grant program has specific criteria for the kinds of projects it funds. These program restrictions are based on the mission of the granting agency. Some programs are only open to applicants from a specific region or state, or of a particular ethnicity or nationality, age range, and so so. The restrictions are detailed in the directories and then fully explained in the application materi-als. Read carefully to know whether or not your project is eligible.

Hot Tip #1

Reference librarians are your friends! Don't by shy; ask for help. Librarians can save you much time and stress. In looking for career information for my own use and for others, librarians have found me great tips, the most up-to-date information, directories, and resources. Searching for information on the Web can at times be like looking for a needle in a haystack, and you don't always know if what you find is the most accurate information. Having the help of a skilled librarian is like having a professional detective on your side.

Beyond public and university libraries, there are specialized grant research libraries across the United States. These libraries house the most detailed, current information on funding opportunities. The Foundation Center in New York City is the main headquarters for a network of cooperating grant research libraries. The Foundation Center publishes helpful guides for grant seekers and it also, along with the cooperating libraries, hosts workshops for grant seekers. Check their website at http://www.fdcenter.org, and see the appendix for more information.

Hot Tip #2

In addition to research in libraries, be on the lookout for grants mentioned in other musicians' bios. Keep a running list—a "tickler" file of the names of these grants so you can either find them on the Web or in a grant directory.

Narrowing the Field—Finding Your "Best Bets"

After researching your options, you should have a list of possible grant programs that seem a good match with your project. The next step is to contact these funding organizations and get the complete program descriptions and application details. Some of this may be online, some not. You can call, e-mail, or write to request information.

Once you have the guidelines and the detailed program restrictions, read them carefully. If your project still seems like a viable match, it's a good idea to call the funding organization and briefly outline your project, to ask specifically about its appropriateness for the program. Grant administrators can be very helpful to you before submitting your proposal. After all, they want to get proposals that are appropriate and well conceived, so talking to you *before* you submit your application is in their interest, too.

Research all your leads. You may find more than one program that fits your project, and applying to several may improve your odds of getting funded.

Hot Tip #3

Don't put all your eggs in one basket. Professional grant writers consider a good success rate to be one in five, having one out of every five proposals sent accepted.

Applying for Grants ■

The meat of a grant proposal is the project statement, a narrative describing the project. It is essentially a compelling argument, a well-reasoned case for *why* the granting organization should fund *your* project.

To be convincing, a project statement should answer the following questions: (This is where the earlier project mapping exercise comes in handy.)

- What specifically do you plan to accomplish through this project?
- What are the expected results, for you, for the community?
- What specifically do you need in order to complete the project (detail money, assistance, work timeline)?
- What evidence do you have to show you are qualified to succeed with this project?
- How does this project match the interests of the funding organization?

Grant Writing: The Inside Scoop

What "slant" do you put on a grant proposal? What do you emphasize? The challenge lies in seeing your proposal from the *funder's* perspective. Emphasize the ways in which your project goals match those of the funder. To be effective, a grant proposal should describe a need or problem, and then outline the proposed project that provides the solution. Your project description should clearly explain whom it will benefit and how. Think: problem, solution, impact. If your project involves a concert series, festival, or teaching program, it's essential to explain in your proposal the needs and benefits from the surrounding community's perspective.

Nitty Gritty

As for the style of writing, you don't need to be overly formal. Instead, write naturally as though you're explaining the project to a somewhat interested potential donor. Be concise. Volume of verbiage will not win you points. Keep in mind that not everyone on a selection panel will be intimately familiar with your specific area of interest. Don't use technical jargon—describe your project in a way that an intelligent, nonspecialist will understand and find compelling.

Beyond writing the proposal project statement, grant applications often call for supporting materials, such as a detailed budget, timeline, letters of reference, demo recordings, and so on. These materials are scrutinized carefully, they're an important part of making your case, so take pains that they represent you well. Each grant program has its own application format, so follow the directions carefully.

Warning: Thoughts to Avoid

Novice grant seekers often make unfortunate assumptions. Don't make the mistake of thinking, "Oh, this application is simply paperwork. I'll just hurry through this, put something down—anything. They probably only care about the recording and letters of recommendation anyway." Wrong! Don't underestimate the importance of the application.

The other mistake grant seekers make is in thinking that grant writing is some mysterious, intimidating skill beyond their reach. It's not, but this thought can prevent some people from even trying. This grant writing mystique can also lead people to contort or even invent a project plan to fit what they imagine the grant program prefers to fund. Funders can easily spot such proposals; they're unconvincing and therefore rejected. Successful grant writing is a straightforward process of making a clear and detailed case for the legitimate match between a proposed project and a funder's mission.

Top Five Reasons Grant Applications Are Rejected

1. Project is inappropriate for the grant program.
2. Late! Didn't meet deadline.
3. Unconvincing project statement. The need addressed, the solution, and the results all must make a compelling case.
4. Didn't follow directions, didn't actually answer the questions asked.
5. Incomplete: missing supporting materials (letter of recommendation, demo, budget, etc.).

How Are Grants Awarded?

Most grant programs use a panel process to select awardees. The granting organization may invite qualified, impartial professionals to serve as panelists. Each panelist receives copies of the applications and supporting materials to review. If there are too many applications for each panelist to review in depth, then the applications are divided into groupings and each panelist is in charge of reviewing and presenting her or his group of applications to the entire panel. Panel meetings are held to discuss the applications and votes are cast to choose the awardees.

A grant program makes an *investment* with each award. Panelists have tough decisions to make. Typically, there are far more deserving and excellent proposals than can be funded. If your proposal is not funded, it's a good idea to call the program officer and ask for feedback on how you might improve your proposal in the future.

True Confessions: Example From the Vault

I've written a number of grants for various projects, and each grant had its own lessons to teach me. But here's my Fulbright grant story. As a grad student, I wanted to study in Paris with the cellist Roland Pidoux. The Fulbright application requirements include two essays, one basically describing the project plan, and one on the applicant's background, life goals, and so on. I wrote my essays and thought I'd done a fairly good job of covering all these points. I asked a friend to read my drafts. He was a Ph.D. candidate in musicology, smart, an experienced writer, and I valued his opinion. I'd always done well in school with writing, so I think I was expecting him to be supportive and encouraging. Boy, was I wrong.

He calmly told me that the proposal was unconvincing, my plan of study wasn't specific enough, and I had not detailed my qualifications. He said it was unfocused and that no one would fund a project described like this. This was a harsh wake-up call. And I will always be grateful. Up to this point, I'd never really considered how important words and writing are to a musician, that communication skills could be so important to one's career.

I didn't get the Fulbright that year. I was rejected and felt very discouraged. But my friend encouraged me to reapply. I rewrote the proposal. I ended up with essays that detailed what is specific to the French school of string playing and how this would enhance my American training. I detailed the repertoire I planned to work on and listed possible performance venues in Paris where I could give recitals. I described my long-term career plans and what a year of study in Paris would contribute to my overall development. I described what I'd done to that date to indicate my track record—festivals, repertoire, degrees, and particular impressive performance venues. And I did get the Fulbright the second time around!

Morals of the Story

1. Get detailed, critical feedback early for your grant proposal draft.
2. Yes, the "paperwork" really matters.

3. The way you describe your goals and projects can have a big effect on the outcome.

4. If you don't succeed at first, try again!

■

Option B?

What happens if your project doesn't fit any grant program? The application deadlines and project time frames may not mesh. It can take several months to a year between applying and receiving either a rejection or an award. If you need a sum of money quickly, you'll most likely be better off organizing a fund-raising campaign instead. The truth is, you are for more likely to be successful raising money from supporters close to you than by "gambling" on the competitive grant process.

Fund-raising 101   ■

People are usually resistant to the idea of doing their own fund-raising. Most are horrified at the thought of asking others for money. They think of this as "begging."

But talk to any experienced fund-raiser and you'll hear a very different perspective. Fund-raising work is all about connecting with people. It's about building relationships, helping people put their interests and values into action for a cause they care about. Like music itself, fund-raising boils down to creating community. A fund-raising campaign can rally individual supporters into a community, a close-knit group galvanized by a cause.

Why Do People Give?

Think about your own actions. Have you participated in, or sponsored someone else in a walk-a-thon? Have you put money in a church collection plate or volunteered as a mentor? Have you ever tutored a child, donated blood, or contributed to some deserving cause? *Why* did you do it?

Chances are there was someone—a friend, family member, or an acquaintance—who invited you to participate and contribute. This person told you about the cause or the project and suggested you get involved. This "recruiter" made it sound appealing. The way it works is, the more the recruiter and the cause matter to you, the more you'll be willing to contribute.

And how did you feel after contributing? You probably felt good! People like to help and they like to see positive results. So when the student you mentor passes an exam, or the church you played the benefit concert for meets its fund-raising goal, you feel proud that you were a part of this process.

When people give time, money, or expertise to a cause they care about, they get something important in return. They get to feel good about themselves. *This* is the return on their investment. Self-esteem is a great reward. As you imagine your future fund-raising campaign, remember that fund-raising is not a one-way transaction. When you ask people to contribute, you're offering them something valuable in return.

It's Personal: People Give Money to People

The first reason why anyone would contribute to your fund-raising campaign is because of her or his relationship with *you*. This is not about being fake or buttering people up. This is about genuine relationships. It's important to keep those close to you informed about your career goals and projects. And you also need to be genuinely interested in them. You need to keep track of *their* interests, careers, families, and plans. Remember, relationships are two-way streets.

"But I Don't Know Anyone With Money!"

As you're reading this, you may be thinking, "I don't know any rich people. The people closest to me either don't have anything to give or won't." The truth is, the vast majority of people in your network have some discretionary funds, money they use on a variety of non-necessities. There are people in your network who could contribute $500 to a cause they believe in without it adversely affecting their finances. For some people, $20 is the limit of their comfort zone, for others, it may be $5,000. So before you give up, read on to consider how you might develop your own fund-raising campaign.

Example: The Quickie Campaign

Maria and Andreas each needed to raise $1,000 to participate in a summer tour with an orchestra going to South America. They had a deadline of one month to raise the money. Their immediate families could not help so Andreas and Maria started thinking about their network, family friends who'd shown interest over the years in their musical development. Maria thought of her family dentist and family lawyer—both had been interested and supportive over the years. Andreas thought of his high school music director. They'd kept in touch and Andreas knew him as a generous fellow who contributed to community charities. These potential patrons were not rich, but all three were well off. Andreas and Maria had a reasonable expectation that these people could afford to and would want to contribute at least part of the needed funds.

Maria and Andreas each called their potential patrons to set up lunch dates, explaining they wanted to catch up and to discuss an opportunity they'd been offered. Maria and Andreas practiced these conversations beforehand. Initially, they both felt awkward and nervous about asking someone directly for money, but after doing some role plays, practicing how to describe the orchestra tour opportunity, imagining talking with these friends of their family, they both were more confident. How'd Maria and Andreas make out? Very well! The conversations were easier than they'd imagined, they each got help from these patrons, and the tour was terrific!

Moral of the Story

If you need to raise a relatively small amount of money (up to $5,000) in a short amount of time (three months or less), look to the folks in your *inner* circle, those closest to you and your family, who already know you well and who can easily be brought up to date on your project and plans. It's easier to ask two people (with good potential) for $1,000 each than to raise your total in $20 incremental contributions. If you have a larger sum to raise and more time to do it, then you can consider expanding your list of potential patrons, cultivating more patrons over time, and asking more people.

Success Factors: The Five "How's"

It's not just about knowing rich people! The success of your fund-raising campaign depends on a number of factors:

- how much money you need to raise
- how much time you have to do this
- how compelling your project is (how appealing it is to your network)
- how you present your project, and
- how you interact with your network.

Overview: The Development Continuum

It's all about relationships. People contribute in proportion to their sense of involvement. The closer you are to people, the more invested they are in your project, the more likely they will want to invest. The development continuum below is a useful way to gage the level of involvement of your supporters. The continuum helps illustrate the process, the how, why, and when people become patrons. This concept comes from workshops that fund-raising gurus David Bury and Steve Procter have presented for the Chamber Music America and Arts Presenters conferences.

The Development Continuum

Levels of relationship:

Ignorance ⟶ Awareness ⟶ Interest ⟶ Commitment ⟶ Ownership

On the chart are five headings for describing the various relationships between you and your supporters. Most to the left is ignorance, the stage for potential supporters, for those who are as yet unaware of you, your music, or your current project. Development work is about moving people, over time, from left to right along the continuum. From awareness or lukewarm interest in you and your career, to deeper involvement, commitment, and ownership. Don't be thrown by the word "ownership." It doesn't mean people in this category "own" your ensemble or your career. Rather, this category is for your closest allies, your inner circle, your advisory board. These are the people who feel a sense of partnership in contributing to your success, those most closely involved in helping you plan and execute projects.

Where would you place members of your network on the continuum chart? At the awareness stage, people may have signed up for your mailing list, attended one or more concert, or bought your CD. At the interest stage, you've gotten to know these people, and in the process, they may have provided you with career ideas, advice, or contacts. At the commitment and ownership stages you've gotten close to these people and they've invested time, energy, or money in you and your career. These folks are your best patron prospects for support ranging from catering a reception, to printing programs, handling publicity, or funding a CD.

Using the continuum chart as a worksheet, write in the names of those in your network inner circle, placing each name under the category appropriate for the level of your relationship. You probably have twenty to twenty-five good contacts, people who've expressed some degree of interest in you and your future. Include your extended family, friends of your family, former teachers, doctors, neighbors, and so on.

To move people along the continuum, you need to invite their participation in support activities appropriate to their level of relationship. After all, it makes no sense to ask people in the "ignorance" category to fund your CD project. However, if you want to cultivate particular contacts now unaware of you, it *is* appropriate to send them an invitation to your concert, or to ask someone in your network to invite them.

You may have friends and family at the "interest" level that you'd like to move towards the "commitment" level. The way to start is with a phone call. Ask to take them out for coffee or lunch, and explain you want to pick their brain about a project you have in mind. It's best to do this in person, so you can get their full attention and reaction to your project. You can think of these as "advising" meetings.

Be prepared—have your project mapped out in written form so that you can describe and show it to your potential patron. Part of the development process is educating your network about your career plans. Non-musicians are often unaware of the costs and procedures of producing concerts, making CDs, or advancing a music career. They don't know why it's important to go to festivals, or why you need a better instrument. Make sure your presentation includes a summary of your track record so far and a description of how this project fits into your overall career plans. Your project map should include a detailed budget of all anticipated costs plus a listing of the resources you already have in place, such as any donated services, space, contributions from others, and the portion of your own savings earmarked for this project.

The goal of these advising meetings is to gather support and ideas, to deepen the level of involvement of your supporters. Fund-raising projects are most effective when they are a group effort, when you pool the talents and expertise of a group. The best case outcome is to have your advisor listen to your project description, get interested, take out a checkbook and say, "How much do you need?" That's wonderful, but it doesn't always happen like this. Instead, your advisor may suggest changes in your project or fund-raising plan, or may refer you to others for additional advice. Or your conversations may yield volunteers for hosting and organizing a fund-raising house concert. The bottom line is, you need to have the meetings to reap the results.

Hot Tip #4

From fund-raising and development professional Steve Procter, "Beyond inviting supporters to lunch, the other powerful development tool is your artistry in action. Everything you do—concerts, school programs, coaching of ensembles, etc.—is a development opportunity. The surest and most powerful way for people to 'get religion' is to see you doing your work. All that's required is that you make a personal invitation."

Hot Tip #5: Think Beyond Cash

In-kind donations are noncash contributions, such as equipment (computers, pianos, PA systems, etc.) or space for rehearsals or performance, or services such as printing, graphic design, website development, and so on. Be creative. Think about the people in your network who might help with your project on a noncash basis. If you have a newsletter, this can be a great medium for requesting in-kind donations, asking for volunteers, or specific service contributions. Newsletters are also great places to acknowledge and thank your growing circle of supporters.

Do It Right!

There's an old saying in fund-raising: You have to have the *right* person ask the *right* prospect for the *right* amount for the *right* reason at the *right* time. If you haven't spoken with your Aunt Ida in ten years and she gets a phone call or letter out of the blue asking her to cough up $3,000, it won't go over well.

"Making the Ask" ■

In the course of your "advising meeting," you'll get a sense of the level of interest of your potential patron. If she or he does not volunteer to contribute, you need to "make the ask." Do some research. Have a specific amount in mind to ask for, appropriate to your supporter's income and to her or his level of interest in your project. The amount should be specific because if you say, "I'd be grateful for whatever you can give" people may give $10 or $20 instead of $200 or $500. Ask family or friends—who know the particular supporter well—what they think an appropriate amount would be. If your potential donor is well off and regularly contributes to community arts organizations, this will inform your thinking.

Practice first. Practice your presentation with a mentor, teacher, or family member. A run-through will help you feel more comfortable in talking about yourself, presenting your project, and in "making the ask." Let's say you plan on asking ten people from your network for donations. Where do you start? Start with whomever you feel most comfortable. With experience, it gets easier.

In your presentation, after you've outlined your project and budget and talked enthusiastically about how it will benefit your career in the long-run, you need to make the ask. You can say something like, "I'm hoping you can assist me with this project. As my budget shows, the total cost is $3,000 and I've already raised $800. I would really appreciate a contribution of $ [appropriate amount]." Then PAUSE—don't fill in the silence. Give your supporter a chance to think and respond. She or he may tell you it's too much but they can give X amount. Or they may say they need to think it over and get back to you, or they may take out their checkbook. Whatever the answer, thank them for their time and interest.

Keep in mind no one "owes" you anything. It's their money to do with as they choose. Essentially, you're presenting a kind of investment opportunity to which your supporters may say yes or no. If the answer is no, it doesn't mean they won't say yes to your future projects. So if you're turned down, you need to let go of feeling resentful. In the end, your deepening relationship with supporters is what matters. It's all about relationships. Think long-range.

Fund-raising and development, when done right, is not about a quick fix for funding one project. It's about your long-term career—and having friends and supporters for the long haul.

Why Are These Meetings Done in Person?

You may imagine that this would be easier—less awkward for you—if done by phone. However, fund-raising is much less effective by phone, mail, or e-mail. In person, you'll get more time and the full attention of your supporter. You want to be able to "read" the response of your potential patron—facial and body language, tone of voice, and so on. Most important, people are much harder to turn down face-to-face, especially when you know them and you've just presented a compelling case for their support.

Real Life

Dilemma: An undergraduate, soprano Charlotte G. had been admitted with scholarship to a summer opera training program in Italy. She was thrilled but didn't have all the funds needed—$2,000 to cover travel, room and board. Charlotte was offered the scholarship in May and the festival was in July. Time was short.

The Plan: Charlotte decided to give a benefit recital back home, in the small town in Maine where she and her family have strong ties. She gave her recital at the high school auditorium, a small venue with good acoustics. She arranged the concert date, venue, and the logistics with the help of her former voice teacher.

The Process: Charlotte talked by phone with some key people back home first, to get ideas and support. At school in Boston, she also sought advice from both the Conservatory's Career Center and the Development Office. And the help of her former teacher, friends and family back home was essential because Charlotte was planning this at a distance.

Charlotte made a detailed list of people to invite: those who knew her and her family well, and who felt invested in her development as a singer. She sent personalized handwritten letters to everyone on the list a month before the performance, updating them on her accomplishments so far and outlining the festival opportunity before her. In the letters, Charlotte explained the importance of this experience, how the training and performance opportunities would contribute to her career. Charlotte included the specifics, explained the budget total, how much she needed to raise, how much she'd gotten as scholarship, and how much she was covering from her savings.

To promote the benefit concert, Charlotte's mom wrote and delivered press releases to the small local newspapers and submitted listings to local church bulletins. The whole family helped spread the word and the excitement about the event, they made posters and most important, they invited people personally.

Charlotte had a great turnout—about one hundred people came and this worked well for the venue. She'd planned a terrific recital program and introduced each piece, engaging the audience. Afterward, there was a reception that family and friends had organized.

Results: Many people contributed at the reception, placing donations in envelopes in a basket. Many others sent checks on the week following the performance. All totaled, Charlotte raised close to $3,000, exceeding her goal!

Follow up: Charlotte sent thank you notes to everyone who contributed, whether it was money, time, expertise, or ideas. She updated them all during and after the festival—sending an e-mail newsletter update. Her net gain was far more than the dollars: Charlotte now has a larger circle of supporters vested in her future.

The Art of the Thank-You

When's the last time you received a handwritten thank-you note? These days, it's so rare that getting one is a special occasion. Memorable. And *that's* why you should write them. E-mail and phone thank-you's just don't pack the same punch. Send thank-you notes to everyone who helps with your projects. They will remember you with good feelings.

You also can acknowledge and thank supporters in your printed concert programs and CD liner notes. Ask them how they'd prefer to be listed, as "Dr. and Mr. John L. Smith," as "Jane and John Smith," or as "Anonymous." If a local business provides you with in-kind donations, ask if they'd like their logo in your concert program or on your posters. If you keep your supporters happy and interested, they will want to stay with you.

Fund-raising Letters ■

We all get direct mail appeals asking us to contribute to a wide range of causes, from local homeless shelters, to the Red Cross, the United Way, to cancer and AIDS research organizations. If you're thinking it'd be a lot easier to just make up a form letter and send it out—think again. The truth is direct mail campaigns have a very small return rate (1–4 percent). Personal face-to-face meetings yield "yes" 50 percent of the time, a much better rate of return. With in-person meetings, you have an even shot at succeeding.

That said, letters are very useful as a tool to reconnect with supporters, to ready them for in-person visits, and to invite them to benefit concerts (as Charlotte did). In a case in which the potential donor is too far away, a very personalized letter can be tailored to the situation. Below is an example of such a fund-raising letter. But note, the reason this letter was appropriate is that there was both a strong family connection and a recent one-on-one meeting. The $500 "ask" was based on what Rachel's family thought would be appropriate for these supporters and this situation.

Thinking beyond Your Current Project

The Development Continuum is an ongoing process. Development work takes time because relationships are built over time, through shared experiences and one-on-one contact. As you add new people to your mailing list, you'll want to find ways to move them along the continuum. Think about what might help potential donors get to know you better, and how you might draw more interested people to your concerts. Steve Procter recommends using "occasional informal newsletters or e-mail updates as a way to maintain and build relationships. These help your friends feel connected to you and your work. Just "tell them the story" about your latest or upcoming concert or project.

Hot Tip #6: Cultivating New Supporters

Get people to sign up for your mailing list and newsletter. Calico Winds, a quintet based in LA, gives out their group's fun refrigerator magnets to all who sign up for their mailing list.

Pay attention to who comes to your concerts. Stay at the reception afterward to meet and greet your well-wishers. These are your supporters and potential patrons. Be gracious—no matter *how* you felt the performance went!

Consider organizing a series of house concerts for your supporters and have them invite potential new supporters. What about master classes, lecture demonstrations, or clinics in your hometown? What about performing a benefit concert for a local community charity for the exposure and contacts, perhaps to later pick the brain of a fund-raising professional?

What about an event that pairs great music and fantastic food? A recital

April 10, 2004

Dear Jane and John,

Thanks so much for coming to my concert last week—it was great to see you! I'm glad we had a chance to visit during the reception and to catch up a little. I was glad to hear Emily's doing so well in Chicago.

I appreciate the interest you've shown in my music and I wanted to fill you in on my current plans. As you know, at the Conservatory I have a wonderful teacher, Donald Weilerstein. He has been very encouraging and is suggesting I apply to several prestigious festivals and competitions next year, including the Young Concert Artists competition in New York City this fall. My teacher is also telling me that I need a better violin. I am past the stage of using a "student" instrument and I need a professional-quality instrument that will allow me to compete successfully in competitions and orchestral auditions. Unfortunately, better instruments are expensive.

The good news is I have found an excellent Italian instrument made in the mid-19th century—it costs $11,000. I have raised $4,000 so far—savings from part-time jobs and contributions from my family. I am contacting close family friends, such as you, to participate in my "new instrument campaign."

In June I'll be back home. I'm planning a "new instrument" benefit concert on June 20, Sunday at 2 pm at the Unitarian Church. I'd love to have you come and I'd love to list your names in the concert program with the others who've contributed to the fund. Would you consider a contribution of $500 towards the purchase of a professional-quality violin? I appreciate your support and interest!

I look forward to seeing you both as well as Emily and Kate this summer, and I will be in touch in the next few weeks.

Best Wishes,

Rachel V.

Rachel V.

Sample fund-raising letter

program of musical bon-bons with an elegant catered dessert buffet-reception. Local caterers might participate or you could do this as a local competition for most elegant dessert. Or what about a musical feast with pieces performed between courses? Use your imagination.

The Moral of the Story

Lack of money or resources need not stop you from succeeding with your projects. Whether you go with seeking grants or the fund-raising route, or do some of both, you will need to be organized, patient, resourceful, and creative. And you'll be far more likely to succeed if you enlist others. Brainstorm for fund-raising ideas with your inner circle. Host a brainstorming party—make it fun!

Summary

For both grant seeking and fund-raising, the main steps for success we've covered in this chapter follow this outline:

Plan: map and articulate your project thoroughly.

Research and respond: understand your prospective supporters and speak to the places your goals and their interest intersect.

Get personal: Establish and maintain face-to-face relationships with the people whose support you seek.

Keep the long view: Think beyond your current project; see it in the context of your long-range career plans so that your actions set the stage for future, continued possibilities.

■ Suggestions for Moving Ahead ■

1. What project (requiring needed funds) are you most wanting to work on? If you have multiple projects, prioritize. Choose the one that would be best to complete first.
2. Map your project, get specific by answering the eight mapping questions earlier in the chapter. If you write the answers down, you'll save yourself work later.
3. List any grant programs you've heard of and are curious about. Besides finding information on the Web, what are the libraries in your area where you could research grant opportunities?
4. Make a list of your supporters, the inner circle of your network. Where would you plot these people along the development continuum?
5. Of the people on your list, whom could you imagine talking to first

about your project, to gain advice? Write out what you would say to describe your project to one of these people.

6. Take it a step further beyond the advice. Choose the person on your list you think would be most receptive to your project. Prepare your presentation. Write out what you'd say as a practice script so you can fine-tune your presentation.

12

Getting It Together: Your Career Package

The focus of this chapter is your complete career package. Maybe you'll be the next Yo-Yo Ma or Renée Fleming, or maybe you'll be one of the vast majority of professional musicians who do not make their living solely from performing. Unless you win a full-time position with a top orchestra, your performance work, especially as an emerging artist, will most likely be part-time. As you're developing your career, you'll still need to put food on the table, pay rent, and take care of yourself, body and soul. How do musicians pull it all together?

Types of Careers ■

Careers come in two basic flavors: traditional and entrepreneurial. Traditional music career opportunities are ready-made jobs for which auditions are held (with orchestras, opera companies, etc.), as well as long-term ensemble residencies at universities. These coveted "traditional" opportunities are relatively few in relation to the applicant pool, so competition is high.

■

Here are a few sobering statistics. According to the National Association of Schools of Music, for the 2002–03 school year, there were over 97,000 students enrolled in music degree programs at the 500+ reporting colleges, universities, and conservatories in the United States. That year there were over 16,000 music degrees granted at these schools. Think about it: 16,000 skilled musicians entering the work force every year. And for those graduates pursuing orchestral careers, according to the American Federation of Musicians, the total number of full-time (or equivalent) positions in major and regional orchestras in the United States is only about 4,500. Audition announcements for positions in the Boston Symphony Orchestra draw

150–300 applicants. Starting salaries for positions in the top five orchestras are at about $100,000, while many regional orchestras pay less than $30,000 a year.

Fortunately, these traditional opportunities, with orchestras, opera companies, or choruses, are *not* the only kind. The other career model is the entrepreneurial one, what's been the main focus in this book. Entrepreneurial musicians create opportunities for themselves. For example, Bang on a Can, the Kronos Quartet, and eighth blackbird are examples of new music ensembles who've carved niches for themselves. They've commissioned works, written grants and raised funds, recorded, and toured. Some have created their own concert series and residencies, and all developed their audiences. The point is: no one *asked* these musicians to form these groups; they did it on their own. Likewise, Boston's acclaimed early music group Emmanuel Music (http://www.emmanuelmusic.org) was founded by conductor/pianist Craig Smith to perform Bach Cantatas as they were intended, as part of the weekly worship service. This group, in residence at their namesake Emmanuel Church, has gone on to record many CDs, tour, and to present multiyear cycles of complete chamber works by Schubert, Schumann, Debussy, and Brahms.

Portfolio Careers

Most musicians have careers that combine both the traditional and the entrepreneurial models. They typically construct layered "portfolio" careers, working several part-time jobs, mixing both traditional and entrepreneurial work. There's an amazing variety in the ways musicians layer multiple projects, combining freelance work, teaching, and various day jobs. This diverse work package can tap into a musician's full range of talents and abilities and make for a satisfying, full life.

Career Profile

Vic Firth, the legendary Boston Symphony Orchestra (BSO) timpanist, retired in 2003 after fifty years with the orchestra. Conductor Seiji Ozawa said Vic was one of the two musicians in the BSO from whom he'd learned the most. Five decades with the same employer sounds like a very traditional career, but this same Vic Firth has had a "side" occupation. His drumstick manufacturing business (http://www.vicfirth.com) has evolved into the leading percussion equipment company in the world.

Vic started making drumsticks because he was dissatisfied with the available equipment. He started by modifying drumsticks, then experimented in making his own. His products are now used and endorsed by classical, jazz, and rock musicians, and his company employs more than one hundred people. Throughout his career, Vic has used a wide range of skills and talents, both as a musician and a successful businessperson. Part of what makes people feel good in life is having the opportunity to develop and use skills to contribute to the greater good. Vic's work as both a performer and entrepreneur has helped thousands of people connect to music.

Finding Your Niche

How do musicians find their niche? How do they make a place for themselves in the professional world? How do they end up with satisfying portfolio careers? Most people experiment. Musicians try out various music-related and non-music projects and part-time jobs. Through trial and error, luck and calculated risks, they explore and test themselves in the professional world. The more exploring they do, the more options they uncover.

Project-based Career Advancement

Music career exploration typically takes the form of projects, from various recording projects, to forming or joining different ensembles, launching concert series or festivals, commissioning works, or starting a private teaching studio. Musicians' careers are often a series of such projects, one leading to the next, through collaborations and freelance work. These projects may last days or years, dovetail or conflict, but they are sustained by the interest and enthusiasm of the participants. From month to month it can seem, to both the musician and to outsiders, that there's no big plan or career direction with these projects because there's no clear cut career "ladder" for musicians. Instead, the connecting threads of interests and skills that run from one project to the next are a kind through line, a sustaining passion. The accumulation of talent, skills, experience, and contacts help musicians advance in their projects, to build them into satisfying portfolio careers.

Building a Portfolio Career

Stephen Beaudoin is a multitalented and entrepreneurial young tenor. While completing his bachelor's degree, he worked as an administrative intern for the Gay Men's Chorus of Boston, working on grant writing and fund-raising projects—a real education for an undergraduate! Stephen then used the skills he developed as an intern to find funding for his own project. He collaborated with Martin Near, a composer colleague, to write an opera dealing with the AIDS epidemic. Stephen applied for a grant from the American Composers Forum and was able to produce the opera at both Roxbury Community College and at the Boston Center for the Arts.

After graduating, Stephen juggled several part-time jobs, including perform-ing with a professional choir, writing classical music articles and reviews for two small Boston-area newspapers, and working at Starbucks—good benefits, flexible schedule—as well as at the American Composers Forum. He then went on to a full-time day job doing development work at a local cultural alliance. This allowed him to hone his skills in grant writing, event planning, donor development, and project pre-sentation. The skills he's developed in his day jobs have helped him with the perform-ing side of his career. Stephen performs regularly with a classical guitarist, and books and promotes these performances. The duo also started their own concert series at a local historic mansion. How'd they do this? They made an appointment to visit the director of the mansion. They presented their idea for starting a series, with program-ming ideas and their press kit. The director loved the concept, gave them an extremely reasonable rental fee for use of the hall, and promised to help with the publicity.

Stephen has found ways to knit his varied interests and skills together to make a busy and satisfying career path. For Stephen, staying flexible and open to new pos-sibilities has brought new opportunities.

Making It Work

For most musicians, whether they are going for a traditional or entrepre-neurial type career, there are times when they need to seek paid employment outside of their performance area. What's typical is that musicians are re-sourceful and creative in finding ways to finance their musician lifestyle. If you are building your repertoire, launching a new ensemble, preparing for au-ditions or competitions, then most likely you'll need to consider ways to earn money while you pursue these projects. As you network, ask musicians what kinds of work they've done outside of performing—you'll be amazed. Ask them what work they liked or didn't and why. Ask what jobs fit well with their musical pursuits. Ask what they'd recommend for you to explore.

Day Job Dilemma: Five Key Considerations ∎

Many musicians struggle with the issue of balancing the need to make a living with the need to pursue their passion. There's no way around it. The process of developing your professional career and income as a performer takes time. Most musicians, at some point in their careers, work day jobs. In looking for the right fit for your work/life balance, here are five key areas to consider:

1. Do you want to work at a day job *within the arts or beyond?* Some musi-cians want to have all of their working hours connected to the arts, to be around others who think and talk like they do. So these musicians

look for day jobs with various arts organizations, or within the recording industry, or with music retailers or music schools.

Other musicians prefer non–arts related day jobs that give them some distance from music. They want to explore other skills and interests, or they find that with a non-music day job, they can conserve their creative energy to be used off the job.

Arts-related Day Jobs

Below are two broad categories of work that many musicians have found complements their performance pursuits.

Music Teaching

includes teaching in a variety of settings:

Public Schools	Private Schools
College-level	Community music schools
Artist-in-residence work	Private studio teaching

Arts Administration

includes work in areas of:

Artist management	Development/Fundraising
Recording industry	Music publishing
Music technology	Music journalism
Public relations/marketing	Arts marketing research
Radio/Television	Music library work
Instrument manufacturing	

Day Jobs Outside the Arts

Many of these jobs have flexible hours or involve contract work that musicians have found compatible with their artistic pursuits. These are just a sampling of the work options for musicians seeking ways to help finance their performing careers. Some of these jobs require very specialized training and experience; others do not. For more ideas, I recommend *Survival Jobs: 154 Ways to Make Money While Pursuing Your Dreams,* by Deborah Jacobson, published by Broadway Books.

Requiring less formal training:	*Requiring more training/experience:*
The old standbys:	Piano tuner
Temp; Waitperson	Personal trainer

House painter	Graphic designer
Nanny	Yoga instructor
Limo driver	Photographer
Telemarketer	Editor
Apartment manager	Alexander teacher
Tutor	Jeweler
Caterer	Court reporter
Proofreader	Paralegal
Car salesman	ESL teacher
Wedding planner	Realtor
Grant writer	Software consultant
Website developer	Computer programmer
Landscaper	Therapist
Carpenter	Locksmith

2. What *skills, experience, and interests* do you have (or want to develop) beyond performing? If you're going to spend a significant amount of time working a day job, it ought to be something you either find interesting, fun, or meaningful. What are you curious about? What are your hobbies? For clues, think about courses you found interesting, organizations you belong to, kinds of books you read, and the type of news stories you follow. Musicians find meaningful and satisfying day jobs in all kinds of settings, including religious institutions, political campaigns, and grassroots community organizations.

   Some go-getter musicians choose day jobs where they can also gain specific skills useful for their own music careers—skills in development, fundraising, marketing, or public relations. Musicians find jobs that provide valuable skills and contacts at many kinds of organizations, such as foundations, or public relations, and marketing firms, for example.

   What kinds of work have you already done and found interesting? Summer jobs and part-time school jobs can often lead to other opportunities. And the skills you're using as you develop your music career (i.e., publicity, fund-raising, booking concerts, and research) may be parlayed into a day job.

3. What kind of schedule, *hours and flexibility* do you want in a day job? Do you need certain nights free for rehearsals and performances? Do you need early mornings for practicing? Many musicians seek work with maximum flexibility. This leads some to start their own businesses, or to work on a contract basis. Other musicians find jobs that dovetail

their music schedules. And depending on the work involved, a company or organization may be able to offer flex time as a benefit, allowing the employee to set her or his own schedule, and not be boxed in to a nine to five schedule. But whatever the situation, in order to balance a day job with a music career, excellent time management skills are required to make it all work (see chapter 10).

4. Do you have *health insurance?* This is one important reason many musicians take part- and full-time day jobs. If your spouse or partner can cover you on her or his health plan, great! If not, you need to get your own coverage. Without it, one hospital visit or unexpected health issue could easily put you in substantial debt. And everyone needs ongoing preventive health care, most especially musicians, who need to keep their bodies in top working order to perform at their best.

Freelance musicians often make do without health insurance, relying on free care programs at local hospitals and clinics. But many musicians are unaware that hospitals by law have to provide the uninsured only the most basic emergency care, not ongoing rehabilitation. This means that without insurance, they'll stabilize you, treat you until you're out of immediate danger, but that's about it, even if you have a serious, life-threatening illness.

For freelance musicians (and all self-employed people), there are various associations that offer members preferred group rate health insurance. Some of the music service organizations that offer health insurance rates are Chamber Music America (http://www.chamber-music.org), ASCAP (http://www.ascap.org), Early Music America (http://www.earlymusic.org), American Federation of Musicians (http://www.afm.org), Music Teachers National Association (http://www.mtna.org), and the Percussive Arts Society (http://www.pas.org). For more ideas, check the Artists' Health Insurance Resource Center at http://www.actorsfund.org/ahirc. In some cases, part-time jobs offer pro-rated benefits, making a not-so-hot salary into a very good deal!

■

Tips on Shopping for Health Insurance

Jack Garrity is an insurance broker who specializes in working with musicians and other independent contractors. The musicians' union in Boston regularly refers their members to Jack, and here's what he recommends for people who're looking for insurance on their own:

"Shopping (and that's the key word—shopping) for health insurance isn't brain surgery but does require some patience and organization. Listed below you'll find what I (try to) do with everyone who contacts me.

Do your homework. Get prices from three companies (if possible). You might start with major national Insurers—Aetna, Cigna and United. Or get quotes through any of the musicians' service organizations or associations. Compare the following nine items:

1. PCP Visits (Primary care physician)—how much per visit? What about for a specialist? Referrals needed?
2. Emergency Room (ER)—how much per admission?
3. Prescriptions (Rx)—co-pay for generics, name brands, or rare name brands?
4. Outpatient Surgery (OPS)—covered 100 percent? Or must a deductible be paid first?
5. Hospitalization—see OPS.
6. Maximum Payout—Is there a limit or cap per accident or policy? Mass. HMOs, for example, are unlimited.
7. Coverage Area—worldwide for emergencies/crisis care? What happens if you are injured outside of your resident state?
8. Network—are the doctors/hospitals acceptable to you?
9. Monthly premium—and, of course, how long is the rate fixed for?

See if you can reduce the monthly premium by dropping the Rx, if not needed, and taking a deductible/co-pay/you pay on the OPS/Hospitalization coverages.

Please note that health insurance is regulated on a state-by-state basis and so procedures, coverage, prices, and applications can vary widely. In Massachusetts, being a small business, for example, a self-employed musician, gets you 'business/commercial/group' rates that are much better than non-business rates. Ask if this is true in your state, too."

Jack @ Diamond Benefits
1-888-635-4402 (Mass. only)
1-781-477-9048 (outside Mass.)

5. *What about the money?* How much income do you actually need each month? To make good choices about work, you need to know how much you're *really* spending each month (not how much you *think* you're spending). If you haven't written out your detailed monthly expenses (chapter 10), it's not too late to do it now! I recommend you track your spending for at least three months, to calculate a reliable monthly average.

Thinking through the five issues above should help you in exploring and considering your work options. In the trial-and-error stage of day job exploration, you can tip the odds of success in your favor if you've thought through your priorities. The rest of this chapter details the two most popular categories of musicians' day jobs: teaching and arts administration.

Teaching Opportunities ■

For many musicians, teaching is a satisfying and rewarding complement to their performance work. At its best, teaching is challenging, creative, and gratifying.

There's a wide range of teaching opportunities, from private studio lessons, to teaching in public schools and private secondary schools, community music schools, colleges, conservatories, and working as teaching artists in residence in a variety of settings. Some musicians find they work particularly well with certain age groups or in master classes, or group lessons. Part of exploring to find your niche may involve sampling a variety of teaching experiences. Below are tips and details on a variety of opportunities.

Private Studio Teaching: Attracting Students through Referrals

The first type of teaching opportunity musicians typically seek is private teaching work and the first question they usually have is, how do I get students? The most efficient way to recruit students is through referrals from local band, orchestra, or choral directors. If you don't already have such contacts, you can research the schools in your area. Find the ones with strong music programs. Ask your colleagues and call the schools to inquire about their programs. Get the names and telephone numbers of the music directors by calling the school's administrative office. Then call the directors and introduce yourself with something like:

> "Hi, my name is Janet Smith. I'm a local violinist. I perform regularly with the ABC Chamber Orchestra, have a master's degree from XYZ School of Music, and am looking to add more private students to my studio. I've heard very good things about your program from parents in the neighborhood. I was hoping to set up a time to come in and meet you. It would be great to hear your students in rehearsal; I'd be happy to do a sectional or coach an ensemble and for you to get to know my teaching a bit, too!"

School music directors are far more likely to refer students to you if they've met you, observed your teaching, and like what they see. Mimi Butler is the author of *The Complete Guide to Running a Private Music Studio* and *The Complete Guide to Making More Money in the Private Music Studio*. She recommends carrying and using business cards everywhere, sending letters each May to local school music teachers about your summer studio, getting involved in local music camps and youth music ensembles, joining professional music organizations, and advertising in an extremely targeted way.

Home Studio or Not?

If you're planning to teach out of your home or apartment consider:

· Is your teaching space appropriately comfortable and professional?
· Is your place in a safe neighborhood and is parking or public transportation an issue?
· If you do use a portion of your home strictly for rehearsing and teaching, you can deduct a portion of your rent and expenses as a legitimate business expense. Consult a musicians' tax specialist to make sure you take all the appropriate deductions (see chapter 10).

An alternative to a home studio is to travel to students' homes, but travel time and scheduling complications usually make this a last resort option. As an alternative, there may be a church, school, or community center in the area where you could establish your private studio. Singers with weekly church jobs as choir section leaders or soloists can often arrange with their choir director to use a room at the church for teaching and rehearsing. And many public schools organize after-school lesson programs using local private lesson instructors. Check out your neighborhood and ask everyone in your network.

Have a Studio Policy

You're a professional, and probably want to be treated as such, so you need to represent your teaching as a *business*. To avoid the frustration of students frequently canceling lessons or forgetting to pay, you'll need a studio policy.

Having a written studio policy that clearly details a payment schedule and cancellation policy will save you many headaches. Private teachers often use monthly or six-week "semester" systems, with students paying in advance for each new block of lessons. And a typical cancellation policy requires two weeks' notice in order to reschedule a lesson. The teacher may schedule an extra week of make-up lessons every three months or so, with one make-up lesson offered to each student. When a parent and student come to meet you initially to discuss private study, that's the time to explain your studio policy and hand the parent a copy.

How Much Should You Charge?

You'll need to find out the going rate for lessons in your area. Ask other musicians and call local community music schools to find out their rates. You should charge an amount that's appropriate to the local rates and to your level of experience. In the Boston area, excellent young musicians with little teaching experience charge $30 per hour, whereas some members of the Boston Symphony Orchestra charge more than $150 per lesson.

How to Develop and Expand Your Skills as a Teacher

Most performers learn to teach by the seat of their pants, with little or no training in pedagogy, music education, or developmental psychology. Typically, performers blindly repeat the way *they* were taught. But not all your students will be like you were as a youngster. A narrow repertoire of teaching methods limits your ability to meet the varied learning styles and needs of your students. You can do better! Below are four ways to boost your abilities as a teacher.

Observe

Find the most experienced, creative, and successful music teachers in your area. Call, introduce yourself, and explain that you're a new teacher and are looking to gain more insights into effective teaching. Ask if you can observe them teach for several afternoons; people are generally flattered and willing to help. It's best to observe teachers working with a range of ages and abilities. And it's good to observe teachers working in a variety of teaching situations, from lessons, to coachings, to classroom situations, so that you can sample a range of options.

Look to see what each teacher focuses on with each student, and how the teacher tailors her or his remarks to each student's personality, learning style, stage of development, and mood that particular day. Most likely, the teachers you observe will spend some time with you afterwards, answering your questions and discussing their approaches to teaching.

Find a mentor

If you hit it off with any of the teachers you observe, you may be on your way to having a longer-term connection, to having a mentor. If the observation is very interesting, ask to continue. And later on, you might ask the teacher to observe *you* teaching a few of your own students, to get feedback. Eventually, a mentor may take you on as her or his teaching assistant. Mentors may refer students to you when their own schedules are full and they may ask you to do some substitute teaching. What's the potential payoff? Great experience on your résumé and references from respected teachers when you're applying for jobs.

Attend master classes

Take every opportunity to attend master classes so that you can observe a wide range of teaching methods and approaches. Is there a conference for your instrument or specialty area? To find out, do a search on the Web. Events such as the National Flute Association annual conference (http://www.nfaonline.org), the International Trombone Association (http://www.ita-web.org), and the annual American String Teachers Association conference (http://www.astaweb.com) often offer multiple master classes with world-class teachers, an incredible opportunity to see how superb teachers approach a range of student abilities and issues.

When observing someone else's teaching, ask yourself, what would *you* focus on with this student? How would you approach the issues? What would you say and what would you ask the student to try again?

Take a class

If you're out of school but live somewhere near a music school, find out it there are pedagogy courses or summer classes for music educators. Or at a university, you might take a course in developmental psychology or a general education course to find out more about how to deal with students at different ages. Some music schools offer specialized summer courses on specific music education methods, such as Kodaly, Orff, Suzuki, Dalcroze Eurhythmics, and Kindermusik. State Universities often have special summer programs of courses leading to Master's degrees in music education. Check http://www.MENC.org or http://www.music.org for more information.

Effective music teachers are constantly improving their skills and experimenting with new approaches. If you stay curious about teaching, you will continually seek out new solutions and your students will benefit. As you improve as a teacher, your reputation will grow and so will your income.

Music Teacher Resources

American Choral Director's Association: http://www.acdaonline.org
American String Teachers Association: http://www.astaweb.com
College Music Society: http://www.music.org
International Association of Jazz Educators: http://www.iaje.org
Kennedy Center's Arts Edge: http://www.artsedge.kennedy-center.org
Music Educators National Conference: http://www.menc.org
Music Teachers National Association: http://www.mtna.org
National Guild of Community Schools for the Arts: http://www.
    nationalguild.org
National Association of Teachers of Singing: http://www.nats.org

NEC Job Bulletin: http://www.newenglandconservatory.edu/career
Suzuki Association of the Americas, Inc.: http://www.suzukiassociation.org

◼

Community Music Schools

Community music schools are institutions that offer after-school, weekend, and evening music instruction to children and adults. These schools hire teachers to give private lessons, coach ensembles, and teach theory, ear training, composition, and other classes. Most instructors are hired part-time, and paid hourly rates with no benefits. In many areas, the majority of such teachers are paid $25–40 per hour. Parents pay tuition by the semester, and the school takes a cut to cover the costs of the facility, advertising, and managing the programs. The advantage for musicians in teaching at these schools is that the organization handles all the scheduling, billing, and provides the facilities. You can find listings of these schools at the National Guild of Community Schools for the Arts http://www.nationalguild.org.

Because many musicians are attracted to these jobs, community music schools often have their pick of qualified candidates experienced teachers with proven track records of success. These schools often do not advertise openings, so musicians apply directly to the schools, sending a cover letter and résumé. Having letters of recommendation from mentors can be advantageous to getting hired.

◼

Annie Fullard of the Cavani Quartet, in relating how her group balances performing and teaching, has described the Cavani as "equally committed to performing and teaching chamber music, as we feel one directly enhances and influences the other." In an article in *American String Teacher* magazine published in November 1998, Fullard says, "Teaching is one of the world's oldest art forms. The more you teach the more you learn—it's a very simple thing."

◼

Private Secondary Schools

These are college preparatory, parochial, and other specialized curriculum schools. Many such schools have music departments with lesson programs, ensembles, music theory classes, and more. Teachers at these schools do not need a particular education degree or teacher certification. Most music teachers at these schools work part-time and are paid an hourly rate for lessons in the $30 to $60 range. Classroom instructors are paid on a different scale on a per class basis. The full-time positions typically include non-music assignments as well. There are teacher placement companies such as Carney, Sandoe, and Associates (http://www.csa-teach.com) that help private school job seekers and employers connect. For listings of private schools in your area, search on the Web or consult the most recent *Peterson's Guide to Private Schools*.

Public Schools

Public school teachers can make good salaries, with excellent benefits and summers off. Starting salaries in the more affluent states are in the low $30,000 range, and salary increases are substantial as teachers gain experience and additional training. Maximum salaries can go to $70,000+. Because of the current shortage of teachers (especially in strings), the public schools hold substantial opportunities for musicians.

To explore this option, ask people in your network for contacts. Observe a class or rehearsal. Check out programs at various schools and for different grades. The teaching experience in public schools can be amazingly varied, depending on the size of the class, grade level, funding of the school, facilities, and the politics of the school's administration.

Public schools hire music teachers to direct band, orchestra, and chorus and to teach group lessons and general music classes. Teaching in the public schools demands abilities beyond musicianship skills. Public school teachers need to have effective teaching methods, understanding of child development stages and learning styles, classroom management skills, and the ability to create and implement lesson plans that meet the school's and the state's education requirements. These are all skills that can be developed through coursework, including evening and summer workshops.

To be hired by a public school, you must have teacher certification, a special license to teach in a particular state. Because of the shortage of teachers, many states have streamlined the certification process to make it easier for people to enter the profession. In Massachusetts, for example, certification is a three-stage process. To get provisional (initial) certification, all you need is a bachelor's degree in the subject you plan to teach, and to pass the state teacher's test, a general knowledge-base test. With provisional certification, you can be hired. Then, to be advanced beyond the probation period to better pay, teachers are required to get further training, additional coursework which can be done in summer courses and seminars. To check out the specifics for certification, contact your state's department of education. For job listings, a good place to check is the Music Educators National Conference, http://www.menc.org, and also your state department of education, as well as any specific school districts you may be targeting, and regional newspaper job listings.

College-level Teaching

College-level music teaching positions are highly competitive with many more qualified and experienced candidates than openings. According to the National Association of Schools of Music, there are roughly 8,500 full-time college level music teaching positions in the United States. One desirable job listing for a college level instrumental or vocal teaching position can yield 100+ qualified applicants. These teaching positions can be extremely varied. Musicians teach at community colleges, liberal arts colleges, and universities where music is an elective, as well as at universities and conservatories where students earn degrees in music.

At the college level, musicians teach private lessons, direct ensembles, and teach a huge range of required and elective courses, master classes, and seminars. Most full-time college level teaching positions involve more than teaching lessons. Typically, a faculty load will include ensemble coaching, master classes, and, depending on the number of studio lessons assigned, teaching one or more classes in pedagogy, music theory, or history.

Generally, the job listings for full-time positions at universities list "doctorate required" or "doctorate preferred." Search committees may consider candidates without the doctorate if they have extensive and successful college-level teaching experience or extensive professional performance experience. At conservatories and highly competitive schools of music, search committees seek artist-teachers with significant national or international reputations and the ability to recruit excellent students.

"Tenure track" jobs at universities are full-time positions with multiyear renewable contracts leading to tenure—guaranteed permanent employment. Candidates in these positions are hired as assistant professors, and if successful, they may, over a number of years, advance in salary and status to the position of associate professor, and finally to full professor with tenure. These types of jobs typically have starting salaries in the low $30,000 to $40,000 range, although the more well-funded schools sometimes compete to hire "star" faculty at much higher salaries.

■

Where to Find Listings for College-level Teaching

Chronicle of Higher Education: http://www.chronicle.com/jobs (search by field: music)

College Music Society's Music Vacancy Listings: http://www.music.org

NEC Job Bulletin: http://www.newenglandconservatory.edu/career subscription e-mail publication, twice monthly listings of teaching, performance, and arts administration openings, plus grants, audition, and competition info

The less competitive opportunities are the part-time positions at schools with smaller music programs. "Adjunct" and "lecturer" positions are part-time and often not well paid. At universities, these positions are often filled by people without doctorates. Working part-time at a college or university is an excellent opportunity to gain valuable experience, and therefore become more marketable for full-time positions at other institutions. Part-time university teaching work can also work well to complement performing activities.

Violist Kenneth Martinson is a member of the faculty resident quartet, the Julstrom, and an assistant professor at Western Illinois University. Formerly he was a member of the Rackham and the Artaria Quartets. Earlier in his career he took part, with the Rackham Quartet, in a Chamber Music America rural residency program with the quartet, living/teaching/performing in King City, California. In an article for Chamber Music America's education newsletter, "Flying Together" in February 2002, Kenneth described the effect of his early teaching experience on his later career: "Teaching 64 string instrument beginners certainly proved to be an immensely valuable experience for me. That year of teaching provided me with enough patience to deal with any student, at any level, for the rest of my life! The experience also forced me to re-evaluate every aspect of my technique from scratch . . . because of my residency experience, I have a rare combination to offer my students: highly developed performing skills and the knowledge I've gained in music education."

Arts Administration Opportunities ■

Beyond teaching, arts administration is the next most popular type of day job for musicians. The term arts administration is a kind of global description for a wide range of "behind the scenes" work in the arts. This work is sometimes referred to as arts management (not to be confused with *artist* management). The term "arts administration" is used most often to describe jobs in the nonprofit sector, administrative jobs with nonprofit organizations such as schools, orchestras, opera companies, festivals, and so on. But the term can also cover a wide range of administrative work in the for-profit sector: with the recording industry, music publishing, and artist management firms.

Arts administrators are the people who make things happen: running concert series, festivals, record labels, arts foundations, and music schools, handling publicity, marketing, fundraising, programming, and more. Many musicians work part- or full-time jobs in arts administration because they want to be part of a larger effort—beyond their work as performers—to help the arts grow in their communities. Many musicians value the opportunity to use the full range of their skills and abilities in service of a worthwhile cause.

Types of Organizations with Arts Administration Job Opportunities

- Performing organizations (symphony orchestras, opera companies, choruses, etc.)
- Presenting organizations (concert series, festivals, venues)
- Arts service organizations (i.e., ASCAP, BMI, American Music Center, Chamber Music America, Opera America, etc.)
- Foundations (state and regional arts councils; private and corporate foundations)
- Arts education institutions (community music schools, conservatories, college music departments, etc.)
- Arts research/consulting organizations (groups that work on audience development, marketing the arts, assessing arts education programs, consulting on management issues for arts organizations)
- Music publishing companies (Belwin Mills, Schirmer, Hal Leonard, Carl Fischer, etc.)
- Radio/TV (includes arts programming and research work)
- Recording industry (major and indie labels)
- Music technology (work in website development, music software development)

Typical entry-level positions in these organizations are administrative assistant jobs: project assistant work, handling correspondence, data entry, database management—the basic office work needed to run an organization. With such jobs, musicians develop office skills and gain valuable experience which can then lead to more advanced, better paying work either at the same organization or others.

The salary range for arts administration jobs is quite wide. Entry-level full-time positions can start at the low $20,000 range. As people develop skills and experience, better pay is readily available. At the high end, top executives at leading symphony orchestras, record labels, and major service organizations routinely earn six-figure incomes.

What Can Come from a Day Job?

Just out of college, French hornist Jean Rife took a clerical position in the textiles department at the Smithsonian in Washington, DC. The important thing about that job was that it was down the hall from the musical instrument collection. Jean became friends with the department members, played their horns, and when they started an early music ensemble, she was right there. Thus began a career-long interest in early music and in playing the natural horn.

Later, Jean moved to Boston, taught part-time in the Weston Public Schools, and took a part-time job at the MIT music library. There, she became friends with the librarian and with the violist Marcus Thompson, who would stop by to talk. During one of their discussions, he mentioned that the woodwind chamber music coach he had hired couldn't come that semester after all. Jean was there to say, "I'll do it!" Marcus hired her, and she's taught at MIT ever since.

These days, Jean's career package includes freelancing, teaching chamber music and horn at MIT, New England Conservatory, and at the Longy School of Music. What makes Jean's career especially interesting is that she is also a yoga instructor and has combined yoga practice with her horn teaching and coaching. Jean first found that yoga was incredibly helpful in her own playing and then, as she incorporated it in her teaching, found it was also a great learning tool for other musicians. In trying to balance her busy life, Jean says, "It requires being clear about your priorities, and these have shifted over the years. I used to do a lot more freelancing but just now, my sixteen year old daughter is my first priority." How does the yoga figure in? Jean says, "Yoga teaches you to be in the present moment so you are always aware that you have a chance to choose." And choosing your priorities and how to live is essential to living well.

Arts Administration Skills

For entry-level arts administration jobs, employers seek candidates with the following:

- Communication skills: verbal and written
- Computer skills
- Ability to handle multiple projects and deadlines
- Organizational skills

- Ability to work well in a team
- Knowledge of the arts

In addition, depending on the organization and the specific job opening, other specialized skills, and experience may be required, such as publicity or fund-raising. To explore arts administration opportunities, check for job postings on the websites of any of the arts organizations in your area. Your state arts agency may provide lists and contacts for these organizations. You can then arrange for informational interviews (described in chapter 2) with staff members at these organizations.

Arts Administration Job Listings

American Symphony Orchestra League: http://www.symphony.org

ArtJob: http://www.artjob.org

Arts Presenters: http://www.artpresenters.org

ArtSearch, publication of the Theatre Communications Group: http://www.tcg.org/frames/artsearch/fs_artsearch.htm

NEC Job Bulletin: http://www.newenglandconservatory.edu/career

New York Foundation for the Arts: http://www.NYFA.org

Check your state arts agency's website (see the appendix) and check your alma mater; many music schools offer job listing publications and online listings

Hornist Debbie Engel has played with the Delaware Symphony Orchestra and with OperaDelaware for the past twenty-three years. Her career "package" also includes working as the orchestra's and opera company's librarian and director of education, overseeing an extensive community outreach program. Plus, she has three teenage children! How does she manage all this? Ms. Engel points out four factors: her supportive family, extreme organization, her faith, and her positive attitude.

The Big Picture

The healthiest approach is to look at the whole of your life as a journey. Life is more than a series of achievements, a tally of accomplishments. As my friend and colleague Derek Mithaug, director of career development at the Juilliard School puts it, "You can avoid years of frustration by focusing now on how to create a journey that will allow you to combine all of your talents and interests. People who create their own paths become the directors of their careers and lives; they are in a position to choose the types of paths they wish to travel."

So, whether you're exploring a day job just to pay bills, or to gain specific know-how, you need to know your priorities, explore your options, and keep an open mind. Talk to lots of people; gather many ideas. And keep in mind that we can't always see how the work we do today will benefit us in the future. Enjoy the journey!

Opportunities in the Music Industry ■

Note: this information was compiled by Mark Broschinsky for the New England Conservatory Career Services Center in 2003. Sources used were MENC (the Music Educators National Conference), *Career Opportunities in the Music Industry*, fourth edition, by Shelly Field; and job listings from the 2003 NEC Job Bulletin. The information is intended to show a range of work opportunities, special training required, and representative salary info. Salaries for various positions can vary widely depending on such factors as level of expertise and geographic location.

Job Title	Salary	Additional Information
Music education		
Private studio	$30–$100/hour teacher	Lesson fee should reflect amount of teaching experience. Beginning teachers in the Boston area frequently charge $30/hr.
Public school teacher (elementary & secondary music teachers)	$20,675–$60,000/year; $30,719/year—average salary for new teachers	Teaching in a public school requires state certification. Schools are supported largely by property taxes so schools in wealthier communities are able to pay more.
Assistant professor (full-time, tenure track position)	$25,000–$50,000/year	Salary depends on the size of the institution, budget, & reputation of the teacher
Instrumental performance		
Orchestral musician	$28,000–$100,000/ year; example: $29,360/ year—Alabama Sym-	This salary range represents a full time orchestra with a season of approximately 40 weeks.

(continued)

Job Title	Salary	Additional Information
	phony (starting salary); $99,580/year—Boston Symphony Orchestra (starting salary)	Other per service orchestras and orchestras with shorter seasons would have a lower salary.
Community orchestras	$0–$70/service; example: $60/rehearsal, $80/performance, Concord Symphony Orchestra (MA)	The salary range reflects or chestras that rely on volunteers and "ringers." Some orchestras offer a scholarship instead of paying for each service.
Military bands & orchestras	$21,000–$77,000/year	Pay scale depends on rank, location, and organization. Some bands also have student loan repayment programs.
Club gigs in Boston and New York (non-classical)	$25–$200/person example: $50/person for 2 sets—Wally's Café; $100–$200/person —Ryles Jazz Club	Depends on reputation of band, how many people attend, and the size of the club.
Church organist/ pianist	$50/service—$50,000/ year	This salary depends on number of hours worked (hours vary from 10-40 hrs/week), size of church congregation, & level of education.

Vocal performance

| Church choir – section leader/soloist | $25–$100/service | Section leaders are generally paid soloist positions whereas members of the choir are generally volunteers. |
| Concert or opera chorus member | $12+/rehearsal; $100+/ performance | Auditions are required for these positions. Résumé and head shot are required for opera company auditions. |

Conducting

| Choir, orchestra or opera conductor | $15,000–$275,000/ year | The higher salaries indicate a position with a major symphony or opera house and a season of approximately 40 weeks. The lower end of the scale represents a part-time position with a smaller organization. |

(continued)

Job Title	Salary	Additional Information
Church choir director	$5,000–$70,000/year	This salary depends on number of hours worked (hours vary from 10-40 hrs/week), size of church congregation, & level of education.

Television, radio, & movie recording (studio work)

Studio musician	Union scale	This type of employment is principally found in Los Angeles, New York, and Nashville. The pay rate varies according to the situation. Generally there is an hourly fee ($50/hour). The fee may be higher if you double or are the group leader.

Composing

Commercial jingle composer	$300–$50,000/ commercial	
TV show composer	$1,000–$5,000/ 30-minute episode	
Film score composer	$2,000–$200,000/film	
Competition prizes	Prizes range from $150–$15,000	International competitions, which attract high profile participants, award the largest prizes.

Instrument making and repair

Instrument maker	$15,000–$65,000/year	Training or apprenticeship programs are required. Pay scale depends on the quality of the work, reputation, and amount of experience
Instrument repair technician	$9–$55/hour	
Piano tuner	$15–$60/hour	

Music communications

Publisher or editor of music books or periodicals	$24,000–$100,000/ year	These positions require strong writing skills. People get started working as interns or assistants
Music journalist	$20,000–$150,000/ year	
Public relations specialist	$21,000–$141,000/ year	

(continued)

Job Title	Salary	Additional Information
Music librarianship		
College, university, conservatory, public library, or orchestra librarian	$18,000–$45,000/year	Some institutions require a graduate library degree.
Music therapy		
Hospitals, psychiatric facility	$16,000–$35,000/year	Requires a degree in music therapy and an internship.
Special education facility	$22,000–$42,000/year	
Clinic for disabled children	$15,000–$70,000/year	
Mental health center	$21,000–$65,000/year	
Nursing home	$17,000–$65,000/year	
Correctional facility	$23,000–$58,000/year	
Private practice	$18,000–$77,000/year	
Arts administration		
Administrative assistant	example: $30,039 — Michigan State University, Department of Music	Associate's degree and 6 months to a year of experience are required. Computer skills are necessary and experience is preferred.
Development associate	example: $34,000 — Lincoln Center for the Performing Arts, NY	Previous experience working with MS Office and database management is required.
Public relations	$30,000–$75,000 example: $45,000–$60,000—Pasadena Symphony	This position is responsible for PR and marketing. 5 years of experience, strong communication skills, and computer skills are required. Salary is based on applicant's qualifications & experience.
Executive Director	$20,000–$250,000 example: $56,000–$75,000—Greater Lansing Symphony Orchestra	Bachelor's degree is required and a master's degree is preferred. Previous experience is required. Salary is based on applicant's qualifications & experience.

■ **Suggestions for Moving Ahead** ■

1. Write out the types of work you've considered doing to support your performing career.
2. Brainstorm by listing other work possibilities you've been curious about. Where can you get more information about these options? (Possibilities: use your network, your school's career center, and alumni office.)
3. What interests or passions would you like to investigate for possible supplemental work opportunities? (Do you like to cook, garden, mentor kids, browse in bookstores, research, etc.?)
4. Make a list of the skills and experience you have now that might lead to supplemental work.
5. Find some role models! Do you know musicians who have "portfolio" careers? Have you talked with them in detail about how they put their work life together? Invite people out for lunch so you can pick their brain about these issues. It's fascinating and inspiring to hear musicians talk about how they got started.

Appendix:
More Resources, Please!

Recommended Resources, Books, Websites, and Organizations Listed by Topic Area ■

Note: For a more extensive list of national, regional, and local arts organizations by topic areas, see the Encyclopedia of Associations *available at most public libraries.*

Career Guides (General)

Do What You Are. Tieger, Paul D., and Barbara Barron-Tieger. Boston: Little, Brown and Co., 1995.

I Could Do Anything If I Only Knew What It Was. Sher, Barbara. New York: Delacorte Press, 1994.

Transitions: Making Sense of Life's Changes. Bridges, William. Massachusetts: Addison-Wesley Publishing Co., 1980.

What Should I Do With My Life? Bronson, Po. New York: Random House, 2002.

Working Identity: Unconventional Strategies for Reinventing Your Career. Ibarra, Herminia. Boston: Harvard Business School Press, 2003.

Competition Information

Concert Artists Guild's Guide to Competitions. New York: Concert Artists Guild, published annually.

Musical America; International Directory of the Performing Arts. New York: K-III Directory Group, published annually and available on CD-ROM.

World Federation of International Competitions: http://www.wfimc.org

Competitions That Lead to Pre-Professional Management

Astral Artistic Services: http://www.astralartisticservices.org
Concert Artists Guild: http://www.concertartists.org
The Pro Musicis International Award: promusicis@aol.com or call 212-787-0993
Young Concert Artists: http://www.yca.org

Directories

Musical America International Directory of the Performing Arts, annual directory, available in print and on CD-ROM

Stearn Directory, annual directory available in print and on CD-ROM

MOD: Music, Opera and Dance annual directory, available in print and on CD-ROM

PAYE: Performing Arts Yearbook for Europe, annual directory, available in print and on CD-ROM

Chamber Music America Directory, New York: Chamber Music America, annual. (Lists professional Groups and services for chamber ensembles; available with membership to CMA.)

American Symphony Orchestra League Directory, annual directory available with membership (for researching soloist opportunities)

Directory of Music Faculties in Colleges and Universities in the United States and Canada (for researching residency, master class, and concerts at colleges)

Festival Information

Artist colonies/retreats: http://www.artistcommunities.org

Festival Finder: http://www.festivalfinder.com

Music, Opera, and Dance in North America. Arts Publishing International Ltd, published annually.

Musical America; International Directory of the Performing Arts. New York: K-III Directory Group, published annually.

Finances

Artists Community Federal Credit Union: http://www.artistscommunityfcu.org
    Loans for arts projects, lines of credit, no-fee savings accounts and IRAs

The National Association for the Self-Employed: http://www.nase.org

The Function of Music

The Everyday Work of Art. Booth, Eric, Naperville, IL: Sourcebooks, Inc., 1999.

Musicking; the Meanings of Performing and Listening. Small, Christopher. Hanover, NH: University Press of New England, Wesleyan University, 1998.

Insurance Issues

Artists' Health Insurance Resource Center: http://www.actorsfund.org/ahirc

Check health insurance rates for members with service organizations such as:

    American Federation of Musicians: http://www.afm.org
    ASCAP: http://www.ascap.org
    Chamber Music America: http://www.chamber-music.org
    Early Music America: http://www.earlymusic.org
    Music Teachers National Association: http://www.mtna.org
    Percussive Arts Society: http://www.pas.org
    Clarion Associates, Inc., musical instrument insurance: http://www.clarionins.com

Job Listings and Audition Listings

Chronicle of Higher Education: http://www.chronicle.com/jobs (search by field: music)
College Music Society's Music Vacancy Listings: http://www.music.org
NEC Job Bulletin: http://www.newenglandconservatory.edu/career
New York Foundation for the Arts: http://www.NYFA.org
Musical Chairs, for overseas audition listings: http://www.musicalchairs.info
International Musician (the union paper): American Federation of Musicians: http://www.afm.org

For Arts Administration Work

American Symphony Orchestra League: http://www.symphony.org
ArtJob: http://www.artjob.org
Arts Presenters: http://www.artpresenters.org
ArtSearch, publication of the Theatre Communications Group: http://www.tcg.org/frames/artsearch/fs_artsearch.htm
NEC Job Bulletin: http://www.newenglandconservatory.edu/career
New York Foundation for the Arts: http://www.NYFA.org
Also: Check your state arts agency's website (see later section in appendix)
  Check your alma mater; many music schools offer job listing publications/online listings

Legal Issues

Volunteer Lawyers for the Arts: http://www.vlany.org
U.S. Copyright Office Library of Congress: http://www.1cweb.loc.gov/copyright

Music Career Guides

Booking and Tour Management. Shagan, Rena. New York: Allworth Press, 1996.
Career Opportunities in the Music Industry. Field, Shelly. New York: Facts on File, 2000.
Composing a Life. Bateson, Mary Catherine. New York: Penguine Plume, 1989.
How to Be Your Own Booking Agent. Goldstein, Jeri. Charlottesville, VA: New Music Times, Inc., 1998
Making Music in Looking Glass Land; A Guide to Survival and Business Skills for the Classical Performer. Highstein, Ellen. Fourth edition, New York: CAG, 2003.
The Performing Artists Handbook. Papolos, Janice. Ohio: Writer's Digest Books, 1984. (out of print).
The Self-Promoting Musician. Spellman, Peter. Boston: Berklee Press, 2000.
Your Own Way in Music. Uscher, Nancy. New York: St. Martin's Press, 1990.

Music Career Advice Online

http://www.newenglandconservatory.edu/career: Click on Carlotta for advice by e-mail
http://www.MusicBizAcademy.com: for straight-talking advice on online self-promotion, recording, etc.
http://www.knab.com: from music business consultant Chris Knab, great info on self-promotion, CDs, radioplay, etc.

http://www.mbsolutions.com: Music Business Solutions for resources, links, articles, newsletter, advice

http://www.menc.org: MENC the National Association for Music Education for careers in music: basic descriptive information on a wide range of professional options, plus job openings for music educators.

New Music Organizations

American Composers Forum: http://www.composersforum.org
American Music Center: http://www.amc.net
Meet the Composer: http://www.meetthecomposer.org
U.S. Copyright Office Library of Congress: http://www.1cweb.loc.gov/copyright

Composers' Rights Organizations

American Society of Composers, Authors & Publishers (ASCAP):
    http://www.ascap.com
Broadcast Music, Inc. (BMI): http://www.bmi.com
SESAC, Inc.: http://www.sesac.com

Orchestral Opportunities

American Symphony Orchestra League: http://www.symphony.org
Conductors Guild: http://www.conductorsguild.org
International Musician (the union paper): American Federation of Musicians:
    http://www.afm.org
Musical Chairs, for overseas audition listings: http://www.musicalchairs.info

Performance Health

Musicians and Injuries site: http://www.eeshop.unl.edu/music.html
Playing (Less) Hurt; An Injury Prevention Guide for Musicians. Horvath, Janet.
    Kearney, NE: Morris Press, 2003
You Are Your Instrument. Lieberman, Julie Lyonn. New York: Huiksi Music, 1991

Presenter Information

Association of Performing Arts Presenters: http://www.artspresenters.org
Chamber Music America: http://www.chamber-music.org
Early Music America: http://www.earlymusic.org
International Society of the Performing Arts (ISPA): http://www.ispa.org
National Assoc. of Performing Arts Managers of America, NAPAMA: http://www.
    NAPAMA.org

Regional booking conferences

Arts Midwest Conference: http://www.artsmidwest.org
Performing Arts Exchange: http://www.southarts.org/pae.htm
Western Arts Alliance Conference: http://www.westarts.org

Publications with CD Reviews

Here are some print and online publications that regularly offer CD reviews. See also *Musical America* and the Indiana University School of Music library's site: World-wide Internet Music resources: http://www.music.indiana.edu/music_resources/journals.html#C. Please note: editors change jobs, offices move, publications change focus. Check first to get all the current information before sending a CD for review.

Andante
56 West 22nd Street
12th floor
New York, NY 10010
(212) 366-9232
http://www.andante.com

American Record Guide
4412 Braddock St
Cincinnati, OH 45204
(888) 658-1907

American String Teachers
ASTA Reviews Editor
4153 Chain Bridge Rd.
Fairfax. VA 22030
http://www.astaweb.com
Quarterly

Choral Journal
American Choral Directors Association
PO Box 6310
Lawton, OK 73506
(580) 355-8161
http://www.acdaonline.org
Monthly

Cello Heaven
Christine Liu
Methodist International Centre
81-103 Euston Street, London NW1 2EZ,
    United Kingdom
deepbluecello@musician.org

The Clarinet
William Nichols, Audio Review Editor
School of Music
Univ. of Louisiana at Monroe
Monroe, LA 71209-0250
wnichols@ulm.edu
http://www.clarinet.org
Bimonthly

Classical Guitar
Tim Panting
1 & 2 Vance Court
Trans Britannia Enterprise Park
Blaydon on Tyne NE21 5NH
United Kingdom
+44 (0) 191 414 9001
Monthly

Classics Today
www.ClassicsToday.com includes extensive CD review coverage

Clavier
(708) 941-2030
Monthly except June-August

Coda Magazine
Stuart Broomer, Coda
161 Frederick Street
Toronto, ON, CA
M5A 4P3
Double Bassist quarterly
http://www.doublebassist.com

Early Music America
Craig Zeichner
Early Music America, Inc.
2366 Eastlake Ave. East #429
Seattle, WA 98102-3399
Quarterly

Early Music Today
http://www.rhinegold.co.uk
44 (0)20 7333 1720

Fanfare Magazine
PO Box 17
Tanafly, NJ 07670
(201) 567-3908
www.fanfaremag.com
Bi-monthly

La Folia
editor@lafolia.com
http://www.lafolia.com

Flute Talk Magazine
200 Northfield Rd.
Northfield, IL 60093
(847) 446-5000
http://www.flutetalkmagazine.com
Monthly (except summer)

Goldberg Magazine
Ediciones Goldberg, s.l.
Plaza Obispo Irurita,
2 - Of. D
31011 - Pamplona
(Navarra-SPAIN)
N.I.F.: B-31599715
(+34) 948 25 03 72
www.goldberg-magazine.com

Gramophone
http://www.gramophone.co.uk
Monthly

International Piano Quarterly
Orpheus Publications Ltd
SMG Magazines Ltd
3 Waterhouse Square
138-142 Holborn
London
EC1N 2NY
UK
44 (0) 181 863-2020
http://www.pianomagazine.com
http://www.classicalmusicworld.com

International Record Review
1 Haven Green
London W5 2UU
Great Britain
44 (0)20 8810 9050
info@recordreview.co.uk

International Trombone Journal
Ed Bahr
1428 Memorial Dr.
Boyle, MS 38730
ebahr@deltastate.edu
Quarterly

International Trumpet Guild Journal
Elisa Koehler
Goucher College Music Dept.
1021 Dulaney Valley Rd.
Baltimore, MD 21204
(410) 337-6293
cdreviews@trumpetguild.org
Quarterly

*International Tuba and Euphonium
    Association Journal*
18880 N. 94th Place
Scottsdale, AZ 85255 USA
(520) 206-6826
newmaterials@iteaonline.org

Keyboard Magazine
(408) 446-1105
Monthly

Music Web
http://www.musicweb.uk.net

Musical America
888-215-6084
info@musicalamerica.com
http://www.musicalamerica.com

Musical Opinion
Published in the UK Quarterly
http://www.musicalopinion.com

New Music Box
American Music Center
30 West 26th Street
Suite 1001
New York, NY 10010
http://www.newmusicbox.com

Piano and Keyboard
(415) 458-8672
Monthly

Saxophone Journal
(508) 473-2228
Bimonthly

Sequenza 21
http://www.sequenza21.com

Soundboard
James Reid

School of Music
University of Idaho
Moscow, ID 83844
jreid@uidaho.edu
Quarterly

The Strad
www.thestrad.com
monthly

Strings
(415) 485-6946
editors@stringletter.com
http://www.stringsmagazine.com
Bimonthly

Tempo
PO Box 171
Herne Bay CT6 6WD
Quarterly

Specific Jazz Publications

Cadence
Cadence Building
Redwood, NY 13769-3104
(315) 287-2852
Monthly

Coda
Box 1002, Stn. "0"
Toronto, Ontario, Canada
M4A 2N4
(416) 593-7230
Bimonthly

Downbeat Magazine
180 W. Park Avenue
Elmhurst, IL 60126
Monthly

Jazz Journal International
1-5 Clerkenwell Rd.
London EC1M 5PA
Tel 0171-608 1348/1362
Monthly

Jazz Times
8737 Colesville Rd, 5th
Silver Springs, MD 20910-3921
(301) 588-4114
Monthly

Jazz Education Journal
Publication for the International Association of Jazz Educators
PO Box 724
Manhattan, KS 66505
(785) 776-8744
Monthly

Jazziz
3620 NW 43rd St.
Gainesville, FL 32606-8103
(352) 375-3705
Monthly

Publicity and Marketing Issues

Getting Radio Airplay. Hustwit, Gary. San Diego, CA: Rockpress Publishing, 1994.
The Musician's Internet; On-line Strategies for Success in the Music Industry. Spellman, Peter. Boston: Berklee Press, 2002
The Self-Promoting Musician. Spellman, Peter. Boston: Berklee Press, 2000.
Six Steps to Free Publicity. Yudkin, Marcia. New York: Plume, 1994.
Words That Sell. Bayan, Richard. New York: McGraw-Hill Trade, 1987.

Recording Issues

How to Make and Sell Your Own Recording, 5th ed. Rapaport, Diane Sward. Englewood Cliffs, NJ: Prentice Hall, 1999.
The Musician's Guide to Making and Selling Your Own CDs & Cassettes. Stanfield, Jana. Cincinnati, OH: Writer's Digest Books, 1997.

Tim Sweeney's Guide to Releasing Independent Records. Sweeney, Tim and Mark Geller. Torrance, CA: Self-Published, 1996.

U.S. Copyright Office Library of Congress: http://www.1cweb.loc.gov/copyright

Residency Work

Artists in the Community; Training Artists to Work in Alternative Settings. Published by Americans for the Arts, Washington, DC: 1996.

The Everyday Work of Art. Booth, Eric, published by Sourcebooks, Inc., 1999.

Giving Cues; Recommended Guidelines for Writing and Designing Performance Materials for Young People. Carr, John, and Silverstein, Lynne, published by the Kennedy Center, 1998.

How to Make Money Performing in Schools. Heflick, David, Orient, WA: Silcox Productions, 1996.

"Resuscitating Art Music" article by John Steinmetz, downloadable at: http://www .mumb.com/artx2.html

Journals

Teaching Artist Journal, Eric Booth editor, 800-926-6579, published by Lawrence Erlbaum Associates: http://www.erlbaum.com

Learning Through Music, produced by the Music-in-Education National Consortium, download articles on residency work: http://www.nec-musicined.org

Singers

American Choral Director's Association: http://www.acdaonline.org

"Aria Ready" The Business of Singing. Kirkpatrick, Carol. Leyerle Publications, 2003.

Early Music America: http://www.earlymusic.org

Backstage, publication for Broadway/Musical theatre work: http://www.Backstage.com

Choral Net, online resource center: http://www.choralnet.com

Chorus America, networking resource: http://www.chorusamerica.org

Classical Singer, magazine/Website, career info: http://www.classicalsinger.com

National Association of Teachers of Singing: http://www.nats.org

Opera America, service organization, publications, workshops: http://www. operaam.org

Opera News magazine, http://www.operanews.com

Stage Presence and Performance Issues

Audition Success. Greene, Don, Ph.D. New York: ProMind Music, 1998

You Are Your Instrument. Lieberman, Julie Lyonn. New York: Huiksi Music, 1991

Performance Success. Greene, Don, Ph.D. New York: Routlidge, 2002

The Relaxation Response. Benson, Herbert, M.D. New York: HarperTorch, Reissue edition, 2000.

Stage Presence from Head to Toe. Hagberg, Karen. Oxford: Scarecrow Press, 2003.

Teaching

Everyone's Guide to Job Searching in Private Schools. Boggess, Laurence. Indiana: Ryanna Books, 1992.

How to Get Your Child to Practice . . . Without Resorting to Violence. Richards, Cynthia V. Provo, UT: Advance Publications, 1985.
Making Money Performing in Schools. Heflick, David. Orient, WA: Silcox Productions, 1996.

Music Teacher Organizations

American Choral Director's Association: http://www.acdaonline.org
American String Teachers Association: http://www.astaweb.com
College Music Society: http://www.music.org
International Association of Jazz Educators: http://www.iaje.org
Kennedy Center's Arts Edge: http://www.artsedge.kennedy-center.org
Music Educators National Conference: http://www.menc.org
Music Teachers National Association: http://www.mtna.org
National Guild of Community Schools for the Arts: http://www.nationalguild.org
National Association of Teachers of Singing: http://www.nats.org
Suzuki Association of the Americas, Inc.: http://www.suzukiassociation.org

Unions

Actors' Equity Association (AKA: Equity): http://www.actorsequity.org
American Guild of Musical Artists (vocalists): http://www.musicalartists.org
American Federation of Musicians (large union, primarily instrumentalists): http://www.afm.org
American Federation of Television & Radio Artists, AFL-CIO: http://www.aftra.org
Screen Actors Guild (SAG): http://www.newsag.org

Work Options

Jobs in Arts & Media Management. Langley, Stephen and James Abruzzo. New York: American Council for the Arts, 1990.
Career Opportunities in the Music Industry. Field, Shelly. New York: Facts on File, 2000.
Survival Jobs; 154 ways to make money while pursuing your dreams. Jacobson, Deborah. New York: Broadway Books, 1998.

Funding Resources

The Foundation Center: http://www.fdncenter.org

Headquarters
79 Fifth Avenue/16th Street
New York, NY 10003-3076
Tel: (212) 620-4230 or (800) 424-9836
Fax: (212) 807-3677

Field Offices

Atlanta
50 Hurt Plaza, Suite 150
Atlanta, GA 30303-2914

404-880-0094

Atlanta Library home page: http://www.fdncenter.org/atlanta

Cleveland
1422 Euclid Avenue, Suite 1600
Cleveland, OH 44115-2001
216-861-1934
Cleveland Library home page: http://www.fdncenter.org/cleveland

San Francisco
312 Sutter Street, Suite 606
San Francisco, CA 94108-4314
415-397-0902
San Francisco Library home page: http://www.fdncenter.org/sanfrancisco

Washington, D.C.
1627 K Street, NW, Third Floor
Washington, DC 20006-1708
202-331-1400
Washington, D.C., Library home page: http://www.fdncenter.org/washington

Cooperating Collections

Cooperating Collections are free funding information centers in libraries, community
foundations, and other nonprofit resource centers throughout the United States that
provide a core collection of Foundation Center publications and a variety of supple-
mentary materials and services in areas useful to grantseekers. Find a Cooperating
Collection near you at http://www.fdncenter.org/collections
Also: The Grantsmanship Center: http://www.tgci.com
Helpful articles and links, publications, classes and training programs available
nationally

Funding Sources on the Web

Arts Grants Opportunities: http://www.booksatoz.com
Arts International: http://www. ArtsInternational.org
Government Agencies: http://www.galaxy.einet.net/galaxy/government.html
National Endowment for the Arts: http://www.arts.endow.gov
National Endowment for the Humanities: http://www.neh.gov
New York Foundation for the Arts: http://www.nyfa.org
University of Washington's List:
http://www.webr.u.washington.edu/~gfis/resources.html

Regional Arts Organizations

These organizations offer regional opportunities for touring, various grants, and technical assistance.

Arts Midwest   612/341-0755
2908 Hennepin Avenue, Suite 200   http://www.artsmidwest.org
Minneapolis, MN 55408-1954   general@artsmidwest.org

Mid-America Arts Alliance
912 Baltimore Avenue, Suite 700
Kansas City, MO 64105
816/421-1388
info@maaa.org
http://www.maaa.org

Mid Atlantic Arts Foundation
201 North Charles Street, #401
Baltimore, MD 21202
410/539-6656
maaf@midatlanticarts.org
http://www.midatlanticarts.org

New England Foundation for the Arts
266 Summer Street, 2nd Floor
Boston, MA 02210

617/951-0010
info@nefa.org
http://www.nefa.org

Southern Arts Federation
1800 Peachtree Street, Suite 808
Atlanta, GA 30309
404/874-7244
saf@southarts.org
http://www.southarts.org

Western States Arts Federation
1743 Wazee Street, suite 300
Denver, CO 80202
303/629-1166
staff@westaf.org
http://www.westaf.org

State Arts Councils/Agencies

These agencies are state funded and provide a range of assistance, grants, and information to residents. Keep in mind that programs change and necessarily reflect a state's economic health and the budget allocated by the legislature.

Alabama State Council on the Arts
334/242-4076
staff@arts.state.al.us
http://www.arts.state.al.us

Alaska State Council on the Arts
907/269-6610
asca@alaska.net

Arizona Commission on the Arts
602/255-5882
general@ArizonaArts.org
http://www.ArizonaArts.org

Arkansas Arts Council
501/324-9766
info@dah.state.ar.us
http://www.arkansasarts.com

California Arts Council
916/322-6555
cac@cwo.com
http://www.cac.ca.gov

Colorado Council on the Arts
303/894-2617
coloarts@artswire.org
http://www.coloarts.state.co.us

Connecticut Commission on the Arts
860/566-4770
http://www.ctarts.org

Delaware Division of the Arts
302/577-8278 (from New Castle County)
302/739-5304 (from Kent or Sussex
    Counties)
delarts@artswire.org
http://www.artsdel.org

*District of Columbia Commission on the
    Arts & Humanities*
202/724-5613
dcarts@dc.gov
http://www.dcarts.dc.gov

Florida Division of Cultural Affairs
850/487-2980
info@florida-arts.org
http://www.florida-arts.org

Georgia Council for the Arts
404/685-2787
gaarts@gaarts.org
http://www.gaarts.org

*Hawaii State Foundation on Culture &
the Arts*
808/586-0300
sfca@sfca.state.hi.us
http://www.hawaii.gov/sfca/

Idaho Commission on the Arts
208/334-2119
idarts@artswire.org
http://www.state.id.us/arts/

Illinois Arts Council
312/814-6750
info@arts.state.il.us
http://www.state.il.us/agency/iac/

Indiana Arts Commission
317/232-1268
inarts@aol.com
http://www.IN.gov/arts/

Iowa Arts Council
515/281-4451
http://www.culturalaffairs.org/iac/

Kansas Arts Commission
785/296-3335
KAC@arts.state.ks.us
http://www.arts.state.ks.us

Kentucky Arts Council
502-564-3757
kyarts@mail.state.ky.us
http://www.kyarts.org

*Division of the Arts, Louisiana Dept. of
Culture, Recreation, & Tourism*
225/342-8180
arts@crt.state.la.us
http://www.crt.state.la.us/arts

Maine Arts Commission
207/287-2724
mac.info@maine.gov
http://www.mainearts.com

Maryland State Arts Council
410/767-6555
marylandstateartscouncil@msac.org
http://www.msac.org

Massachusetts Cultural Council
617/727-3668
web@art.state.ma.us
http://www.massculturalcouncil.org

*Michigan Council for Arts and Cultural
Affairs*
517/241-4011
artsinfo@michigan.gov
http://www.michigan.gov/hal

Minnesota State Arts Board
651/215-1600
msab@tc.umn.edu
http://www.arts.state.mn.us

Mississippi Arts Commission
601/359-6030
http://www.arts.state.ms.us

Missouri Arts Council
314/340-6845
moarts@mail.state.mo.us
http://www.missouriartscouncil.org

Montana Arts Council
406/444-6430
mac@state.mt.us
http://www.art.state.mt.us

Nebraska Arts Council
402/595-2122
nacart@synergy.net
http://www.nebraskaartscouncil.org

Nevada Arts Council
775/687-6680
http://www.dmla.clan.lib.nv.us./docs/arts

New Hampshire State Council on the Arts
603/271-2789
http://www.state.nh.us/nharts

New Jersey State Council on the Arts
609/292-6130
http://www.njartscouncil.org

New Mexico Arts Division
505/827-6490
http://www.nmarts.org

New York State Council on the Arts
212/627-4455
helpdesk@nysca.org
http://www.nysca.org

North Carolina Arts Council
919/733-2111
http://www.ncarts.org

North Dakota Council on the Arts
701/328-3954
comserv@state.nd.us
http://www.state.nd.us/arts

Ohio Arts Council
614/466-2613
http://www.oac.state.oh.us

Oklahoma Arts Council
405/521-2931
okarts@tmn.com

Oregon Arts Commission
503/986-0082
oregon.artscomm@State.OR.US
http://www.oregonartscommission.org/
    main.php

*Commonwealth of Pennsylvania Council
    on the Arts*
717/787-6883
http://www.artsnet.org/pca/pca.html

Institute of Puerto Rican Culture
787/725-5137
http://www.icp.gobierno.pr

Rhode Island State Council on the Arts
401/222-3880
info@risca.state.ri.us
http://www.risca.state.ri.us

South Carolina Arts Commission
803/734-8696
jguinn@arts.state.sc.us
http://www.state.sc.us/arts

South Dakota Arts Council
605/773-3131
sdac@stlib.state.sd.us
http://www.state.sd.us/deca/sdarts

Tennessee Arts Commission
615/741-1701
http://www.arts.state.tn.us

Texas Commission on the Arts
512/463-5535
front.desk@arts.state.tx.us
http://www.arts.state.tx.us

Utah Arts Council
801/236-7555
http://www.arts.utah.gov

Vermont Arts Council
802/828-3291
info@arts.vca.state.vt.us
http://www.vermontartscouncil.org

Virginia Commission for the Arts
804/225-3132
http://www.arts.state.va.us

Washington State Arts Commission
360/753-3860
http://www.arts.wa.gov

*West Virginia Division of Culture &
    History*
Arts & Humanities Section
304/558-0220
http://www.wvculture.org

Wisconsin Arts Board
608/266-0190
http://www.arts.state.wi.us/static/
    aboutus.htm

Wyoming Arts Council
307/777-7742
wyoarts@artswire.org
http://www.wyoarts.state.wy.us

Index